REFIGURING MIMESIS

Representation in early modern literature

REFIGURING MIMESIS

Representation in early modern literature

EDITED BY
JONATHAN HOLMES
AND ADRIAN STREETE

UNIVERSITY OF HERTFORDSHIRE PRESS

First published in Great Britain in 2005 by
University of Hertfordshire Press
Learning and Information Services
University of Hertfordshire
College Lane
Hatfield
Hertfordshire AL10 9AB

British Library Cataloguing in Publication Data
A catalogue record for this book is available from the British Library

ISBN 1-902806-35-2 paperback

Design by Geoff Green Book Design, CB4 5RA
Cover design by John Robertshaw, AL5 2JB
Printed in Great Britain by Antony Rowe Ltd, SN14 6LH

Contents

Contributors

VANCE ADAIR teaches in the Department of English Studies at the University of Stirling. He has published numerous articles on Shakespeare and critical theory and is currently completing a book that considers the relationship between subjectivity and enjoyment in Shakespearean drama.

CHRISTIAN BILLING is Lecturer in Drama at the University of Hull. His research and publication focuses on the body in performance in early modern English drama. He is the Artistic Director of Mamamouchi's Miscreants, an all-male production company dedicated to the gender-political interrogation of early modern English drama. He is currently completing a monograph on the relationship between anatomical science and the human body on the early modern English stage.

JOHN DRAKAKIS is Professor of English at the University of Stirling. His many publications include *British Radio Drama* (CUP, 1981), *Shakespearean Tragedy* (Longman, 1992), *Antony and Cleopatra* (Macmillan, 1994) and *Tragedy* (with Naomi Conn Liebler, Longman, 1998). He is the editor of *Alternative Shakespeares* (Routledge, 1985 and 2002) and several editions of Shakespeare plays and is the general editor of the New Critical Idiom series (Routledge). He is currently completing the Arden 3 edition of *The Merchant of Venice.*

GABRIEL EGAN is Senior Lecturer in English at Loughborough University and his research spans original staging of early modern drama, theatre history, and modern critical, cultural and editorial theory. He is author of *Shakespeare and Marx* (OUP, 2004) as well as the forthcoming *Green Shakespeare: From Ecopolitics to Ecocriticism* (Routledge, 2005).

PETER HOLLAND is McMeel Family Chair in Shakespeare Studies in the Department of Film, Television and Theater, University of Notre Dame, USA. From 1997 to 2002 he was Director of the Shakespeare Institute and Professor of Shakespeare Studies, University of Birmingham. Among his publications are *The Ornament of Action: Text and Performance in Restoration Comedy* (CUP, 1979) and *English Shakespeares: Shakespeare on the English Stage in the 1990s* (CUP, 1997) as well as editions of Wycherley and numerous Shakespeare plays. He is the editor of *Shakespeare Survey*, a general editor (with Stanley Wells) of *Oxford Shakespeare Topics*, the general editor of the Redefining British Theatre History series and the editor (with W.B. Worthen) of the first volume in that series, *Theorizing Practice: Redefining Theatre History* (Palgrave, 2003).

JONATHAN HOLMES is Lecturer in Drama at Royal Holloway, University of London. His main research interests are in the field of early modern rhetoric and aesthetics. He has published articles in several journals including *Shakespeare Survey* and *New Theatre Quarterly*, and is the author of '*Merely Players*'? *Actors' Accounts of Performing Shakespeare* (Routledge, 2004). He also works as a theatre director.

PAUL INNES is Lecturer in Literature in the Department of Adult and Continuing Education at Glasgow University. He has also taught at the Universities of Stirling, Strathclyde and Edinburgh, and held a British Council Lectureship at the University of Warsaw from 1992 to 1995. He is the author of *Shakespeare and the English Renaissance Sonnet: Verses of Feigning Love* (Macmillan, 1997).

MONIKA SMIALKOWSKA is Research Fellow at Doncaster College and holds a Ph.D. from the University of Gloucestershire. Her main interests lie in the field of early modern literature, particularly the court masque, and theorising popular and high culture. She has published several articles in those areas.

ROGER STARLING is a doctoral candidate in the Department of English and Comparative Literary Studies, University of Warwick, where he is completing a dissertation on Shakespeare and the question of mimesis.

He is the editor of a special issue of *Angelaki: Journal of the Theoretical Humanities* entitled 'Inventions of Death: Literature, Philosophy, Psychoanalysis' (2002).

ADRIAN STREETE is Lecturer in English at the Queen's University of Belfast. He has published work on Marlowe, Shakespeare, Nashe, Calvin and early modern sign theory in journals such as *Literature and History* and *Literature and Theology*. He is currently working on a book on early modern religion, subjectivity and drama.

POONAM TRIVEDI is Reader in English, Indraprastha College, University of Delhi, India. She has published articles on women in Shakespeare, the performance of Shakespeare in India, and on Indian theatre traditions. She is co-editor of a collection of essays, *India's Shakespeare: Translation, Interpretation and Performance* (The University of Delaware Press, 2004) and currently she is working on a book on the performance of Shakespeare in India.

Foreword
Hamlet *and Auerbach*

Peter Holland

Hamlet Seems, madam? Nay, it is. I know not 'seems'.
'Tis not alone my inky cloak, good mother,
Nor customary suits of solemn black,
Nor windy suspiration of forc'd breath,
No, nor the fruitful river in the eye,
Nor the dejected haviour of the visage,
Together with all forms, moods, shapes of grief,
That can denote me truly. These indeed seem,
For they are actions that a man might play;
But I have that within which passes show,
These but the trappings and the suits of woe.[1]

As Hamlet describes to his mother the difference between his feelings and the forms of social and theatrical representations of grief, he establishes a paradox – almost a crisis – of representation: on the one hand, a set of external behavioural events codified into stereotypical activities that are conformable with forms of mimetic conventions; on the other, an announcement of internalised event, ostended as being recognised as emotion but only evidenced through a form of speech, something that is itself an action that men – and occasionally women – not only "might play" but, now for centuries, have indeed been playing.

Representation at this moment is defined in terms both of "show" and the antithesis to show, that which "passes" it. Indeed, in the First Folio text (1623), the emphasis on and rejection of "show" is even more apparent, for where in the Second Quarto (1604/5) Hamlet talks of "shapes" (or rather *chapes*) of grief, in F1 he speaks of "shewes of griefe", now anticipating and therefore underlining the opposition with "that Within, which passeth show".[2] The textual variant is enticing in the context of this collection of essays but few editors of *Hamlet* have adopted it, preferring Q2's sense of the outsides, the externalised manifestations of grief, those characteristically visible outlines that combine with "forms" as exemplifications of "moods", preferring too to delay the sudden performative self-consciousness of the player playing for two more lines – even though over-emphasis might equally be seen as only too apparently part of Hamlet's behavioural representational mode at this point.[3] The double show demonstrates the centrality of spectacle, of forms of mimetic display, defined as indistinguishable from the performable.

In his rejection of such ambivalencies, Hamlet codifies an inner, one which of course he represents as other to the forms of appearances, the modes of moods which become, in a kind of proto-rejection of Stanislavskian feeling, a superficies of emotional state against which that inner can be posited. The inner now "passes" show and the verb takes on a rich range of possible meanings, a semantic field of opportunity in which the inner both goes beyond, surpasses and exceeds the outer (*OED v.* 34-8) and also passes it by "without attending to" it, neglecting and disregarding the triviality of anything that can be within the purview of the performative (*OED v.* 29.a, with citations from *King John* and *Coriolanus*). Not an early modern sense but so potent now would be the aim of *passing* as racial or gendered other, playing on the inevitable lack of clarity, of assurance, whether the show is a show or something which itself may be an unperformed real. It turns Hamlet's inner into a momentarily confusing representation of *show*, for that is indeed what happened: Hamlet can only speak of that within but can never – could never – prove it, turn it into an inner known beyond the subject in a way that would be visible beyond the forms of language, forms which here – as throughout the play – carry the suspicions endemic to the social structures of language itself in its inability to show beyond its verbal show, to collapse its separation from a posited real.

But the verb *pass* will also travel across the play into a noun, ending in those passes that are part of the fencing, from the "pass of practice" that Claudius recommends Laertes to use (IV.vii.137), to "the pass and fell incensed points / Of mighty opposites" that Hamlet, unknowingly, invokes in reporting the deaths of Rosencrantz and Guildenstern (V.ii.61–2), and the "dozen passes" of the fencing wager that Osric reports (V.ii.162). Hamlet will finally turn noun back into verb, inviting Laertes, "I pray you pass with your best violence" (V.ii.302, = *OED v.* 24), not knowing that this is not a representation of violence, the show of death that fencing is supposed to be but actually, really, unperformably the violence that will result in Hamlet's death, a death which he then performs and stages, not least in giving Fortinbras his "dying voice". That within Laertes turns the show of fencing, its spectacle of aggression controlled by rules and appearances, into something other, from representation into presentation, from a mimetic play into the thing that is played on. As the word *pass* traverses the play so it defines the impossibility of fixing the limits of passing, the negation of constricting the antithesis as absolute, for that which passes also infects and becomes that which it passes, mimesis shading uncontrollably into that of which it is representational.

Why then does Hamlet wear black in his first scene? He chooses to set against the truth, the unplayable of emotion the inadequacy of the all too playable, the "customary suits of solemn black" which are only – merely – "the trappings and the suits of woe", creating an equivalence of these suits which are of black and of woe. Why bother to use these means, for him contemptible in their irreconcilability with that state of grief he claims he knows he feels? Hamlet both performs and denies his performance, donning his costume of customary suits, an outfit that writes (note the extraordinary choice of adjective in that "inky cloak") his grief in its colouring, inscribing its meaning of commitment to the shades in its shade but doing so through those means that he questions for their truth. Hamlet's performance is both mimetic and as representation also a denial of mimesis.

An account of *Hamlet* as mimetic space would then need to engage with the interpenetration of the performable by or with the unperformable, that which passes show, and the passage in the play with which I began would open out into the broadest cultural manifestation of the forms of early modern social representation, the display of mimesis as process, the becoming mimetic, which Hamlet would wish, were it not necessarily impossible, to contrast in its imperfection, its vulnerability to untrue representation, with that imagined, spoken of but undemonstrable set of sensations of grief, the feelings which generate the tears, the bowed head or the sighing which, like that which is spoken of, is *only* (whatever that might mean here) a show.

My account of the speech would then have led outward to an early modern anxiety which the essays in this collection explore and my method so far is itself a game of mimesis, for in moving from a small passage from a major text to a figuring of a culture's construction of its form of representation, its methods of mimesis, I am deliberately representing – performing a mimesis of – Erich Auerbach's *Mimesis*, the text whose investigation of 'The Representation of Reality in Western Literature' (its subtitle) underpins and is still the crucial source of tension/resistance to these essays.[4] As a student I belonged to a generation still pervasively influenced by Auerbach. In my first year as an undergraduate, it seemed that every teacher recommended *Mimesis*, less for its argument than as a model for imitation, an encouragement to a mimesis of *Mimesis* of whose jokey ironies they seemed oddly unaware.

As model, of course, the text also defined a certain presence and denial of its own historical status as academic text. In some respects the culmination of the great tradition of German philology, itself even now largely unrecognised in Anglophone culture as the crucial academic progenitor of cultural studies, *Mimesis* was unable to replicate the forms of discourse out of which it emerged and for which it yearned. Written during the Second World War in Istanbul where Auerbach had taken an academic position, in exile as a Jew fleeing Germany, the book is doubly divorced from its origins, both geographically and methodologically. The German philological tradition depended on its display of learning in a culture of reference, learning as footnotes, but, as Auerbach explained in the moving final passages of the book, both the moment and the place of writing made it impossible to connect with such a tradition: Istanbul's "libraries are not well equipped for European studies" and the war meant that "[i]nternational communications were impeded" so that "I had to dispense with almost all periodicals, with almost all the more recent investigations, and in some cases with reliable critical editions of my texts" (p. 557). In a sense, *Mimesis* could not be the learned text it wished to be – and which would have meant that, if it had been able to be, it would probably never have been written, been achieved: "If it had been possible for me to acquaint myself with all the work that has been done on so many subjects, I might never have reached the point of writing" (p. 557). As Auerbach's reply to his critics, 'Epilegomena to *Mimesis*', demonstrates,[5] Auerbach yearned for the panoply of academic learning as much as he continued to yearn for a return to Germany.

If on the one hand early modern performance is that kind of show that Hamlet disdains, it could also be celebrated as the trope of *imitatio*, that imitation so strongly recommended throughout the period as a model for writing through models, acknowledging the finest writing by imitating it, an imitation that was perceived as the sincerest form of flattery. In another place, in another play, imitation could also be the sincerest sign of grief, everything that for Hamlet it is not:

> I my brother know
> Yet living in my glass; even such and so
> In favour was my brother, and he went
> Still in this fashion, colour, ornament,
> For him I imitate.
>
> (*Twelfth Night*, III.iv.389–93)

Viola's customary suits are a deliberate imitation of her brother's outfits, her outline mimicking his as a sign of her loss of him, her yearning to be the twin, the other that is also the self, what the mirror (*my glass*) shows as both self and not-self, as Viola and Sebastian. The mirror resists death: seeing her brother as herself in the mirror, Viola knows – but what kind of knowledge can her awareness of the doubleness of this representation (self and not-self) provide and guarantee? – that he lives as her.

The opposition of Hamlet's costumes of performable representation and Viola's fashion as imitation also imitates that rethinking of the mimetic that Derridean analysis would offer against that humanist philological tradition of which Auerbach stands as exemplar. Edward Said, in his account of Auerbach, is tentative over what to make of Auerbach as a Jew; his phrasing is strikingly awkward here: "Auerbach's Jewishness is something one can only speculate about since, in his usually reticent way, he does not refer to it directly in *Mimesis*".[6] But Auerbach was Jewish and one has no need to "speculate" about Auerbach as a Jew – or does Said mean by "Jewishness" a degree of being a Jew, how much of a Jew Auerbach was? – but how his Jewishness appears might also be apparent through his method, itself a mimesis of Jewishness. There is a wonderful convergence of the close textual analysis that is the very basis of German philology and the even closer analysis of *torah* that is the very basis of

Jewishness as religious practice. *Mimesis*'s method, its beginning in each chapter from the exacting close reading of a passage, might look in an English context like the inheritance of I.A. Richards and the doctrine of 'Practical Criticism' and I am sure that those repeated recommendations of *Mimesis* that I heard in Cambridge were based precisely on that assumption. But in another light, it is an exposition of the cultural meaning of a text in ways that led in the Jewish tradition to an understanding of the divine word and in a philological tradition to an understanding of the otherness, historical and geographical, of other cultures. Derrida's rethinking of mimesis as representation, in its celebration of language as the limit, is also, of course, part of the same Jewish tradition even as it seeks to reconstruct the terms with which that tradition operated.

Since Auerbach and Derrida are two kinds of fathers whose presences are engaged with throughout these essays, it seemed necessary to write this Foreword in terms of Hamlet, the character who negotiates so painfully with the presence of his father in a play so demandingly full of fathers and sons locked into analogous patterns. As the essays traverse both early modern culture and its progeny – as well as the history of accounts of that culture and its engagements with its own histories – they do so in the full awareness of their performance and of the impossibility of ever finding that within, even as they show that which they have uncovered. We can no longer write with the confidence that Auerbach manifests on every page of *Mimesis*, even though we must write in the knowledge of, as well as against, the confidence in the functioning of representational practices of which he so brilliantly wrote.

Foreword

1. William Shakespeare, *Hamlet*, ed. Harold Jenkins (London: Routledge, 1982), I.ii.76-86.
2. Q2's chapes was emended to 'shapes' in Q3 (1611).
3. Incidentally, I have never heard an actor use Q2's wonderful form of address to Gertrude here: not 'good mother' (from F1), but 'coold mother' (i.e. cold or cooled), an adjective which is certainly aggressive but also appropriate.
4. Erich Auerbach, *Mimesis: The Representation of Reality in Western Literature*, trans. Willard R. Trask (Princeton, NJ: Princeton University Press, 1953).
5. Included as an appendix in the 2003 50th anniversary edition of Trask's translation, with a preface by Edward Said (Princeton, NJ: Princeton University Press, 2003), pp. 559-74.
6. Ibid., p. xvii.

INTRODUCTION

Refiguring mimesis: representation in early modern literature

Jonathan Holmes and Adrian Streete

THE EARLY MODERN period is characterised by a crisis of representational practice. Fuelled by the iconoclastic impulses of reformed religion and in conjunction with profound, and often aligned, political, technological and economic changes, the literary achievements of the period negotiate an acute cultural engagement with the discourses of representation. Over the last three decades, early modern studies have witnessed a proliferation of subtle critical articulations dealing with aspects of this crisis that have been as productive as they have been controversial. In the main, scholarship has sought to delineate both the contours of the early modern subject and its representations in relation to a careful historicism as well as a materialist analysis of cultural production. Studies in the field have productively examined, for example, the interconnections between the stage and colonial expansionism, cross-dressing, theories of language, the market place and religious sectarianism to name but a few.[1] By borrowing from continental philosophy and sociology, scholars working in these areas have also effected a decisive shift within the discipline and connectedly in notions of disciplinarity itself. No longer are the theatre and theatrical practice understood as belonging to an exalted realm of literary and aesthetic invention that somehow stands aloof from all other forms of cultural production. Rather, the theatre can be seen as a site where early modern culture interrogated the manifold representational practices used to make sense of a rapidly changing world.[2]

At the same time continental thought has itself responded to our own late capitalist crisis in representation, conveniently labelled by the umbrella terms post-structuralism and postmodernism.[3] This response has broadly been characterised by a move away from theories of artistic or authorial expressivity popularised by the legacy of Romanticism, and a renewed interest (logical in retrospect) in the much older concept of mimesis. Whether it is in the post-Frankfurt School writing of Theodor Adorno, the rehabilitation of Emmanuel Levinas's work through that of Jacques Derrida, of the concentrated explorations of René Girard, the often-misrepresented work of Jean Baudrillard, or recent developments in the work of Derrida himself, mimesis is firmly back on the philosophical agenda. However, despite these theoretical advances, it remains the case that in the Anglo-American critical tradition mimesis is all too often taken for granted, both as a term and as a concept. This state of affairs may be in no small part due to geography. It is noticeable that, despite the continuing and rigorous resurgence of continental interest in mimesis, Anglo-American critical thought, with the notable exception of the writing of Judith Butler, has thus far been largely diffident in its views on the topic. Only very recently, in the work of the sociologist Graham Ley, the classicist Stephen Halliwell and the philosopher Kendall Walton, has this subject begun to be discussed in any real depth.[4] This near-silence is perhaps most glaring in our own field, early modern studies: glaring because of the ubiquity (explicitly and otherwise) of the concept in writing across all discourses of the early modern period. Robert Weimann and Roger Starling are so far notable by the singularity of their work in this area. Indeed, for Weimann, this neglect of the mimetic raises some important questions. As he has argued in his 'Afterword' to the recent second edition of *Alternative Shakespeares*:

> In Anglo-American Shakespeare criticism, this concept [mimesis] is usually employed in a sense that is virtually synonymous with 'imitation' and even 'representation'. But today, is there not a stringent need to make distinctions that question the (neo)Aristotelian domestication of what mimesis stood for?[5]

Weimann makes a crucial point. In the first place, critical work in early modern studies concerned with the mimetic is often lacking in a certain conceptual and historical rigour. If mimesis is to be used as a 'catch-all' term, encompassing notions as diverse as 'imitation' and 'representation', then we also need a sharper historical and critical awareness of the interconnecting valences of these terms. The alternative, as Weimann conceives it, is that as a critical and philosophical term mimesis remains a domesticated trope of an unreflective critical practice. To take what is perhaps the most pervasive example, the assumption that mimesis stands for an epistemologically transparent 'reflection of reality' remains almost unconsciously ingrained in much critical discourse. In this respect, the shadow cast by Erich Auerbach's seminal study *Mimesis: The Representation of Reality in Western Literature* is a long one. For although Auerbach in fact challenges the idea that mimesis simply 'reflects' reality, too often his book has been co-opted in the service of a more traditional, referential model of mimesis. To this end, it is the project of a number of contributors to this volume to refigure this Auerbachian hegemony by re-focusing, as Auerbach himself did, on the irreducibility of the mimetic as a philosophical idea.[6]

Nevertheless, it would be unfair to say that the conceptual vagueness identified by Weimann is solely a feature of contemporary critical concerns and divisions. Early modern writers and thinkers also faced remarkably similar conceptual difficulties. Certainly it is the case that early modern texts are fascinated to the point of obsession with the relationship between their own status as artefact and that of the world they claim to represent. Whether in the commonplace dramatic preoccupation with meta-theatre and the familiar poetic employment of metaphors of role playing and theatricality; in the reliance of music on imitation (in both the technical and general understanding of the word) and that of visual art, of self-reflexive knowingness, the ubiquity of the concern with mimesis and its various cognates in the period threatens at times to become overwhelming. The fascination is perhaps most clearly exemplified in the numerous sophisticated attempts to theorise these art forms that begin to emerge in Europe during the fifteenth and sixteenth centuries. In England, this movement gave rise to one of the most celebrated statements of poetics, Sir Philip Sidney's magnificent *A Defence of Poetry*, written in the 1570s but not published until several years later.

Famously, when it comes to dealing with mimesis, Sidney's text does not really offer the kind of conceptual clarity that we might expect. Sidney writes that "Poesy therefore is an art of imitation, for so Aristotle termeth it in his word mimesis, that is to say, a representing, counterfeiting or figuring-forth – to speak metaphorically, a speaking picture – with this end, to teach and delight."[7] The first word that we might draw attention to here is 'imitation'. Here Sidney is drawing upon an Aristotelian rhetorical term *imitatio* that during the period was, in theory at least, separate from mimesis. This word and the practice that it implies would have been familiar to most early modern schoolchildren since *imitatio* refers, as Brian Vickers notes, to "the use of models in learning to write, from the elementary stages of language-learning to advanced composition".[8] In short, *imitatio* implied the self-conscious imitation of literary models and forms. Understood in this way, *imitatio* is considered successful if it engendered some affective response to the text in the auditor or reader: it was perhaps for this reason that theories of *imitatio* and of mimesis were often intertwined. Still, if Sidney's definition had ended here, then it would have resembled countless other descriptions of the period. However, as intimated, he goes on to align the practice of *imitatio* with that of mimesis, which he defines as "counterfeiting" or "figuring-forth". Understood in this way, it seems that mimesis refers to a kind of imitation, but one that imitates the world (broadly conceived) rather than literary forms.

What this shows is that, historically, while it was certainly possible to make distinctions between terms like 'mimesis', 'imitation' and 'representation', equally it would not do to labour these distinctions. Indeed, we might even say that Sidney's understanding of mimesis represents a conceptual hybridity that accounts for a variety of representational practices. To this end, it is noticeable, if unsurprising, that English writers since *A Defence of Poetry* have used 'mimesis', 'imitation' and 'representation' mixed, as in Sidney, with a soupçon of 'invention', more or less interchangeably. Certainly the contributors to this volume are not unaware of the competing meanings of these terms in both early modern and contemporary discourse. But, we suggest, it is the very conceptual hybridity of the mimetic, broadly conceived, which animates all of the essays contained here. By stretching the very idea of the mimetic in both critical and historical terms, the contributors demonstrate the ongoing theoretical viability of mimesis for early modern studies, as well as potentially new directions that such enquiries might take. For this reason, Weimann's point that mimesis is often "reduced to what the socially distinct, and distinctly limited, cultural demands and interests of the dominant Renaissance poetics allowed"[9] requires some adjustment. Undoubtedly there were dominant conceptions of what the term mimesis meant in the early modern period. Nonetheless, there was also a surprising degree of flexibility in discussions of the term. Influenced no doubt by the lessons of the new humanist philology, writings on this subject also evince a growing awareness that the ancients were far from being agreed on the mimetic, an awareness, interestingly, that has also animated some of the most exciting contemporary theoretical work in the field.

The term mimesis is first found in Book Three of *The Republic*, in which Plato is famously concerned to quash the unhealthy and unseemly consequences of mimetic behaviour. For Plato, the mimetic is bound up with speech and action, a connection that was to become central to rhetorical theory in the West. As he asks: "Is not to assimilate oneself to another person in speech or manner to '*represent*' the person to whom one is assimilating onself?"[10] The problem with such resemblance is that by imitating another there is a real risk of catching "the infection in real life".[11] Mimesis, in other words, is contagious, a Platonic idea that Jacques Derrida has famously expanded upon.[12] Moreover, mimesis threatens social stability. Plato's Guardians are discouraged from taking the part of the old, the young, women, slaves, the wicked or the mentally disturbed: "Our Guardians must recognize that there are men and women who are mad and bad, but they must not represent them in poetry or drama."[13] In terms of the political realm and its proper maintenance, an engagement with mimesis distances the individual still further from the form of the good from which, according to the theory of forms, we are all already removed. This tension between aesthetic richness and ethical corruption lingers, in varying degrees of mediation, through the genealogy of Neo-Platonist thought up to the early modern period and beyond. In contrast Aristotle, in what may well have been a response to Plato, configures mimesis differently. As he notes in his *Poetics*, "the objects that the imitators represent are persons engaged in action".[14] For Aristotle, an engagement with personality or character, with ethos, is not required; instead of action, praxis is the subject of the mimetic act. Crucially, this removes ethical content from the process of mimesis itself and places it on the action that is the subject of this process: "imitation is differentiated – by the means, by the objects, and by the manner of presentation".[15] Therefore, whether or not mimesis is ethical depends on what is being imitated. The process itself is neutral, a rhetorical act rather than a moral one.

This distinction in the classical articulation of mimesis has further complicated the understanding and reception of an already troublesome concept. Not the least difficult implication has been confusion as to the degree of literal resemblance and verisimilitude required; pictorial art as we understand it did not exist in classical Athens, and yet simplistic notions of imitation as an accurate and recognisable depiction of a subject have become attached to visual art more securely than any other discourse. Both Aristotle and Plato, however, emphasise behavioural or in some sense performative mimesis, applicable more to drama, poetry and music (and later the novel) than to so-called fine art. Once this has been grasped, the claim that much modernist or postmodernist art is non-mimetic because it does not literally resemble something, or because it does not start from an ontological premise, becomes less tenable. Indeed, this sense of a performative mimesis is central to the work of Kendall Walton. Walton states that engagement with a work of art operates as a game of imaginative make-believe in which the work is used as a prop in the creation of a fictional world, in which we then participate. He explains:

> Representations are things possessing the social function of serving as props in games of make-believe … A prop is something which, by virtue of conditional principles of generation, mandates imaginings … Propositions whose imaginings are mandated are fictional, and the fact that a given proposition is fictional is a fictional truth.[16]

Mimesis is a formal and psychological necessity in the construction of any artefact and in the involvement of the spectator in the world established by that artefact. Mimesis, rather than a formal element of a particular kind of artefact (the subset misleadingly called 'representational'), is a central element – indeed, arguably the central element – in the production of all art. Mimesis is what separates the artefact from the world that manufactures it, and is therefore itself the product of labour, of practice, rather than an ephemeral rhetorical device. Such an understanding also points to the fact that mimesis is produced by, but at the same time also produces, ideology. So if, as a number of our contributors suggest, the mimetic calls into question the subject's relationship between artefact and world, then by attending to the mimetic, we are also forced to confront those ideological structures that produce and mediate the phenomenon that we clumsily, if not inaccurately, call 'reality'.

This fundamental performativity of mimesis, its existence in *praxis* rather than *ethos*, has been consistently the focus of twentieth-century theoretical reflections on the subject. In his monumental work *Aesthetic*

Theory, Theodor Adorno locates the debate firmly against the background of the rise of Modernism and the consequent crisis of representation: "If the question as to the future of art were not fruitless and suspiciously technocratic, it would come down to whether art can outlive semblance."[17] It becomes clear that for Adorno this outliving is not only possible but also the inevitable position of all art, as "the mimesis of artworks is their resemblance to themselves".[18] Art operates in a continually self-reflexive chain of imitation that allows Adorno also to reclaim music as a mimetic art form (one of the central aims of his project), as in this way it becomes unavoidably mimetic of itself. Music since the Enlightenment has been excluded from mimesis by virtue of its obvious inability to depict the world in terms of recognisable resemblance; Adorno's move, in addition to the inherent performativity of classical mimesis, allows us perhaps to see music differently, as operating more closely to other art forms than has recently been acknowledged. Intriguingly, this is in itself a return to the early modern, in which music theory – following Pythagoras and Boethius – clearly began from the assumption that music was a mimetic art just as were sculpture or poetry. This view is clear in the work of Zarlino and Galilei (father of the astronomer) in Italy, and Thomas Morley and Thomas Campion in England.[19]

A different kind of return to past models is evident in the quasi-anthropological structures of mimesis established by René Girard. Girard also searches out the behavioural dimension of the concept, thinking of mimesis in terms of a pre-Socratic and ritualistic formulation. He constructs the mimetic act as one of rivalry, in which the imitator mimics the model because she or he wishes to appropriate that which the model possesses, prompting the model to redouble their appropriative act – so effectively mimicking their imitator – and so "each becomes the imitator of his own imitator and model of his own model".[20] In Girard, mimesis is understood as a model of control, interestingly inverting the fears of Plato as to its subversive dangers, though the polar opposition between imitator and model thereby established is clearly susceptible to critique. Such a critique is offered by Philippe Lacoue-Labarthe, who contrastingly sees the mimetic poet as one who "presents himself as what is not, exposes himself as other than he is, and depropriates himself".[21] Importantly, this act of depropriation is in itself figured as the cause of Plato's concern with mimesis. As part of his radical re-reading of Plato, Lacoue-Labarthe characterises mimesis as feminised: "what is threatening in mimesis is feminisation, instability, hysteria".[22] This same threatening, mimetic effeminacy can, according to Lacoue-Labarthe, be found throughout *The Republic*, from Socrates' initial, paranoid prohibition of the Cronos myth, with its castration complex, through to the final linking of transvestism, madness and mimesis at the end of Book Three.

While Lacoue-Labarthe has identified gender as a mimetic concern, it is in the work of Luce Irigaray, who sees Plato's Cave as womb,[23] and Judith Butler that the connections between gender and mimesis have been most intricately developed. For example, in positing that "there is no gender identity behind the expressions of gender; that identity is performatively constituted by the very 'expressions' that are said to be its results",[24] Butler develops an understanding of mimesis that is at once social and artistic. More importantly, she reverses the accepted relationship between model and imitator, in which it is assumed that 'reality' is prior and originary and therefore also a source of truth, and the artefact or 'expression' is subordinate and pale. Instead Butler collapses the distinction, implying that a receptor traces a false model for the imitator when in fact there is only the imitation; the sense of 'that which is imitated' is false. The influence of Derrida for this line of thought is palpable, as Butler extends the deconstructive play of signifiers without origin to the performative mimesis of gender. The sense of continuous self-reflexivity and, in the broadest sense, performance, is central to modern interpretations of mimesis. Again, we note that the idealist critical assumption that sees mimesis as an unproblematic 'representation of reality' can no longer be unequivocally sustained. This realisation also has profound implications for our understanding of subjectivity, a central concern of this volume. For example, in his book *The Imaginary Institution of Society*, the philosopher Cornelius Castoriadis outlines a theory of representation that brings together this refigured conception of mimesis as well as the centrality of the subject. In the first place, Castoriadis rejects the traditional notion that mimesis offers a 'representation of reality' that is then perceived by the subject. He notes that: "Representation … is not a painting hung within the subject decked out with various kinds of *trompe-l'oeil*, or else itself an immense *trompe-l'oeil*."[25] Instead, representation is a much more uninscribed phenomenon:

> Representation is perpetual presentation, the incessant flux in and through which anything can be given. It does not belong *to* the subject, it *is*, to

> begin with, the subject … Representation is precisely that by which this 'us' can never be closed up within itself, that by which it overflows on all sides, constantly makes itself other than it 'is', posits itself in and through the positioning of figures and exceeds every given figure.[26]

As Castoriadis concludes:

> Representation is not tracing out the spectacle of the world, it is that in and through which at a given moment a world arises. It is not something that provides impoverished 'images' of 'things' but that of which certain segments take on the weight of an 'index of reality' and become 'stabilized' … as 'perceptions of things'.[27]

A Derridean perspective of free-playing signifiers, each colliding with and manufacturing others, or a Butlerian view of expressive performativity is equally apposite for an investigation into a period of protean science and mutable disciplinary boundaries, in which each discourse is a wondrous reforming of another. But in Castoriadis's formulation, we see the foregrounding of the subject as the location of a refigured mimetic art and a reconstituted conception of selfhood. As we will see, this is also an elision that responds to the figuration of early modern theatrical discourse and contemporary theoretical praxis.

Viewed with such a light, we can begin to understand the early modern period as a site of a much more fluid, dialogic and complex mimetic art than had previously been assumed. The famous early modern trope of the microcosm, for example, in which each artefact and each individual is a miniature example of the universe itself, becomes revivified when examined through the lens of twenty-first-century mimesis. Indeed, our two opening essays by Roger Starling and Vance Adair both focus on a play, Shakespeare's *Richard II*, which is well known for its complex exploration of this trope. Starling's essay draws productively upon the work of Philippe Lacoue-Labarthe in his examination of the mirror in *Richard II*, arguing that the 'modernity' of Shakespeare's mimetic practice is to be found in its radical (de)constitution of the subject. In Starling's work, the king's subjectivity is an essentially mimetic position, one that impacts more upon the political constitution of the state than on the king himself. Adair's essay shares many of the concerns articulated by Starling, but his Derridean analysis of the play takes as its point of departure the idea of the address in *Richard II*. For Adair, the play disrupts a connection between sign and referent, central to classical accounts of the mimetic, and in doing so opens to question the very possibility of 'history' itself. By disrupting the category of mimetic referentiality, both of these essays point to fertile new connections between a broadly deconstructive critique of mimesis and early modern subjectivity. Gabriel Egan's essay, on the other hand, looks to re-examine the physical *space* of the early modern theatre. In his broadly historicised reading of representational practice, Egan teases apart the connections between classical mimetic ideals and the bathetic descent suggested by the theatrics of Ben Jonson in particular. The possibility of multiple levels of representation raised in Egan's essay is also taken up by Paul Innes in his reading of *Julius Caesar*, which focuses on the problematic of both structure and 'character' in the play. Innes argues that the drama is not in any simplistic way 'about' Julius Caesar, but is instead concerned with a multiplicity of mimetic discourses, discourses that disrupt traditional character-based readings as well as the famed 'double structure' of the play.

If the first four essays are firmly located in the interface between the early modern and post-structuralism, Poonam Trivedi's essay represents a shift in discursive focus towards the post-colonial. In it, she provides a reading that examines the impact of the Western theatre upon nineteenth-century India. Trivedi contrasts pre-colonial representational discourses in India with the mimetic assumptions that the colonial theatre brought with it. However, the mimeticism engendered by this clash has also led, argues Trivedi, to a hybridity of representational practice that might even be appropriated as part of "the decolonising process" in contemporary Indian culture. The political import of the mimetic is also raised in Monika Smialkowska's essay on the power, or otherwise, of the elite aristocratic voice in the court masque. Smialkowska suggests that, far from straightforwardly 'reflecting' the ruling elite's self-image, the mimetic methods of the masque are much more complex than is often assumed in recent critical work on the topic. Reflections and the difficulties therein also animate the next essay in the volume by Christian Billing. Drawing upon early modern theories of reflection, Billing explores the trope of the mirror before moving on to a discussion of the way in which gender becomes a refracted discourse in contemporary representations of Mary Frith, discussing in particular *The Roaring Girl.* The focus of the penultimate essay by Adrian Streete is a very different play by Thomas Middleton, *The Revenger's Tragedy.* In his essay, Streete examines the connections between the discourses of political resistance and iconoclasm in early modern culture before going on to offer an iconoclastic reading of the play, one predicated upon the disavowal of the material sign. Materiality, but this time of the musical kind, also animates the final essay by Jonathan Holmes. Holmes understands early modern music as a mimetic art, and in his discussion of John Donne's poetry and its relationship to music he offers a subtle reconfiguration of Donne's mimetic theory, a complex schema that draws upon Plato, Aristotle, Boethius and Augustine, and which attests to the richness of early modern mimesis. Indeed, it is because of this richness that the contributors to this volume suggest that it is time to refigure the question of mimesis. The essays contained herein interpret a newly invigorated critical debate individually and demonstrate a fertile and subtle awareness of its complexity in the early modern period. As all the contributors suggest, mimesis during the period is characterised above all by the startling intellectual dexterity and imaginative boldness with which it is expertly discussed in prose and skilfully incorporated into the dramatic work of the time. This volume begins for the first time in English to accord this richness the attention it merits, and to initiate the rehabilitation of one of the central theoretical issues of this or any other period.

Introduction

1. Some of the most important of these studies include: Stephen Greenblatt, *Renaissance Self-Fashioning: From More to Shakespeare* (Chicago and London: University of Chicago Press, 1980); Alan Sinfield, *Literature in Protestant England 1560-1660* (London and Canberra: Croom Helm, 1983); Francis Barker, *The Tremulous Private Body: Essays on Subjection* (New York and London: Routledge, 1984); Catherine Belsey, *The Subject of Tragedy: Identity and Difference in Renaissance Drama* (London and New York: Methuen, 1985); Terry Eagleton, *William Shakespeare* (Oxford: Blackwell, 1986); Jonathan Dollimore, *Radical Tragedy: Religion, Ideology and Power in the Drama of Shakespeare and his Contemporaries*, 2nd edn (New York and London: Harvester Wheatsheaf, 1989); Martin Elsky, *Authorizing Words: Speech, Writing and Print in the English Renaissance* (Ithaca, NY and London: Cornell University Press, 1989); Debora Shuger, *Habits of Thought in the English Renaissance: Religion, Politics and the Dominant Culture* (Berkeley, CA: University of California Press, 1990); Joel Fineman, *The Subjectivity Effect in the Western Literary Tradition: Essays towards the Release of Shakespeare's Will* (Cambridge, MA and London: MIT Press, 1991); *Alternative Shakespeares*, ed. John Drakakis (London and New York: Routledge, 1992); Jean Christophe Agnew, *Worlds Apart: The Market and the Theater in Anglo-American Thought, 1550–1750* (Cambridge and New York: Cambridge University Press, 1993); Linda Charnes, *Notorious Identity: Materializing the Subject in Shakespeare* (Cambridge, MA and London: Harvard University Press, 1993); *Political Shakespeares: Essays in Cultural Materialism*,

ed. Jonathan Dollimore and Alan Sinfield (Manchester: Manchester University Press, 1994); Laura Levine, *Men in Woman's Clothing: Anti-Theatricality and Effeminization* (Cambridge: Cambridge University Press, 1994); Linda Gregerson, *The Reformation of the Subject: Spenser, Milton and the Protestant Epic* (Cambridge: Cambridge University Press, 1995); Katherine Eisaman Maus, *Inwardness and Theater in the English Renaissance* (Chicago and London: University of Chicago Press, 1995); Robert Weimann, *Authority and Representation in Early Modern Discourse*, ed. David Hillman (Baltimore, MD and London: Johns Hopkins University Press, 1996); Huston Diehl, *Staging Reform, Reforming the Stage: Protestantism and Popular Theater in Early Modern England* (Ithaca, NY and London: Cornell University Press, 1997); Richard Hillman, *Self-Speaking in Medieval and Early Modern English Drama* (Basingstoke: Macmillan Press, 1997); *Post-Colonial Shakespeares*, ed. Ania Loomba and Martin Orkin (London and New York: Routledge, 1998); Michael Neil, *Issues of Death: Mortality and Identity in English Renaissance Tragedy* (Oxford and New York: Oxford University Press, 1998); *Shakespeare and Modernity: Early Modern to Millennium*, ed. Hugh Grady (London and New York: Routledge, 2000); *Philosophical Shakespeares*, ed. John J. Joughin (London and New York: Routledge, 2000); Ania Loomba, *Shakespeare, Race, and Colonialism* (Oxford: Oxford University Press, 2002).

2. For an excellent recent reading that seeks to recuperate the category of the aesthetic within early modern studies, see John Joughin's 'Shakespeare, Modernity and the Aesthetic: Art, Truth and Judgment in *The Winter's Tale*', in Grady, *Shakespeare and Modernity*.
3. See Alex Callinicos, *Against Postmodernism: A Marxist Critique* (Cambridge: Polity Press, 1989); Terry Eagleton, *The Ideology of the Aesthetic* (Oxford: Blackwell, 1990); Fredric Jameson, *Postmodernism, or, The Cultural Logic of Late Capitalism* (Durham, NC: Duke University Press, 1991).
4. See Graham Ley, *From Mimesis to Interculturalism* (Exeter: University of Exeter Press, 1999); Stephen Halliwell, *The Aesthetics of Mimesis: Ancient Texts and Modern Problems* (Princeton, NJ: University of Princeton Press, 2002); Kendall Walton, *Mimesis as Make-Believe* (Cambridge, MA: Harvard University Press, 1990); and also Timothy Murray's excellent collection *Mimesis, Masochism and Mime* (Ann Arbor, MI: University of Michigan Press, 1997), which presents sixteen essays on the subject by leading French thinkers.
5. Robert Weimann, 'Afterword', in *Alternative Shakespeares*, ed. John Drakakis, 2nd edn (London and New York: Routledge, 2002), p. 236.
6. In many respects, A.D. Nuttall's *A New Mimesis: Shakespeare and the Representation of Reality* (London and New York: Methuen, 1983) can be viewed as a distinguished excrescence of this traditional referential model of mimesis in early modern studies.
7. Sir Philip Sidney, 'A Defence of Poetry', in *English Literary Criticism*, ed. Brian Vickers (Oxford: Clarendon Press, 1999), p. 345.
8. Ibid., p. 22. See the 'Introduction' to Vickers's book for a more detailed discussion of the distinction between imitation and mimesis in the period.
9. Ibid.
10. Plato, *The Republic*, trans. Desmond Lee (London: Penguin, 1987), p. 92.
11. Ibid., p. 95.
12. See Jacques Derrida, 'Plato's Pharmacy', in *Dissemination*, trans. Barbara Johnson (London: Athlone, 1981).
13. Ibid.

14. Aristotle, *Poetics*, trans. James Hutton (New York and London: W.W. Norton, 1982), p. 46.
15. Ibid. p. 47.
16. Walton, *Mimesis*, p. 69.
17. Theodor Adorno, *Aesthetic Theory*, ed. and trans. Robert Hullot-Kentor (London: Athlone, 1997), p. 101.
18. Ibid., p. 104.
19. See: Zarlino, *Institutioni Harmoniche* (1558); Thomas Morley, *A Plain and Easy Introduction to Practical Music* (London, 1597); Thomas Campion, *Observations in the art of English Poesie* (London, 1601).
20. René Girard, 'Mimesis and Violence', in *The Girard Reader*, ed. James G. Williams (London: Crossroads, 1996).
21. Philippe Lacoue-Labarthe, *Typography: Mimesis, Philosophy, Politics*, ed. Christopher Fynsk (rpr. Stanford, CA: Stanford University Press, 1998, originally published in French in 1979), p. 133.
22. Ibid., p. 129.
23. See Luce Irigaray, *Speculum of the Other Woman* (Ithaca, NY: Cornell University Press, 1985).
24. Judith Butler, *Gender Trouble* (London: Routledge, 1990), p. 25.
25. Cornelius Castoriadis, *The Imaginary Institution of Society*, trans. Kathleen Blamey (Cambridge: MIT Press, 1998), p. 331.
26. Ibid.
27. Ibid., pp. 331-2.

CHAPTER ONE

"Scenes from the life of one who is suited for nothing": Shakespeare and the question of mimesis

Roger Starling

> We are all framed of flaps and patches and of so shapelesse and diverse a contexture, that every peece and every moment playeth his part. And there is as much difference found betweene us and our selves, as there is betweene our selves and other. *Magnum rem puta, unum hominem agere. Esteeme it a great matter, to play but one man.*
>
> The sacred writ pronounceth them to be miserable in this world, that esteeme themselves. *Dust and ashes* (saith he) *what is there in thee, thou shouldest so much glory of?* And in another place, God had made man like unto a shadowe, of which who shall judge, when the light being gone, it shall vanish away? *Man is a thing of nothing.*
>
> (Michel de Montaigne, *Essays*, trans. John Florio)

Scene one

AT THE CLIMACTIC MOMENT of the well-known deposition scene in Shakespeare's *Richard II*, the beleaguered king interrupts his accusers to request that a mirror be brought "hither straight", in order that "it may show me what face I have, / Since it is bankrupt of his majesty" (IV.i.255–7).[1] Professing to satisfy their demands and read the accusing articles "When I do see the very book indeed / Where all of my sins are writ" (IV.i.264–5), he seizes the mirror and gazes with apparent self-pity at the spectacle of his own reflection:

> Give me that glass, and therein will I read.
> [RICHARD *takes the glass and looks in it*]

No deeper wrinkles yet? Hath sorrow struck
So many blows upon this face of mine
And made no deeper wounds? O flatt'ring glass,
Like to my followers in prosperity,
Thou dost beguile me! Was this face the face
That every day under his household roof
Did keep ten thousand men? Was this the face
That like the sun did make beholders wink?
Is this the face which faced so many follies
That was at last outfaced by Bolingbroke?
A brittle glory shineth in this face,
As brittle as the glory is the face,
[*He shatters the glass*]
For there it is, cracked in an hundred shivers. (IV.i.266–79)

Critics of this passage, after duly remarking the emblematic significance of the mirror, have typically focused on the subsequent exchange between Richard and Bolingbroke, in which the antagonists provide conflicting interpretations of the significance of Richard's performance. Surprisingly, perhaps, since their struggle has so far been predominantly political, the exchange is concerned not with issues of kingship and usurpation, but with the nature of performance itself: that is, with theatrical representation or mimesis. For Richard, who concludes his speech with the injunction "Mark, silent king, the moral of this sport: / How soon my sorrow hath destroyed my face" (IV.i.280–1), his performance is the enactment of an unseen grief: a means of unveiling or bringing to light what would otherwise remain hidden or concealed. For Bolingbroke, on the other hand, Richard's performance is purely histrionic: his sardonic rejoinder, "The shadow of your sorrow hath destroyed / The shadow of your grief" (IV.i.282–3), not only points out the artifice of his conceit, but also seizes the opportunity to cast aspersions on the authenticity of Richard's grief. In other words, whereas Richard subscribes to a poetics of theatrical presence (of truth in the mode of *aletheia* or unconcealment) in which 'things' are literally revealed through the efficacy of outward signs, Bolingbroke responds with a counter- or anti-theatrical poetics (of truth in the mode of *homoiosis* or adequation) in which appearances or fictional presentations in general are measured against the truths they ostensibly (re)present.[2] Initially, then, it would appear that we are presented with a choice: a choice between Richard's theatrical iconophilia, in which truth is presumed to inhere in its figural or mimetic unveiling, and Bolingbroke's sceptical iconoclasm, in which truth is a matter of rational calculation or discernment.

For critics of *Richard II*, such issues have for the most part been subordinated to a preoccupation with character, through which the question of theatrical representation or mimesis is almost invariably referred to the stylised antics of the self-deposing player-king. Certainly the traditional iconography of the mirror – as an attribute of *Vanitas* in medieval iconography and, in a tradition that commences with Plato's *Republic*, as a figure for mimetic representation in general – lends itself to an unequivocal association with Richard, an impression that is reinforced throughout the play by his persistent self-preoccupation and frequently remarked faith in an ideal, Cratylitic correspondence between signs and their referents.[3] It is for this reason that one of the play's most recent editors can interpret the shattering of the mirror as a "climactic *coup de théâtre*" that functions on two distinct levels: as an instance of Richard's "extravagant escapism" through which he "narcissistically evades a reality he himself has invited" (the mirror as a property of *Vanitas*); and as an instrument of "deeper insight" into the "fragility and impermanence" of his own being (the mirror as a reflector of truth).[4] In both cases, however, what the mirror invariably reflects is aspects of Richard himself, an assumption that not only reinforces traditional interpretations of his character, but also authorises the recurrent opposition between Richard's histrionic verbosity and Bolingbroke's plain-speaking pragmatism. Indeed from this perspective, the 'moral' is apparently clear: the shattering of the mirror marks an irrevocable passage from the self-centred narcissism and theatrical ostentation of Richard's residual medievalism to the demystified realities of modern political governance. But is this in fact what the scene shows us?

Indeed on closer inspection, things are perhaps not so clear. To begin with, it remains to be determined why critics of *Richard II* have for the most part implicitly sided with Bolingbroke (at least as regards the interpretation of the mirror scene), or why Richard, in the lines immediately following, lends credence to Bolingbroke's interpretation in terms that, contrary to Richard's ostensible iconophilia, point out the discrepancy between outward "shadows" and his "unseen grief" (IV.i.287). Indeed why, to return to the passage above, does Richard ask for the mirror in the first place? Why does he (or, perhaps more to the point, why does Shakespeare) feel compelled to quite literally *hold up the mirror*? And why, given his theatrical proclivities, does Richard perform the ultimate – albeit theatrical – iconoclastic gesture of shattering the reflective surface? Is there perhaps more to this mirror, and indeed to Richard, than meets the eye?

Scene two

Critics of *Richard II*, to the extent that they ponder such questions, have not been slow in once again referring them to the question of Richard's character, which is invariably assumed to conform to the subjective requirements of continuity and development (the term 'subject', from the Greek *hypokeimenon*, 'that which lies beneath', presupposes the property or self-consistency of an underlying or subjacent foundation). Consider, for example, the interpretation of the mirror scene referred to above. As noted previously, Richard, in breaking the mirror, is presumed to experience "a moment of deeper insight into his own nature":

> It [the mirror] becomes for him 'the very book … Where all [his] sins are writ' … and the means of disclosing, as through a glass darkly, 'the tortured soul' … that lies beneath the youthfully handsome and as yet unwrinkled countenance. The brittleness of the glass symbolizes for Richard the fragility and impermanence of life itself and links up thematically with the 'hollow crown' speech of 3.2 with its effect of expanded consciousness and deepened self-perception.[5]

Even discounting the element of sentimental fantasy informing this account of Richard ("youthfully handsome and as yet unwrinkled countenance"?), we might still ask how in this politically charged and conspicuously public scene – in which, as a consequence, we can be certain of *precisely nothing* with respect to Richard's ethos or identity as a speaker – it is possible to *verify* that this is indeed a personal and deeply felt speech? Or that it is in any way disclosive not simply of Richard's alleged 'character' (that is, of Richard, precisely, as a *character*) but of *anything at all* pertaining to the consistency or self-identity of a subject? Unless, perhaps, there is *already* a mirror – an *invisible* mirror – fixedly, if not permanently, in place?

To address such questions, let us, for the moment, take leave of that decidedly public context in which Richard is ostensibly revealed, and consider instead his reflections within the intimate retreat of Pomfret, the castle where he is eventually imprisoned. For it is here, far from the public gaze, that Richard not only enters alone, but also provides privileged access to his ostensibly 'subjective' interiority by means of his first, and indeed only, soliloquy. Listen, then, as this most conspicuously public of performers commences his solitary meditation:

> I have been studying how I may compare
> This prison where I live unto the world;
> And for because the world is populous,
> And here is not a creature but myself,
> I cannot do it. Yet I'll hammer it out.
> My brain I'll prove the female to my soul,
> My soul the father, and these two beget
> A generation of still-breeding thoughts:
> And these same thoughts people this little world
> In humours like the people of this world.
> For no thought is contented.
>
> (V.v.1–11)

Even when alone, and at least notionally off-stage, Richard's thoughts tend almost immediately to the condition of theatre. Not only, for example, does Richard's fanciful conceit rely implicitly on the topos of the *theatrum mundi*, but the speech as a whole, in fact, recalls nothing so much as writing a play: with his "still-breeding thoughts" quite literally 'peopled' through their own 'subjective' birth and autonomy, and thus reflecting in microcosm the world that Richard himself inhabits. And those thoughts, too, acquire an element of theatrical verisimilitude by virtue of their discontent, and to that extent resemble the similarly discontented "humours" that populate the world at large. It is as though Richard, instead of turning simply inward, turns curiously inside out, such that his inner life or character, revealed through the mirror of his soliloquy, mirrors or is mirrored by the "humours" of those around him. Indeed Richard, who, as king, was formerly the 'mirror' of his subjects, is now their mirror in a different sense: as though the mirror, once shattered, has not so much disappeared as begun to proliferate endlessly: its fragments reflecting other fragments in an infinite *mise-en-abîme* of discontented and indeterminate 'subjects'.

Thus, no longer at the centre of a system that he himself centred,

Richard, as he ruminates on the vicissitudes of time and fortune, continues to proliferate. Not, this time, into the discontented multitude reflected in his "little world", but rather, in a further elaboration of the *theatrum mundi* topos, into a discontinuous series of roles or theatrical personae:

> Thus play I in one person many people,
> And none contented. Sometimes am I king;
> Then treason makes me wish myself a beggar,
> And so I am. Then crushing penury
> Persuades me I was better when a king.
> Then am I kinged again, and by and by
> Think that I am unkinged by Bolingbroke,
> And straight am nothing. But whate'er I be,
> Nor I, nor any man but that man is,
> With nothing shall be pleased till he be eased
> With being nothing.
>
> (V.v.31–41)

A consideration of this passage will make clear that, despite appearances to the contrary, none of these roles is entirely chosen by Richard 'himself'. Rather, those roles or personae, whether real or fanciful, are received from the Other (or, as we will see, from *others*).[6] And the mark of this otherness is ultimately the inscription of an irreducible finitude: that curious instability by which one role succeeds and displaces another in a movement that writes, re-writes and thus, in a movement that is both creative *and* destructive, (de)composes or (de)constructs the 'subject'. Indeed, the "nothing" on which Richard broods is precisely the nothing that determines the 'subject' as mortal: mortal in the sense not only of a 'properly' finite being, but also with regard to an 'original' lack or infirmity – what Richard calls "discontent" – that destines the 'subject' to an ineluctable insufficiency or 'desistance'.[7] The 'subject', thus determined as mortal, can only accede to selfhood – if indeed it ever can – through the assumption of roles or models that precede it. Thus Richard, in brooding upon this vain and hapless theatre, broods upon the nothing of which he is composed, which is the nothing to which he is destined. But who, then, is Richard?

Scene three

Richard's shattering of the mirror is assumed by many critics to inaugurate a new mode or discourse of subjectivity not only in *Richard II* but also within the Shakespearean corpus more generally. The subject, previously imagined as an ideal, specular unity in which truth coincides with appearance, is renounced through Richard's iconoclastic gesture in favour of an alternative conception in which the subject is presented in terms that are more conspicuously modern.[8] Whereas in the earlier conception the subject was entirely subsumed by its role, in the modern version the subject is marked by an increase of self-consciousness that assumes the form of a gap or inner distantiation between role and subject. Richard, in this reading, is the inheritor of a mode of subjectivity widely associated with Montaigne, and to that extent anticipates Shakespeare's elaboration of the problem in *Hamlet*, in which this sense of alienation is extended even to Hamlet's own self-representations.[9] Indeed, what is common to each of these prototypical modernists is a preoccupation with the subject that seems always on the verge of dissolution: a dissolution, as we have seen, into a multiplicity of roles or guises, of which none are properly subjective.

Appearances, however, can be deceiving. Indeed, this alleged or ostensible 'modernity' marks the irruption within literary and philosophical discourse of the ancient Greek problem of mimesis: the problem, precisely, of theatrical representation, mimicry, impersonation.[10] It is customary, at least within literary studies, to think of mimesis as a synonym for representation, in the sense of realism or verisimilar reproduction, as in the subtitle of Erich Auerbach's influential study entitled *Mimesis: The Representation of Reality in Western Literature*.[11] Yet this sense, which derives from Plato and Aristotle and, philosophically speaking, is the forerunner of Richard's emblematic mirror, is ultimately misleading, even although it has exerted, and continues to exert, an incalculable influence on literary and philosophical thinking. This sense of mimesis as representation is not only, perhaps, the most familiar or traditional definition, but it is also a definition that dissimulates an older, more archaic, or pre-philosophical one. Thus, according to Jacques Derrida:

> If we go back to *mimésis* 'prior' to the philosophical 'decision,' we find that Plato, far from linking the destiny of art and poetry to the structure of

> *mimésis* (or rather to the structure of all of what people today often translate – in order to reject it – as re-presentation, imitation, expression, reproduction, etc.), disqualifies in *mimésis* everything that 'modernity' makes much of: the mask, the disappearance of the author, the simulacrum, anonymity, apocryphal textuality.[12]

The 'modernity' to which Derrida is referring is first of all that of the Parisian artistic and intellectual avant-garde of the late 1960s and early 1970s, and in particular the sophisticated textual theorising associated with Roland Barthes, Michel Foucault, the Tel Quel group and others. What Derrida is suggesting here, however, is that in their haste to overturn the conventions of literary representation (which was regarded, in the Paris of the late 1960s, as the ideological equivalent of a repressive system of political representation) they succeeded not in getting rid of the oppressive weight of tradition so much as returning to an earlier literary-philosophical problem which the interpretation of mimesis as representation simply functioned to occlude. They returned, in other words, through the radical elaboration of a post-Mallarméan poetics, to one of the founding problems of Western philosophy.

What, then, is the nature of this problem? As Derrida suggests, mimesis has been traditionally defined as belonging to the order of representation as a consequence, first of all, of its delimitation in Book Ten of Plato's *Republic*, where it was defined as the imitation of phenomenal appearances (and thus at a proportionately greater remove from the ideal truth of the Ideas), and its subsequent rehabilitation in Aristotle's *Poetics*. Thus, Derrida argues:

> whether or not Plato condemns *mimésis* as imitation, he poses the question of poetry by determining it as *mimésis*, thus opening the field in which Aristotle's *Poetics*, entirely subsumed under that category, will produce *the concept* of literature that reigned until the nineteenth century.[13]

Yet as Derrida points out, "If we go back to *mimésis* 'prior' to the philosophical 'decision'" – prior, that is, to the delimitation of mimesis as imitation in *The Republic*, Book Ten – we find an earlier, more archaic definition in the discussion of the pre-Platonic *lexis* (that is, the complete set of verbal resources available to the poet or rhapsode) that appears in Book Three. In this context, mimesis is defined specifically in terms of dramatic impersonation, that is, when the poet or rhapsode speaks in the voice of another, as opposed to *haple diegesis*, or simple narration, when discourse is presented *in propria persona* (that is, through the poet's own or proper person).[14] Thus whereas in the latter case the speaker's words can be verified (at least theoretically), in the former they are anonymous or 'apocryphal': the author disappears, or is occluded, by the voice or identity she or he assumes. Thus, the poet is a kind of actor: and actors, for Plato, are inscrutable. Or, as Duncan observes in *Macbeth* following the disclosure of Macdonald's treason: "There's no art / To find the mind's construction in the face" (I.iv.12–13).

The significance of this will become apparent once it is recalled that Platonic metaphysics depends precisely on being able to distinguish between two modes of repetition: 'good' mimesis, which faithfully repeats or 'imitates' the truth of the Ideas; and 'bad' mimesis, which repeats in the absence of either truth or knowledge.[15] In other words, to the extent that Platonism, and indeed all subsequent metaphysics, is predicated on the ability to differentiate between 'good' mimesis and 'bad' mimesis, then Platonism *is implicitly confounded by the actor*, whose 'imitation' is insusceptible to verification (of truth as either *aletheia* or *homoiosis*).[16] Indeed rather than being a local or specialised instance, the actor, on the contrary, discloses precisely the 'internal' duplicity or undecidability of the *mimeisthai*, which Platonism wishes to divide in two. Thus, within any repetition – within any (re)presentation whatsoever – inheres the irreducible possibility of an absence or default of truth, which is the risk, ultimately, of a confusion, loss of identity, dispropriation, madness: in short, a *general* instability.[17]

The implications of Derrida's account of Plato, with particular attention to *The Republic*, have been pursued most rigorously by Philippe Lacoue-Labarthe, who interprets the subsequent history of literature and philosophy, up to and including Nietzsche and Heidegger, in terms of a properly philosophical effort to contain its destabilising effects. In particular, Lacoue-Labarthe adduces in *The Republic* a rivalry or mimetic *agon* between philosophy and mimesis, concerning which Socrates, in the course of Plato's dialogue, is perfectly explicit. Yet the neglect of this rivalry by subsequent commentators (and, in particular, Heidegger) has resulted in what Lacoue-Labarthe perceives as an uncritical acceptance of the denigration of mimesis in *The Republic*, Book Ten.[18] Thus, by refusing to take seriously the motives behind the Platonic denigration, Heidegger himself proves an unwitting participant in the very metaphysics he is seeking to limit. In what, therefore, does this metaphysical investment consist? And why does the critical or philosophical problem of mimesis point specifically towards the threat or vertigo of a general instability?

In Lacoue-Labarthe's view (who, in this respect, follows Heidegger's lead), Western metaphysics is precisely committed to the use of onto-typological fictions (types, models, exemplars) in order to impose meaningful coherence through the mastery or elimination of difference. In the periods leading up to the era of modern technology, these fictions were transcendental, as in the case of the Platonic *eidos* or the Christian God. In the modern period, however, which should be understood as 'modernity' in the broadest sense from Descartes to Nietzsche, these transcendental fictions, in keeping with the Heideggerean problematic of the 'completion' of metaphysics in technology, are displaced by their human-centred counterparts such that, in modernity, the type will always consist of a figure of humanity: Oedipus, for example, in the case of psychoanalysis, or the worker in the case of Marxism.[19] In other cases these types will consist of models or figures of community, or the 'essence' of a people or race, as in, most notoriously, the ideology of National Socialism. It is Lacoue-Labarthe's view that the use of onto-typological fictions, most catastrophically realised in the horror of Nazi Germany, constitutes the realisation of a philosophical-political tendency in Western thinking in general, in which the political has been conceived as the privileged sphere for the *fictioning* of beings and communities.[20]

For Lacoue-Labarthe, this understanding of the political task, which is evident, for example, in the formulaic recitation of the ancient Greek *paedia*, as well as in concepts such as *Gestaltung* (configuration, fashioning) and *Bildung* (formation, constitution, education, etc.), is itself a form of mimetic supplementation, one that depends precisely on an understanding of mimesis derived from Aristotle's *Physics*.[21] Here Aristotle writes that "on the one hand, *techne* accomplishes what *phusis* is incapable of effecting; on the other hand, *techne* imitates *phusis*"[22] It is this specifically apophantic ('shows' [*phainei*] 'forth' [*apo*]) interpretation of mimesis, by which a being or entity is presumed to reveal itself in its essence (truth, once again, as *aletheia*), to which Lacoue-Labarthe takes exception, discounting as it does the more nuanced and indeed highly problematic character of mimesis evident, however indirectly, in the text of Plato's *Republic*. There is no question, within the confines of a brief article, of doing justice to the intricacy and complexity of Lacoue-Labarthe's reading, informed as it is not only by a painstaking analysis of the figurative and discursive strategies of Plato's text, but at the same time by a complex and often difficult account of Plato's subsequent reception, specifically in the writings of Heidegger and René Girard. By way of summary, however, we can note the following features:

1. In the text with which we are concerned ('Typography'), Lacoue-Labarthe commences by staging the problem of "philosophical madness": that is, both madness as a philosophical problem, as a problem *for* philosophy; and madness, on the other hand, as that which inevitably befalls philosophy itself: that is, of philosophy not necessarily as a kind of madness in itself (although this is no doubt open to question), but towards which philosophy is in some way destined. We might speak, then (although Lacoue-Labarthe refrains from this), of the *tragedy* of philosophy: that is, of its pre-destination to a kind of tragic dissolution.

2. Philosophy, in general, has maintained two distinct strategies with regard to mimesis: the one, exemplified by Heidegger's reading of Plato, consists, as noted above, of a straightforward acceptance of its determination as a mode of inferior copying in *The Republic*, Book Ten; the second, exemplified in this instance by the work of Girard, consists in the expectation of a revelation or disclosure of mimesis in its essence: that is, the presentation or truth of the means of presentation (or in other words, a presentation of the 'essence' of mimesis that would be otherwise unaffected by the mimetic supplement).

3. What these two strategies have in common is what Lacoue-Labarthe regards as a properly philosophical attempt to master or contain mimesis and its destabilising effects, effects which are perfectly legible in the text of *The Republic* (of *The Republic*, precisely, as a *text*). For what Lacoue-Labarthe points out, in keeping with the arguments first presented by Derrida, is that *The Republic* itself is a pharmaceutical or therapeutic device for 'capturing' or staging the mimetic by *reducing* it to the figure of imitation. Plato, in other words, *holds up a mirror to mimesis* that consists in artfully determining mimesis (mimicry or theatrical presentation) as specular or visual imitation: a mirror, in other words, that makes a mirror of mimesis.

4. This staging, for Lacoue-Labarthe, although it necessarily betrays the non-identifiable or non-presentable 'essence' of mimesis as ungrounded or theatrical mimicry, is nonetheless absolutely necessary to secure any identity whatsoever. For this reason: that mimesis, rather than being

simply a matter of secondary imitation or copying, is itself 'original', and that this 'originary representation', severed from the determination of truth (since mimesis, as Plato surmised, is necessarily secondary as well), is precisely the abyssal 'ground' of the mimetic. It is for this reason that mimesis 'itself' has no essence or property, but rather consists – or, as Lacoue-Labarthe puts it, "de-sists" – in the appropriation and destabilisation of everything supposedly proper. Hence "the only recourse, with mimesis, is to differentiate it, to identify it. In short, to *verify* it", which nonetheless would not fail to betray its 'original' and irreducible impropriety.[23]

5. Mimesis, in this view, confirms – and displaces – what Lacoue-Labarthe refers to as "typography": the 'composition', 'stamping' or indeed *structuring* of the subject through the use of onto-typological models or fictions. Indeed 'character', in this view, is always struck from the outside, and derives from the "always anterior circulation of discourses", which not only renders the subject susceptible to the imprint of typological fictions, but at the same time loosens or unsettles them.[24] There is thus:

> as Lacan would say, a 'preinscription of the subject' in the structure or order of the signifier that marks the symbolic order's first domination of the subject. But the 'subject,' traversed from the very beginning by a multiple and anonymous discourse (by the discourse of others and not necessarily that of *an* Other), is not so much (de)constituted in a cleavage or simple *Spaltung* [splitting] – that is, in a *Spaltung* articulated simply in terms of the opposition between negative and presence (between absence and position, or even between death and identity) – as it is splintered or dispersed according to the disquieting instability of the improper.[25]

Whence, in other words, from this 'originary' non-identity or impropriety, "the obsession with appropriation that dominates through and through every analysis of mimesis, of mimetism", and, more specifically, with the question or obsession with the 'subject' that informs, from Plato to the present, every thought and every discourse on mimesis. For indeed:

> What is threatening in mimesis, understood in these terms, is exactly that kind of pluralization or fragmentation of the 'subject' provoked from the outset by its linguistic or symbolic (de)constitution: an effect of discourses, the 'self'-styled 'subject' always threatens to 'consist' of nothing more than

a series of heterogeneous and dissociated roles, and to fraction itself endlessly in this multiple borrowing.[26]

Thus, "the mimetic life" – which is precisely to say, any 'subject' – is irreducibly composed of "*scenes from the life of one who is suited for nothing*" – that is, of a potentially infinite proliferation of 'identities' that are ultimately both in-adequate and non-revealing: *non-mirroring*, in other words, if by this term is meant the absence or default of truth as either *aletheia* (unconcealment) or *homoiosis* (adequation).[27]

It is for this reason, finally, that philosophy, which since Plato has always been in envious competition with the tragic, is pre-destined to a kind of tragic (that is, mimetic) dissolution, because the only way of 'capturing' or verifying mimesis is to enter into implicit competition with the mimetic: that is, to exceed the mimetic at its own game. And this staging of the mimetic, this 'play', is the very stuff of theatre: of desire, first of all, and of rivalry, disguise, confusion of identities, madness, conflict and eventual death. The mirror, in other words, invariably 'captures' or exposes philosophy as the rival – the dissimulated double – of mimesis.

And so what, then, of 'literature'? It is no accident, in the first instance, that Platonic philosophy set itself up as the rival of tragic theatre, of all genres the one in which the poet is least present in his discourse, and therefore the least responsible or accountable. And poets, in Plato's view, are a threat to the philosophical order of his ideal republic precisely because of their tendency to propagate mimetic fictions, in other words 'bad' examples, models of lewd or licentious behaviour, of irreverence towards the gods, unmanliness, dishonour, madness or dispropriation in general: not only, in other words, fictions that are insufficiently grounded in truth, but which serve in Plato's view to incite desire – *mimetic* desire, the contagious and excessive imitation of models – and thus with the consequent threat of instability, in terms of the displacement of the rational faculties of the soul and the outbreak of rivalry or violent competition in the *polis*.[28] 'Good' mimesis, the 'proper' imitation of heroes, models of virtue, truth, knowledge, etc., is threatened, as in the case of Platonism more generally, by the permanent possibility of a *general* or unrestricted mimesis.

It is for this reason, as Girard surmised, that tragic violence aims to effect a cathartic or sacrificial remedy for dangers of excessive imitation.

Yet while for Girard the selection of the victim or tragic scapegoat is entirely arbitrary – tragedy being in this instance perceived as a purely representative or vicarious solution to the problem of mimetic dissolution – the victim is, according to Lacoue-Labarthe, entirely in keeping with the 'origin' of mimetic disorder. It is thus entirely necessary that, if the cause itself is the fictional or mimetic nature of 'subjectivity', then the victim – the tragic hero – should be none other than the *representative* of general or 'originary' mimesis. Hence the victim:

> is always, whatever his status, a *mimos*. That is, in effect, anyone at all, but a 'just anyone' who signals himself (if we can use this kind of expression) as 'such,' who exhibits 'his' non-identity, who brings along in 'his' history (Oedipus) or 'his' function (the king), in 'his' *ethos* (the fool) or 'his' trade (the actor, the artist), the dreaded evidence of the primal status and undivided rule of mimetic confusion.[29]

The representative, in other words, the *mimetician* par excellence, will always be the one who shows or exhibits himself as, simultaneously, everything and nothing: the representative of that disquieting plasticity or malleability – the aptitude, precisely, for assuming all characters or roles – which is precisely that of an 'originary' absence or default of identity. Indeed the victim, in other words, will not only be the one who, manifestly or visibly, *redoubles the mimesis*, but who, in his very (absence of) 'nature', makes visible the unsettling suspicion that representation itself – mimesis – is primal.[30]

It is for this reason – the representative nature of the scapegoat – that tragedy itself was regarded by Plato as justifiably threatening: for not only does it function by putting into circulation those models or examples it otherwise seeks to expel, but its efficacy is necessarily confined to the scenic or specular order. The victim, in other words, *is* representative, not only of a general instability of absence of identity, but at the same time a representation in the sense of a theatrical fiction. Tragedy, in effect, can only *mime* the expulsion of what it vainly and endlessly repeats. It necessitates, in Plato's view, a stronger, philosophical antidote, just as, for example, the dominant conception of 'literature' has tended in general to conform to a post-Aristotelian concept of imitation, that of truth or fidelity to nature: mimesis, in other words, not only as the mirror of nature, but a mirror that (artfully) conceals or secretes itself, that disappears or otherwise veils or withdraws itself, through the reflection or (re)presentation of an otherwise absent truth:[31] the mirror, in short, as a *figure* – a trope, certainly, but also, and in a precise sense, a *model* or *type* – of mimesis.

Scene four

The extent to which Shakespeare's plays incorporate a diverse range of mimetic activity in terms of both performance and subject-matter has been the subject of numerous important studies.[32] What has yet to be grasped, however, is the extent to which their astonishing 'modernity' derives precisely from the ancient problematic of mimesis, as glimpsed, most formidably perhaps, by Plato, and as expounded in texts by Derrida and Lacoue-Labarthe. As I have attempted to make clear, the force of this problematic lies primarily in its delineation of the mimetic (de)constitution of the 'subject', a topic that would have been well known to Shakespeare and his contemporaries, as the theory of exemplarity or 'emulation'.[33] According to this theory, the purpose of literary activity is the production of models or examples of conduct: positive models as an incitement to virtuous or heroic conduct; the negative as means of public admonishment and censure. What this theory assumes, therefore, is a 'plastic' or malleable 'subject': an *actor*, in short, with an aptitude for all roles or characters, who is consequently in need of a stamp of identity or imprint of form: a *type* – ethos or character – struck from without, which derives "from the always anterior circulation of discourses".[34] Shakespeare, by presuming to write in an era conspicuously marked by the revival of classical learning, is thus, so to speak, *imprinted* with the theory of exemplary types.[35]

Yet according to a well-documented line of transmission, Shakespeare is not simply the inheritor or passive recipient of such theories, but a dramatist who explores the nature and paradoxes of exemplarity in ways that are in many respects similar to the humanist and post-humanist experimentalism of such writers as Montaigne, Rabelais and Cervantes.[36] In each case, their experimentalism derives, either wholly or in part, from their ability to exploit, within the context of a highly self-conscious and self-reflexive mode of literary productivity, the indeterminacy of the textual or mimetic supplement (that is, the inherent instability of the relationship between *verba* and *res*).[37] Indeed writing, in this period, seems precisely to exploit a seemingly endless quest for rules, methods of composition, exemplary authors, texts and authorities of all kinds, while at the same time revelling conspicuously in the tendency of writing and indeed all language to depart from, exceed and subvert the prescribed norms. Exemplarity, in other words, was a method of governing, or attempting to govern, the inherent instability and unruliness of discourse: the ability, on the one hand, for writing to act as a mirror of truth by *seeming* to reflect or refer to objects beyond itself (and thus, so to speak, *miming* truth through the pretence of unmediated presentation or reference) and on the other hand by managing, just as effortlessly, to divest itself of its ostensibly presentational or referential ground and to function instead as an instrument or medium of pure or ungrounded representation: a *general* mimesis, in other words, and thus the locus of an irreducible instability or default of truth.

That writing, so to speak, is in want of truth corresponds within the Shakespearean corpus as a whole to a preoccupation with the inherent instability or pre-maturation of the 'subject', a 'subject', as we have already seen, who only accedes to selfhood or subjectivity proper by means of an exemplary figure or model of imitation: by means, precisely, of an artistic or mimetic supplement. But, as Lacoue-Labarthe points out, there is a law that governs the process of supplementary *imitatio*, the 'mimetological law' par excellence, which states that, in order for selfhood to be achieved, *imitatio* must rid itself of *imitatio*.[38] The subject, in other words, can only appropriate itself as such not simply through the acquisition of a model, but by concealing (from itself) the fact of its imitation. Whence the fiction, for example, of self-formation or 'apophantic' subjectivity through which the subject, rather than assimilate the pre-existing roles or models to which its pre-maturation condemns it, comes to itself, reveals itself, by discarding inappropriate models or types (examples, in other words, of 'bad' mimesis) or, conversely, when a seemingly proper or integral subject experiences, through a series of extraordinary and unfortunate circumstances, an unexpected loss or withdrawal of 'self'.

These are, quite obviously, the respective patterns of Shakespearean comedy and tragedy: *A Midsummer Night's Dream*, for example, in which the notably malleable lovers experience an almost dizzying exchange of roles and partners before assuming their 'proper' characters or identities (involving, precisely, the potentially tragic topoi of confusion, rivalry, instability of identity, dispropriation, madness, etc.); or *Hamlet*, in which the loss of a paternal model or exemplar triggers an 'internal' crisis of identity affecting both Hamlet and all of Denmark. As well, both of these plays depict theatre in terms that are conspicuously belied by the events on stage. In *A Midsummer Night's Dream*, the lovers and courtiers are assembled at the beginning of Act Five to watch a performance of 'Pyramus and Thisbe' in which they observe, in non-recognition, many of the roles and actions they themselves had recently performed; while Hamlet, as part of the revenge action, aims to catch "the conscience of the King" (III.i.582) by holding up a mirror that reductively distorts the identities of Claudius and Gertrude (that 'reveals' them, precisely, as allegorical types or figures).[39] Theatre, in other words, is not only regarded in these plays as a conspicuously restricted activity – an activity confined to a demarcated space of exemplary, and exemplarily *visible*, performance – but also depends for its efficacy on the displacements and distortions of representation. Comedy, in other words, permits the on-stage audience to celebrate the imminent consummation of its 'proper' civility in collective non-recognition, while tragedy consists in the spectacle of a conspicuously public 'discovery' facilitated by theatrical indirection.

Elsewhere, to confine ourselves simply to these two plays, there is evidence of the *mimos* and his fate: in Bottom, most notably, who wishes to 'play all the parts' in the performance of 'Pyramus and Thisbe', and in the supernatural figure of Puck, whose theatrical impersonations and manipulative trickery serve not only to facilitate the action but also to provide a meta-theatrical commentary for the benefit of an equally blind and unsuspecting audience (looking on, that is, in non-recognition – like the on-stage audience in Act Five – at the antics of their own mimetic doubles). In *Hamlet*, the *mimos* is Hamlet himself, the "glass of fashion and the mould of form" (III.i.152), whose tragic dissolution is marked by an increasing proliferation of indeterminate and unstable roles and identifications (a question, once again, of conflict, rivalry, confusion of identities, madness, dispropriation, etc.).[40] It is as though Hamlet, having lost his enabling model or exemplar, supplements the ensuing lack through a succession of temporary replacements: by attempting, in other words, to 'fix' his inherent instability while compulsively exhibiting or acting it out. And just as the (absence of) truth is veiled in *A Midsummer Night's Dream*, the nothing to which Hamlet is destined is made clear by the fateful convergence through which, anterior to the main action, Hamlet receives his 'identity'.[41] If comedy, in other words, is a mirror that veils the (absence of) truth, tragedy, in this case, is a distorting mirror that at the same time paradoxically unveils: *Hamlet*, by centring itself on Hamlet's self-centred absence or loss, discloses his much-discussed 'subjectivity' as a shattered and yet 'revealing' reflection: a succession, more precisely, of "*scenes from the life of one who is suited for nothing*".

Scene five

And so what, then, of Richard? It should be apparent by now that the 'trick of the mirror' is to 'fix' the general instability (of truth, identity, subjectivity, etc.) by means of a supplementary distortion through which it assumes the *appearance* of that which is otherwise absent.[42] The mirror, in other words, although associated with the attempt, from Plato to the present, of 'capturing' the destabilising play of mimesis (and thus, to that extent, an *anti-mimetic* instrument), is, at the same time, disconcertingly 'productive' as well: a figure – albeit a dissembling one – of that same or general mimesis. Why, then, is Richard, and indeed Shakespeare, concerned to hold up the mirror? And who, after all, is Richard? Returning briefly to the scene of Richard's deposition, it should be noted, in the first instance, that Richard specifically requests that a mirror be brought in direct response to the demand, urged by Bolingbroke and Northumberland, that he read aloud the accusing articles, and in doing so, presumably, that he acknowledge their truth. It is, in other words, a scene or playlet orchestrated by his opponents, who either assume or would like it to appear that Richard is unquestionably guilty. It is as though, in other words, Richard's crimes are to his opponents *so readily apparent* they might just as well be inscribed on his features. As Richard remarks, "I'll read enough / When I do see the very book indeed / Where all my sins are writ, and that's myself" (IV.i.263–5). The mirror is requested not simply in order for Richard to inspect them for himself, but rather to make a spectacle of doing so, and thus make a spectacle of his opponents. Richard, in other words, holds up the mirror not so much to himself, but to 'himself' as a mirror of Bolingbroke. His histrionics are indeed assumed, but they are assumed for reasons that have little or nothing to do with Richard's alleged 'character'. They are assumed, rather, to point out the deliberately theatrical machinations of that most ostensibly non- or anti-theatrical of politicians: a mirror, precisely, *for* Bolingbroke. In other words, *Richard himself is the mirror*: the one who is both everything and nothing. Consequently, 'his' character is nothing other than the character(s) of those around him, whose 'discontented humours' – ambition, narcissism, vanity and, above all, a susceptibility to theatrical gestures – he serves to make strikingly visible. What stirs, then, behind the shattered glass is none other than ourselves: everyone and no one. But who 'we'?

Chapter One

The epigraphs to this paper are taken from 'Of the Inconstancie of Our Actions' and 'An Apologie of *Raymond Sebond*' in *Montaigne's Essays*, transl. John Florio, 3 volumes (London: J.M. Dent, 1965).

1. William Shakespeare, *Richard II*, in The Norton Shakespeare, ed. Stephen Greenblatt and others (New York and London: W.W. Norton, 1997). Unless noted, all subsequent references to the plays of Shakespeare are to this edition.
2. The terms *aletheia* and *homoiosis* figure prominently in Heidegger's delimitation of Western metaphysics. For a consideration of these terms with respect to the problem of mimesis (and the consequent unsettling of Heidegger's account of the metaphysical destiny of the West), see Jacques Derrida, 'The Double Session', in *Dissemination*, trans. Barbara Johnson (Chicago: University of Chicago Press, 1981), pp. 173-–285, esp. pp. 192–3; and Philippe Lacoue-Labarthe, 'Typography', in *Typography: Mimesis, Philosophy, Politics*, ed. Christopher Fynsk (rpr. Stanford, CA: Stanford University Press, 1998), pp. 43–138. The argument that follows makes constant (albeit often implicit) reference to the interpretation of mimesis by Derrida and Lacoue-Labarthe.
3. On the significance of the mirror, see Ernst Robert Curtius, *European Literature and the Latin Middle Ages*, trans. Willard R. Trask (Princeton, NJ: Princeton University Press, 1973), p. 336; Herbert Grabes, *The Mutable Glass: Mirror-Imagery in Titles and Texts of the Middle Ages and English Renaissance*, trans. Gordon Collier (Cambridge: Cambridge University Press, 1982); and Robert S. Knapp, *Shakespeare – The Theater and the Book* (Princeton, NJ: Princeton University Press, 1989), pp. 27–34. With respect to mirrors, multiple perspectives and subjectivity in *Richard II*, see also Ernest B. Gilman, '*Richard II* and the Perspectives of History', in *A Curious Perspective: Literary and Pictorial Wit in the Seventeenth Century* (New Haven, CT: Yale University Press, 1978), pp. 88–128; Scott McMillin, 'Shakespeare's *Richard II*': Eyes of Sorrow, Eyes of Desire', *SQ* 35 (1984), pp. 40–52; Joel Fineman, *Shakespeare's Perjured Eye: The Invention of Poetic Subjectivity in the Sonnets* (Berkeley, CA: University of California Press, 1986), p. 211 and pp. 303-4; Christopher Pye, 'The Betrayal of the Gaze': Theatricality and Power in Shakespeare's *Richard II*', *ELH* 55 (1988), pp. 575–98; Ned Lukacher 'Anamorphic Stuff': Shakespeare, Catharsis, Lacan', *SAQ* 88 (1989), pp. 863–98; Sandor Goodhart, 'Being Nothing': Kings, Mirrors and Subjects in Shakespeare's *Richard II*', in *Sacrificing Commentary: Reading the End of Literature* (Baltimore, MD: Johns Hopkins University Press, 1996), pp. 42–93; Richard Hillman, *Self-Speaking in Medieval and Early Modern English Drama: Subjectivity, Discourse and the Stage* (Basingstoke: Macmillan, 1997), p. 108; and Hugh Grady, *Shakespeare, Machiavelli, and Montaigne: Power and Subjectivity from Richard II to Hamlet* (Oxford: Oxford University Press, 2002), pp. 58–108.
4. Charles R. Forker, 'Introduction', in William Shakespeare, *King Richard II*, ed. Charles

R. Forker, The Arden Shakespeare, Third Series (London: Thomson, 2002), p. 38.

5. Ibid.
6. This difference, although seemingly minor, marks an important moment in Lacoue-Labarthe's reading with/against the psychoanalytic theory of Jacques Lacan. See, in particular, 'Typography', pp. 128–9.
7. On the 'desistance' of the 'subject', see Philippe Lacoue-Labarthe, *Heidegger, Art and Politics: The Fiction of the Political*, trans. Chris Turner (Oxford: Blackwell, 1990), pp. 80–3; and Lacoue-Labarthe, 'Typography', p. 129. See also Jacques Derrida, 'Introduction: Desistance', in Philippe Lacoue-Labarthe, *Typography*, pp. 1–42. I return to this issue at greater length later in the chapter.
8. See, in general, the critical pieces dealing with entries under *Richard II* that are detailed in n. 3 (above).
9. For a recent discussion of relations between Shakespeare and Montaigne, see Grady, *Shakespeare, Machiavelli, and Montaigne*, esp. pp. 109–25.
10. For recent accounts of mimesis and its significations from ancient Greece to the present, see Gunter Grebauer and Christoph Wulf, *Mimesis: Culture – Art – Society*, trans. Don Reneau (Berkeley, CA: University of California Press, 1992); and Stephen Halliwell, *The Aesthetics of Mimesis: Ancient Texts and Modern Problems* (Princeton, NJ: Princeton University Press, 2002). Despite their respective merits, neither of these studies addresses the question of mimesis in relation to the problematic of subjectivity. For more specific accounts of mimesis in pre-Platonic Greece, see Eric A. Havelock, *Preface to Plato* (Cambridge, MA: Harvard University Press, 1963), esp. pp. 20–35; and Penelope Murray (ed.), *Plato on Poetry* (Cambridge: Cambridge University Press, 1997), esp. pp. 3–6.
11. Erich Auerbach, *Mimesis: The Representation of Reality in Western Literature*, trans. Willard R. Trask (Princeton, NJ: Princeton University Press, 1953).
12. Derrida, 'Double Session', p. 186 n. 14.
13. Jacques Derrida, 'Plato's Pharmacy', in *Dissemination*, trans. Barbara Johnson (Chicago: University of Chicago Press, 1981), pp. 61–171, p. 138 n. 63.
14. For an important discussion of the implications of this distinction, see Lacoue-Labarthe, 'Typography', pp. 132–7.
15. See Derrida, 'Double Session', p. 186 n. 14, and 'Plato's Pharmacy', for further elaboration in relation to the problematic of writing.
16. For discussion and elaboration of this point, see Lacoue-Labarthe, 'Typography', pp. 132–7.
17. This point is intimated, rather than developed, in the epilogue to Derrida's 'Plato's Pharmacy', which dramatises, through a mimetic presentation of 'Plato', the impossibility of closure intrinsic to Plato's metaphysics. See also Lacoue-Labarthe, 'Typography'.
18. For discussion of Heidegger's 'unacknowledged mimetology' for his politics and thinking in general, see Lacoue-Labarthe, *Heidegger, Art and Politics*; Philippe Lacoue-Labarthe, 'Transcendence Ends in Politics', in Fynsk (ed.), *Typography*, pp. 267–300; and Lacoue-Labarthe, 'Typography'.
19. See Philippe Lacoue-Labarthe, 'Oedipus as Figure', *Radical Philosophy* 118 (2003): 7-17. This problematic derives ultimately from Heidegger's work on nihilism in relation to Ernst Jünger. See Martin Heidegger, 'On the Question of Being', in *Pathmarks*, ed. William McNeill (Cambridge: Cambridge University Press, 1998), pp. 291-322. See also Lacoue-Labarthe's elaboration of this topic in 'Typography'.

20. See Lacoue-Labarthe, *Heidegger, Art and Politics.*
21. Lacoue-Labarthe, *Heidegger, Art and Politics*, pp. 80–5. As Lacoue-Labarthe notes elsewhere, 'Aristotle' functions here "not as the name of a doctrine, but the site of a generative schema, a matrix, the index of a historico-theoretical constraint" ('Diderot: Paradox and Mimesis', in Fynsk (ed.), *Typography*, pp. 248–66, p. 255). My use of the term 'supplement' and its variants here and throughout this paper are intended to refer to the logic of supplementarity outlined by Jacques Derrida. See *Of Grammatology*, trans. Gayatri Chakravorty Spivak (Baltimore, MD: Johns Hopkins University Press, 1976), pp. 141–64.
22. Aristotle, *The Physics*, trans. Francis M. Cornford (Cambridge: Cambridge University Press, 1957), vol. 1, p. 173. Cited by Philippe Lacoue-Labarthe, 'Hölderlin and the Greeks', in Fynsk (ed.), *Typography*, pp. 236–47, p. 238. For an account of the implicit duality of Aristotle's statement, see Lacoue-Labarthe, 'Diderot: Paradox and Mimesis', pp. 255–6.
23. Lacoue-Labarthe, 'Typography', p. 116.
24. Ibid., p. 128.
25. Ibid.
26. Ibid., p. 129.
27. Ibid.
28. This, of course, is the basis of the well-known theory of 'mimetic desire' formulated by René Girard. As summarised by Lacoue-Labarthe, Girard maintains that "every desire is desire for the desire of the other (and not immediately for the desire of any object); every structure of desire is triangular (entailing the other – mediator or model – whose desire desire imitates); every desire is thus from its inception infused with hatred or rivalry. In short, the origin of desire is mimesis – mimetism – and no desire is ever forged that does not at once desire the death or the disappearance of the model or 'exemplary' personage that gave rise to it. This is why, for Girard, '*mimesis* meets violence and violence redoubles *mimesis*.' This is also why, in general, every culture (every society whatsoever) is built violently on the ground – and thus the threat – of a *generalized* state of competition" ('Typography', p. 192). As in the case of Heidegger, Lacoue-Labarthe's account of mimesis is elaborated both with and against the analyses of Girard. For a critical discussion of Girard's 'system', see Lacoue-Labarthe, 'Typography', pp. 102–17.
29. Lacoue-Labarthe, 'Typography', p. 116.
30. Ibid., p. 115.
31. For a concise account of the implications of the metaphysical interpretation of mimesis for the history of criticism and poetics, see Derrida, 'Double Session', p. 186 n. 14.
32. A comprehensive list of studies relevant to this issue would no doubt run to many pages. What is important to point out, however, is that there is currently no full-length study of which I am aware that takes into account the complex interplay in Shakespeare's theatre between mimesis as a 'theory' of subjectivity – that is, as both an implicit and explicit topic of presentation – and as the means by which the 'theory' is presented. The work that might have come closest in this regard, although no doubt developed in different terms, is Joel Fineman's *Shakespeare's Will*, which was left incomplete at the time of his death. For some indication of the possible range of Fineman's discussion, see his earlier essay, much influenced by Girard, entitled 'Fratricide and Cuckoldry: Shakespeare's Doubles', in *Representing Shakespeare: New Psychoanalytic Essays*, ed. Murray M. Schwartz and Coppélia Kahn (Baltimore, MD: Johns

Hopkins University Press, 1980), pp. 70-109; *Shakespeare's Perjured Eye*, esp. pp. 297–307; as well as the various fragments collected in *The Subjectivity Effect in Western Literary Tradition: Essays toward the Release of Shakespeare's Will* (Cambridge, MA: MIT Press, 1991). In this regard, René Girard's study, *A Theatre of Envy: William Shakespeare* (New York: Oxford University Press, 1991), is, although valuable, deficient with respect to the representational aspects of mimesis highlighted by Lacoue-Labarthe.

33. On the theory of exemplarity, see Timothy Hampton, *Writing from History: The Rhetoric of Exemplarity in Renaissance Literature* (Ithaca, NY: Cornell University Press, 1990); and, for the 'emulation' of literary models as the basis of the early modern theory and practice of writing, Brian Vickers (ed.), *English Renaissance Literary Criticism* (Oxford: Clarendon Press, 2003), pp. 1–55.
34. Lacoue-Labarthe, 'Typography', p. 128.
35. As noted by both Hampton and Vickers (see n. 66), the revived concepts of exemplarity and *imitatio* were the basis of early modern literary and political theory, the two, in this period, being virtually indistinguishable. It is in these terms, too, that it is possible to detect important parallels between the theory of exemplarity and Heidegger's poetico-political programme. I pursue the question of the political in Shakespeare with respect to the problem of mimesis in the context of a forthcoming study.
36. On this topic, see Terence Cave, *The Cornucopian Text: Problems of Writing in the French Renaissance* (Oxford: Clarendon Press, 1979); and Hampton, *Writing from History.*
37. See, for discussion of this point, Derek Attridge, 'Puttenham's Perplexity: Nature, Art, and the Supplement in Renaissance Poetic Theory', in *Literary Theory/Renaissance Texts*, ed. Patricia Parker and David Quint (Baltimore, MD: Johns Hopkins University Press, 1986), pp. 257–79; and Cave, *The Cornucopian Text.*
38. Lacoue-Labarthe, *Heidegger, Art and Politics*, p. 79.
39. See, on this point, Knapp, *Shakespeare – The Theater and the Book*, p. 29. As Knapp points out, 'The Murder of Gonzago' "mirrors by distorting" Claudius and Gertrude as "*exempla* of two commonplace sins, murderous ambition and feminine inconstancy", p. 29.
40. As the text makes clear, the figure of Hamlet as an exemplary prince is dependent upon a prior, mirroring relationship with the image of his heroic father. There is thus, for Shakespeare, an 'originary' imbrication of what Lacan terms the Imaginary and the Symbolic, in which, for Hamlet, the collapse of the former results in the disintegration of his position within the latter. The consequence is that the 'identities' of both Hamlet and Denmark, which were previously secured through an identification with Hamlet senior, are not only subject to mimetic dissolution, but expose in retrospect the extent to which such identities are themselves irreducibly theatrical.
41. I refer here to the temporal coincidence, fateful for both Hamlet and Denmark in general, that unites the slaying of Fortinbras of Norway by Hamlet senior, the birth of Hamlet, and the gravedigger commencing his work. See *Hamlet*, I.i.79–106 and V.i.130–7. Here, among other things, we learn that Denmark, in its violent differentiation from Norway, is founded on an "emulate" (I.i.82) or mimetic rivalry (deferred or dissembled in *A Midsummer Night's Dream*) that returns to haunt both Hamlet and the state.
42. On the 'trick of the mirror', see Lacoue-Labarthe, 'Typography', pp. 87–95.

CHAPTER TWO

"'Tis in reversion that I do possess": speculation and destination in Richard II

Vance Adair

Looking awry

ON THE AFTERNOON of Saturday 7 February 1601, the eve of the abortive Essex rising, eleven close associates of the ill-fated Earl attended what many critics believe to have been a specially commissioned performance of Shakespeare's *Richard II* at the Globe theatre. Six months after the rebellion, while perusing documents in the Tower of London, Queen Elizabeth chanced upon a file entitled 'Richard II' before remarking famously, "I am Richard II; know ye not that?"[1]

While attempts to establish the veracity of any causal relationship between Shakespeare's play and the Essex rebellion have been an enduring topic of critical debate,[2] in more recent years the connection between the staging of Shakespeare's play and the Queen's identification with the deposed monarch appears to have crystallised into historical fact. In the hands of Stephen Greenblatt and Jonathan Dollimore, for example, both narratives are adduced as evidence of nothing less than the counter-hegemonic potential of the Elizabethan theatre. If contemporary scholarship remains blasé about the political threat posed by *Richard II*, a reproachful Greenblatt claims that:

> in 1601 neither Queen Elizabeth nor the Earl of Essex were so sure: after all, someone on the eve of a rebellion thought the play sufficiently seditious to warrant squandering two pounds on the players [...] and the Queen understood the performance as a threat.[3]

Similarly, Jonathan Dollimore is quite unequivocal in reading the performance of Shakespeare's play as "a famous attempt to use the theatre to subvert authority" arguing that "Queen Elizabeth afterwards anxiously acknowledged the implied identification between her and Richard II".[4] In short, even though Essex's rebellion fell short of the mark, the subversive import of Shakespeare's play ultimately found its true addressee.

In this chapter I would like to argue that insufficient attention has been paid to the way that *Richard II* is a text that is repeatedly caught up in the very problems of the address, of the destination and, ultimately, of the thrust or project of history itself. Whither is writing destined? What kind of speculation, implicit in all classical accounts of mimesis, accompanies the idea that a text (however circuitously) 'arrives' somewhere? In his earliest published text Jacques Derrida argues that history involves "postal and epistolary reference or resonance of a communication from a distance [...] so that a return inquiry is asked on the basis of a first posting":[5] history, then, not as a sedimentation of acquired experiences so much as an openness to receiving and placing calls, to taking up and sending on. This *retroactive* constitution of a text's sense would seem to bear upon the way that a text, in its historical necessity, is always modified, transformed, traversed, separated from itself and returned to its outside by all those works that might seem only to come after it. Maurice Blanchot goes further in his suggestion that every text constitutively is an *open* space of deferred reciprocity between reading and writing. That is to say, a text is always open, "its sense always open both in arrival, to come and in a process of retroactive constitution by the accidents of its 'future'".[6]

Let us hold these issues in suspense for the moment to reconsider a famous exchange that actually takes place in Shakespeare's *Richard II.* In an effort to console the Queen's grief at her husband's recent departure for Ireland, Bushy initiates discussion of a similar logico-formal paradox. Bushy adapts the popular Renaissance motif of anamorphosis which, heuristically at least, offers itself as a useful allegory for the Queen's predicament:

> Each substance of a grief hath twenty shadows,
> Which shows like grief itself, but is not so.
> For sorrow's eye, glazed with blinding tears,
> Divides one thing entire to many objects,

Like perspectives, which, rightly gaz'd upon,
Show nothing but confusion; ey'd awry,
Distinguish form. So your sweet Majesty,
Looking awry upon your lord's departure,
Find shapes of grief more than himself to wail,
Which, look'd on as it is, is nought but shadows
Of what it is not [...].

(II.ii.14–23)

Initially, Bushy compares the elusive source of the Queen's presentiments of woe to the *trompe-l'oeil* of a sharpened perspective glass (ll.16–17) which, because of its uneven surface, multiplies and distorts the thing that it reflects. Labouring the analogy, Bushy argues that only when it is looked at from a prescribed angle ("ey'd awry") will it be possible for the Queen to discern the equally phantasmal quality of her grief.

Almost imperceptibly, however, Bushy implies another reading of anamorphosis that seems to dispute this logic. While conventional wisdom on anamorphosis would have it that an object can "distinguish form", i.e. be grasped visually, only if it is viewed from aside, Bushy appears to *depart* from his own thesis by advising the Queen that her "looking awry upon your lord's departure, / Finds shapes of grief more than himself to wail" (ll. 21–2). In other words, Bushy's argument itself becomes split and redoubled here in his paradoxical suggestion that the Queen is "looking awry" at Richard's departure precisely because she fails to "look awry". It is in the Queen's response that we find a much more pithy account of the logical paradoxes that are exposed in this (non) figure of anamorphosis. Impassive to Bushy's suggestion that her grief is in fact without foundation, the Queen develops the exhortation to "look awry" into the strange time of another detour, that of the *future anterior*:

[...] nothing hath begot my something grief,
Or something hath the nothing that I grieve –
'Tis in reversion that I do possess –
But what it is that is not yet known what,
I cannot name; 'tis a nameless woe, I wot.

(II.ii.36–40)

This idea that "nothing" can beget something is also, of course, central to

Jacques Lacan's extended consideration of anamorphosis in so far as it illuminates the retroactive dynamic of desire in the constitution of subjectivity. For Lacan, the anamorphic stain that appears to distort and temporarily undermine the consistency of so-called reality is analogous to the function of what he calls "the gaze as object *a*". What is peculiar about this object is the fact that it is, strictly speaking, a semblance, a nothing which takes the form of something only when it is apprehended by a sideways glance that constitutively *produces* it, *après coup*, as the (belated) "cause" of desire.[7] The Queen's suspicion that "'Tis in reversion that I do possess" (l. 38) provides a strangely eloquent gloss on Bushy's bungled excursus on anamorphosis: for it is precisely in this difficult sense of 'reversion' as 'a past that is yet to come' that subjectivity comes to be situated in the signifying chain.

Strictly speaking, the speech appears to suggest, there is nothing that precedes the movement of reflection since this movement itself 'posits its presuppositions' and produces the retroactive illusion according to which its object was given in advance. Following Derrida we could say that the logic of Bushy's speculations confounds the principles of classical mimesis in so far as they suggest that "the mime imitates nothing, reproduces nothing, opens up in its very origin the very thing [it] is tracing out".[8] The destination that is speculated upon here, rather, is one that is contingent upon a subject that (constitutively) lacks its own place: "As though on thinking on no thought I think, / Makes me with heavy nothing faint and shrink" (II.ii.31–3). Subjectivity finds itself inscribed here in a movement of some disjointing, disjunction or disproportion: as a 'cause' that eschews any nostalgia for the security of a point of departure. Opining to Bushy that she is unable to determine a "cause" (II.ii.6) of her grief, the Queen can only articulate her predicament through reference to the anachronism of how, in some uncanny sense, she perceives herself to be late with respect to that which has already happened to her in the future:

> [...] methinks
> Some unborn sorrow ripe in Fortune's womb
> *Is coming towards me*, and my inward soul
> With nothing trembles; at some thing it grieves;
>
> (II.ii.9–12 emphasis added)

Simultaneously anticipated *and* summoned from a single coming that exceeds figuration, the Queen appears to be in thrall here to a strange kind of telepathy which, according to Jacques Derrida, is also the constitutive ground of (im)possibility that haunts every telecommunication system whatever its content, form or medium.[9] Without deferral, nothing begins. In a speech which, like the play itself, gains its rhetorical power by adopting what can only be described as 'an apocalyptic tone', throughout *Richard II* this essentially ambivalent aspect of that which is to 'come' also becomes (and keeps on coming as) the tonal figure of a radical otherness that, following Derrida, may be described as deriving "only from the other, from nothing that may be an origin or a verifiable, decidable, presentable, appropriable, identity".

As its more familiar legal provenance implies, 'reversion' is concerned with inheritance in prospect: it yields, it brings back and *comes back* in a way that violates the very idea of an initial investment. Including the two mentions it receives in *Richard II* the term 'reversion' occurs only three times in Shakespeare's plays. Significantly, the third reference is to be found in *I Henry IV* where, doubtful of any improvement in their political fortunes, Hotspur is reassured by Douglas that there

> [...] now remains
> A sweet reversion – we may boldly spend
> Upon the hope of what is to come in.
>
> (IV.i.53)

Denoting at the same time that which is still to come and, in a more difficult sense, something that ostensibly 'remains' as the retroactive product of this speculation, reversion here seems to imply an understanding of the remainder as that which precedes its own temporal genesis. In a text where, as we shall see, the question of the mimetic fidelity of the mirror is the focus of considerable anxiety, Bushy's meditations on the perspective glass come to trouble conventional assumptions about mimesis and temporality. There is no simple reference here. Rather, following Derrida, it is more the case that "We are faced then with mimicry imitating nothing; faced, so to speak, with a double that doubles no simple, a double that nothing anticipates, nothing at least that is not itself already double."[10]

The recursive trajectory announced in the term 'reversion' returns us inevitably (and appropriately) to Queen Isabel's account of the anamorphic gaze, whose object is similarly revealed to be a mirage retroactively invoked by a surplus that forever exceeds the determination of presence. Considered within the context of a play like *Richard II*, which ultimately becomes ensnared by the logical confusions that arise when the law of "fair sequence and succession" (II.i.199) is placed in jeopardy, this apparently dialectical (and invisible) sleight of hand also constitutes the dramatic and, I would like to suggest, *traumatic* conditions of its putatively historical narrative. *Richard II* is a drama of de-positioning that consistently defies the logic of 'position' as such. Bearing within itself the recursive trajectory of that which is both rejected *and* withheld, the text's historical project is impelled under the aspect of a curious auto-affection which I will read alongside Jacques Derrida's analysis of that more contemporary myth of origins and filiation, the Freudian *fort/da*. In what follows I'd like to suggest a number of the ways that *Richard II* problematises classical accounts of mimesis in so far as it is a text that speculates on itself, comes back to itself, without ever leaving a scene of inheritance that is, ultimately, also a scene of writing.

Post

Richard II seems always to have an eye turned toward the future. With an air of resignation that is inexplicable given that his fate is far from decided, Richard somewhat precipitously invites his audience to "sit upon the ground / And tell sad stories of the death of kings" (III.ii.155–6). Similarly, after his deposition Richard's concern once again is with posterity, requesting that the Queen

> In winter's tedious nights sit by the fire
> With good old folks, and let them tell thee tales
> Of woeful ages long ago betid;
>
> (V.i.40–3)

Frequently telling its tale through the telling of tales that somehow postdate it, historical verisimilitude in *Richard II* is concerned less with a strategy of re-writing than of *overwriting* a text that increasingly comes to convey the impression that it is prior as well as posterior to any singular event. Simultaneously gathering itself together only to disperse itself again, *Richard II* shares much in common with a more contemporary myth of filiation and symbolisation: the Freudian double *fort/da* that, according to Derrida, "conjugates into the same genealogical (and conjugal) writing the narrated *and* the narrating of narrative".[11] This recursive movement is perhaps most conspicuously disclosed in the surfeit of doubling in the text, where *Richard II* bends itself even to the vertiginous and unfathomable limits of that which is "doubly redoubled" (I.iii.80). Famously, not only does the King himself come to engage in a dialogue with his own shadow, castles too are "doubly portcullis'd" (II.ii.65), Bolingbroke is charged with a "double wrong" (III.ii.215), Richard is on the lookout for "double tongues" (l. 21), the bows of soldiers are possessed of "double-fatal yew" (l. 117) and, in parting from Anne, Richard laments how he is "doubly divorc'd" (V.i.72).

Bearing in mind James Calderwood's observation that *Richard II* is "a divorcing play",[12] it is also the case that the text itself moves forward by doubling back through the detour provided by an original exclusion. In fact, *Richard II* increasingly comes to pose itself as it deposes itself, in so far as 'depositioning' becomes, strictly speaking, something that the text itself *performs*. If doubling raises the troubling suggestion that there can only ever be an essential duplicity without an original, bibliographical efforts to negotiate an authentic version of the text largely come to rest, appropriately, on the 'deposition scene'. Critical debate over the 'origins' of the scene in the light of its reappearance in the fourth quarto of 1608 inevitably turns upon the unacknowledged suspicion that the origin is always already an addition. Either the scene is assumed to be a 'later' addition to the text[13] or something that already existed in performance. Despite John Jones's confident assertion that "the fourth quarto merely restores what was there at the start", the deposition scene is already the site of an overwritten erasure, de-positioning the origin as an effect that is produced *ex post* by a text that falls short of itself from the start.[14] In other words, what is simultaneously at issue and disavowed in these editorial disputes – with its stockpiling of additions and subtractions (both of which amount to the same thing in a differential order) – is that, in Derrida's words, any temptation to go "back from the supplement to the source must recognize that there is a supplement at the source".[15]

According to Jean-Luc Nancy every nostalgia for a primal scene is coterminous with a 'storytelling' that tries to remain innocent of another scene: that of writing itself. In an argument that is evocative of the metaleptic scenography of *Richard II*, Nancy argues: "We know the scene: there are men gathered around, and someone telling them a story …

They were not gathered before the story, it is the telling that gathers them … It is the story of their origin."[16] There is a subtle yet crucial displacement at work here: the origin of the 'nation' cannot be sought in stories; it is the very act of narration that constitutes an origin aporetically in an impossible moment of foundation and legitimation.

In the beginning there was the 'post'. That is to say, it is precisely in so far as the founding moment is always already mobilised by this *post* that the nation narrates and produces its effects of legitimacy through repetition. In so far as we can consider *Richard II* a text that is, in this particular respect, uniquely concerned with the institutional politics of the 'Nation', both at a diegetic level *and* as the traumatic narrative origin of Shakespeare's history plays, it is also the case that it can only acquit this task problematically: through certain postal effects that challenge any view of history as a narrative where events conform to a tidy seriality. In an argument that provides added significance to the occasion of Aumerle's purloined letter in the play, Geoffrey Bennington argues that "if the nation was not troubled by the necessary possibility of the letter's not arriving, then the state would be absolute and have no relation to any outside: it could not strictly speaking be a nation […] it would have no history, and thus no narration".[17]

In short, my point is that throughout *Richard II* it is the very idea – central to classical accounts of mimesis – of there being an initial and initiating point of departure that the text simultaneously invokes and renders most enigmatic. It is in Gaunt's elegiac speech, however, where both the nation and narration most obviously and ineluctably come into contact with a certain postal effect. In Gaunt's famous evocation of England as "This other Eden, demi-paradise" (II.i.40–68; 42) nothing less than a myth of national origins appears to be endangered by Richard's financial mismanagement. Venerating England as the product of a strange kind of auto-genesis, "This fortress built by Nature for herself / Against infection" (II.i.43–4), Gaunt's metaphors also repeatedly make appeal to a logic of the boundary in an attempt to quarantine the nation from any relation to an outside, as "in the office of a wall, / or as a moat defensive to a house" (ll. 46–7).

It is, however, precisely this erosion of the boundary that clandestinely renders possible any movement of a 'return' to origins. The very idea of a retreat before the boundary, of that which England must ambivalently "beat back", is also secretly called for by the very institution that patrols it.

It is at the end of his speech that Gaunt's speculations upon the multiple senses of the term 'boundary' come into closest proximity with the scene of writing:

> England, *bound* in with the triumphant sea,
> Whose rocky shore *beats back* the envious siege
> Of wat'ry Neptune, is now *bound* in with shame,
> With inky blots and rotten parchment *bonds*;
>
> (II.i.61–4)

The threatened erasure of the boundary here gives rise to another kind of insolvency; that of a bond which simultaneously binds and detaches (dispatches) identity from itself in an athetic movement that, according to Derrida, is unthinkable outside consideration of what he calls the "postal principle". In *The Post Card: From Socrates to Freud and Beyond*, Derrida discusses the topology at work in the lexicon of the boundary as, precisely, "collapses of the coastline", an essential divisibility that is accompanied by "strategies of approach and overflow, strictures of attachment, *places of reversion*, strangulation, or *double bind*" (emphasis added).[18] In one episode that has a more explicit bearing on writing, the Duke of York urges his son to show him the contents of a letter dismissed by his wife as "nothing but some band that he is ent'red into":

> Bound to himself? What doth he with a bond
> That he is bound to? Wife, thou art a fool.
> Boy, let me see the writing.
>
> (V.ii.65; 67–9)

It is precisely this enigmatic syntax of binding/unbinding – as a movement that does not have at its disposal the unified space of a figure – that also concerns Gaunt. Asphyxiating itself on the economy of its own reserves, Gaunt's conviction that England "Hath made a shameful conquest of itself" (II.i.66) and that the "state of law is bondslave to the law" (l. 113) indicates what kind of double bind is involved when difference infiltrates the origin: England's identity is so indebted to itself ("leas'd out" – l. 59) that any return (owed) to itself merely 'amounts' to a further expropriation of itself. Mortgaged to the perfidies of the signifier, in the image of "inky blots" we find a striking suggestion of how, turning away from itself, Richard's 'England' now occupies a relation of belonging that is without interiority: like writing, it is constitutively bound to (for) itself only by acceding to the threat of its own erasure.

Long before Richard's 'formal' deposition, then, Gaunt draws attention to an originary violence of writing as the agent of a "usurpation [that] has always already begun".[19] This suggestion that writing alienates identity from essence, that it eats away at the entire scene of inheritance with its "rotten parchment bonds" (l. 64) is especially ironic in a play that, as Jonathan Goldberg has so powerfully argued, cannot repress its "relationship to an emerging textuality".[20] Derrida's reading of the paradigmatic scene of Freud's *fort/da* (with its own interminable movement of binding/unbinding) also argues that questions of "inheritance ... of genealogy, of the paradoxes of nomination, of the king"[21] are tied to a telematics of the post that constitutively unmoors identity from every assured destination.

I would also like to suggest that this movement of self-division that is the focus of censure both legitimises and negates the 'myth of origins' so conspicuously staged throughout the scene. Closer examination reveals how Gaunt's narrative is remarkable precisely in the way that it so often violates the genealogical axioms of continuity, tradition and providentialism in the speech that some critics have read unproblematically as a redaction of Elizabethan ideology. For example, in a particularly sinuous contamination of present and past tenses Gaunt admonishes Richard that

> ... had thy grandsire with a prophet's eye
> Seen how his son's son should destroy his sons,
> From forth thy reach he would have laid thy shame,
> Deposing thee before thou wert possess'd,
> Which art possess'd now to depose thyself.
>
> (II.i.104–8)

In Gaunt's fantasy the scene of inheritance once again gives way to a complex pattern of forward and recursive loops. The image of the grandfather as one who comes "forth", who, through a teleological paradox, is simultaneously posed both before and after his grandson, bears a striking resemblance to Derrida's analysis of the Freudian scene of inheritance. According to Derrida, grandson Ernst's 'calling himself back' and Freud's 'posting' himself, writing to himself from a position not yet existing, point not beyond the pleasure principle so much as to a 'postal principle' that both disorders and gives rise to every genealogical model whatever its content or medium. So too in Gaunt's speech we find this double conjugation of annulment and return – of posing and deposing, possession and dispossession – that confounds the very logic of position as such. Already something of a *revenant* himself, even Gaunt's solicitation of a 'beyond' in the guise of a prophet is caught up in this contradictory movement of a 'coming back' that annuls its own ostensible grounds of possibility; of that which has barely come to leave when it is going to come back: "Methinks I am a prophet new inspir'd, / And thus expiring do fortell of him" (II.i.31–2). So too in Gaunt's description of Richard as "my brother Edward's son", and in his lament that Edward's "son's son should destroy his sons" (II.i.105) we find an equivocal syntax of the possessive and the genitive function that is not merely an artefact of grammar. This dissemination or threatened erasure of filiation is hinted at throughout the text: the Duchess of Gloucester relates to Gaunt as "thy sometimes brother's wife" (I.ii.54); speaking to Mowbray Richard refers to Bolingbroke as "our cousin, cousin" (I.iv.20) and addresses Gaunt as "brother to great Edward's son" (II.i.121). Harry Berger Jr.'s astute observation that *Richard II* repeatedly comes up against "a structural flaw in the very notion of mimesis, [that] is magnified by confusion in the paternal deployment of the genealogical principle",[22] may be glossed with the further suggestion that the text's ascending and descending trajectories inscribe this capacity for dissemination as the very thrust of its historical project. With England's indebtedness to "rotten parchment bonds" it is, specifically, writing that threatens to throw into disarray this genealogical principle that, as Derrida has argued, has long since been the safeguard of classical models of mimesis. Writing, in other words, becomes orphaned; "being nobody's son at the instant it reaches inscription, [it] scarcely remains a son at all and no longer *recognizes* its origins, whether legally or morally".[23] And yet, as I would like to argue in more detail, it is the text's very lexicon of doubling, binding and reversion that gives rise to history in a way that would not be possible "if the place of the letter were not divisible from the start".[24]

The step (not) beyond

Whither, then, are we led by such speculations? Let us risk a leap forward to *I Henry IV* where Hal's delinquent behaviour is compared, significantly, to that of Richard who is described as "The skipping King, [who] ambled up and down, / With shallow jesters, and rash bavin wits" (III.ii.60–1). This idea of a degenerate and tottering monarch is developed further in an image that presents Richard as someone who was, quite literally, a pushover, who would "stand the push / Of every beardless vain comparative" (ll. 66–7). In a footnoted reference to this sobriquet of "The skipping King" the Arden editor of the play remarks somewhat imperiously that "There is nothing like this behaviour in *Richard II*."[25]

Let us take a step back. If *Richard II* discloses a certain recursive and athetic trajectory that we have been discussing in terms of the problematic of the 'postal principle', the text is no less emphatically caught up (possibly even ensnared) in the thematics and the lexicon of the step, a rhetoric of *going* or *aller* that is also of interest to Derrida under the rubric "of the way or the a-way, of the near and the far, of all the frameworks in *tele-*, of the adestination [...]".[26] Time and again *Richard II* advances a rhetoric of the 'step' as that which simultaneously registers and then hollows out the very distance that it is ostensibly called upon to measure. Indeed, the entire text returns time and again to this strange separating movement that frequently finds itself on the curvature of a return, so that each step of the drama is as much retentional as it is protentional. As Richard's vacillation in the deposition scene, his re-signing, perhaps demonstrates most vividly – "Ay, no; no, ay" (IV.i.201) – to say the word 'not' of anything is still to speak and to leave in language that trace of one's approach (through negation) to the other. Holding together the double movement of approach and distancing that skews and displaces the determination of presence, the term *pas* in both Derrida and Blanchot is, rather, a composite term – simultaneously an adverb ('not') and a noun ('step') – whose overall movement exceeds the simple opposition either of affirmation or negation. This recursive trajectory whereby a step forward is somehow coterminous with a movement back is, we should recall, also the focus of Gaunt's conceit when the play kicks off as he attempts to reinscribe Bolingbroke's exile into the appeasing words of a poetic fancy:

> The sullen passage of thy weary steps
> Esteem as foil wherein thou art set
> The precious jewel of thy home *return*.
>
> (I.iii.265–7)

Do we not find here, in the necessarily ambivalent image of the "foil", an explicit association between the idea of 'speculation' as a venturing forth and as that which is constitutively allayed and delayed through the detour of a (specular) return? Implying, in other words, that a slippage occurs between identity and destination, Gaunt's metaphor encapsulates neatly both senses of "foil" as the rival which impedes self-reflection and also that which becomes the surface for a relayed appropriation of identity.

More specifically, this speech also obliges us to consider Jacques Lacan's seminal account of the mirror as that which, far from serving the exemplary function of mimesis as a moment of seamless reproduction and reflection, is in fact a site of radical ambivalence. According to Lacan the ego erects itself (*stands* by itself) only by *anticipating* itself on the basis of an irreducible 'stepping' behind itself. In so far as the text, as we shall see, encounters repeatedly the mimetic problems that accompany every attempt to 'pose-oneself-before-oneself',[27] as Richard's de-position scene illustrates perhaps most dramatically, we should bear in mind Lacan's assertions that the subject learns to hold itself straight, upright, by spatially identifying with the specular image. In a text that is manifestly concerned with the re-establishing of rights and property, *Richard II* makes legible a certain preoccupation with the feet as procuring the necessary space(s) for such *restitution*, a term which, according to Derrida, also implies "placing the subject upright again, in its stance, in its institution".[28] We may go so far as to claim that *Richard II* also evidences a certain orthopaedic anxiety in that it so consistently assumes this necessity of establishing the subject in an upright position.

Early in the text Mowbray sues for his rights to the King by invoking a term that is crucially concerned with the question of the subject's optical erection. Refuting Bolingbroke's charges Mowbray claims that "I am disgrac'd, impeach'd, and baffl'd here" (I.i.170). In (appropriately) a footnoted reference the Arden editor glosses the term "baffl'd" as a chivalric custom that "is used when a man is openly perjured, and then they make of him an Image paynted *reverted* with his heles upwarde".[29] From Richard's initial inquiry into whether there is "some known *ground* of treachery" (I.i.2) in Bolingbroke's appeal, the entire scene encodes a syntax of throwing down and taking up so that any grounds for appeal rest, quite literally, on whether the combatants are in full possession of their feet: Mowbray agrees to meet Bolingbroke "were I tied to run afoot [...] Where ever Englishmen durst set his foot" (I.i.53, 66), a challenge that is later modified in his promise to "hurl down my gage / Upon this overweening traitor's foot" (ll. 146–7). Even the King's intervention is implicitly punned upon as a reference to footwear:

> *Richard* Norfolk, throw down we bid, there is no boot
> *Mowbray* Myself I throw, dread sovereign, at thy foot.
>
> (I.i.164–5)

From Bolingbroke's initial (and ultimately specious) "farewell" to "England's ground" as a "mother" and "nurse that bears me yet!" (I.iii.306–7) we can discern an increasing preoccupation in the text with what Derrida calls "[a] fundamental subjectivity of the ground [...] along with this *pas de contact* (this *pas de sujet*) which rhythmically raises the adhesion of a march/walk/step".[30] "Look not to the ground", Richard at one point exhorts his dwindling band of supporters, "Yea favourites of a king, are we not high?" (III.ii.87–8). By contrast, when he is later imprisoned in the Tower, the recently deposed King is enraged by reports that his horse has conveyed Bolingbroke to the coronation "So proudly as if he disdain'd the ground": "Would he not stumble? Would he not fall down, / Since pride must have a fall, and break the neck / Of that proud man that did usurp his back?"(V.v.83; 87–9). The incidence of the "fall" here not only involves an alternation between high and low; the very threat of usurpation itself is also connected with an implied threat to the very availability of a "ground". Bearing in mind Richard's instruction that Northumberland "Tell Bolingbroke, for yon methinks he *stands*, / That every stride he makes upon my land / Is dangerous treason" (III.iii.91–3), the figure of the ground again appears to be something that is instituted rather than simply revealed through its adhesion to a certain step.

While *Richard II* variously implies a necessity of the step, of that which is closest to the ground, this step also threatens the very institutional stability of the ground as such: i.e., as something that is, in a radical sense, always already in the process of being usurped. So it is that we find an embattled Richard trying to resist attack on his kingdom by enlisting the help of "heavy-gaited toads" that will "lie in their way, / Doing annoyance to the treacherous feet / Which with usurping steps do trample thee" (III.ii.15–17). Again, it is around this question of the step, of the gait – especially in a text where "forbidden legs" that have "dared to touch a dust of England's ground" (II.iii.89–90) kick off the tragedy proper – that

Richard's fall comes to be implicated, quite literally, in what is *simultaneously* both a strange and pedestrian kind of movement: "[...] shoes are what you let fall. Particularly old shoes. The instance of the fall, the fallen, or the downfallen [...] You let something fall like an old shoe [...] The remainder is also this lowness."[31] That is to say, the question of the step in *Richard II* also rigorously concerns this speculative threshold, the separation or interval that speculation properly crosses over: "It passes over, it is beyond measure. It goes beyond the observable and the *visible*."[32] And is this not also the 'beyond' that Maurice Blanchot characterises as endemic to all writing? For Blanchot writing is indissociable from this step (*pas*) toward the not (*pas*) that is forever beyond (*au delà*), precisely in so far as writing exposes the decision of a lack that marks itself only by a surplus without place, that is impossible to assign to *a* place.[33] With the *step/not* – the possible identification of an intangible edge – the crossing of the line becomes a problem. Nowhere is this more evident than in the inconclusive trial between Mowbray and Bolingbroke. Poised to "set forward" into combat, Richard, inexplicably, commands that the appellants "return back to their chairs again" (I.iii.117; 120). Once again, the destination that this implied step renders possible has a form of advance that does not consist in passing, traversing or transiting, but rather which 'sets forward' in a movement of negation that the step is obliged to take back at the very next step.

Back

We will permit ourselves a slight detour at this point in order to suggest that the word 'back' disseminates throughout *Richard II* as a kind of tonal figure for this problem of what, precisely, it might mean either to take back or to come back. In this respect we are concerned with that ubiquitous 're-' in re-presentation, re-production and re-flection that is central to all mimetologism. Derrida discusses, as that which both threatens *and* inscribes the possibility of every arrival, this strange complicity between the word 'back' and the question of the destination in his claim that "There is only the *back*, seen from the back, in what is written [...] Everything is played out in retro."[34] In *Richard II* the word 'back' also assumes the burden of this equivocal spacing, of that which writes/is written. Like the step (*pas*), 'back' signals a certain trace of alterity whose movement is no longer determinable according to a linear and indivisible line. If, as

Nicholas Royle so patiently argues, there is "the incursion and recursion of the word 'back' whenever the prefix 're-' is in operation",[35] 'back' becomes the (postal) signature of the question of the 're-' in general: of a turning back that has no reality that is signifiable prior to this very turn in re-turning. Most strikingly, perhaps, it is the aborted contest between Mowbray and Bolingbroke that gestures toward this spacing. Instructing the combatants to "return back to their chairs again" (I.iii.120), Richard's use of 'back' here appears to be placed in a strangely superfluous kind of relation to 'return'. Simultaneously coming and going, moving literally "from one side to the other turning" (V.ii.18), the supplementary twists and turns of Richard's language are only further compounded by the neutralising syntax of his request that the combatants "Withdraw with us ... While we return these dukes what we decree" (I.iii.121–2). 'Return', 'back', 'again', 'withdraw': all of these terms clear an undecidable path that opens on to nothing other than the moment of de-cision itself, to "what we decree". The entire scene returns back to nothing apart from further effractions that serve only to expose the very enigma of this 'return'. Commanding Mowbray to "Return again" (I.iii.178) after having decreed the "hopeless word of 'never to return'" (l. 152), this ambivalence also comes to contaminate the very sense of Mowbray's leave-taking: "Farewell, my liege. Now no way can I stray / Save *back* to England all the world's my way" (ll. 206–7). How are we to understand (indeed, to follow) this recursive syntax? A perplexed Arden editor of the play heroically glosses the meaning as " I can never go astray now, except in returning to England; I am free to wander anywhere in the world."[36] In other words, what coming back amounts to here is, paradoxically, an arrival at the departure, an arrival that departs essentially from itself. We might also recall here how "York thrives to beat back Bolingbroke" (II.ii.143), or Gaunt's description of England's shores as that which "beats back the envious siege" (II.i.62), and, in what is perhaps the most strangely articulate comment on this double movement, the Queen's lament that hope is "a *keeper back* of death" (II.ii.70).

As a drama of seemingly interminable supplementary twists and turns, *Richard II* comes to implicate writing in an essential de-positioning that, along with Derrida, we might read as the original modality of the speculative itself. The 'play' appears never to advance anything that it does not immediately take back, "without ever positing anything which remains in its position [...]".[37] In particular Richard is frequently given to "saying what he does *as* he does it".[38] That is to say, the unusually large number of performative speech acts in *Richard II* also gravitate implicitly around this tension of the *fort/da* as that which is similarly always in the process of describing in advance the scene of its own description. Simultaneously posing and deposing, positing and depositing itself in the a-way of increasingly diminished returns, E.M.W. Tillyard's famous view of the text as "static"[39] may now be read not merely in terms of neutralisation, but as a movement immanent to the text – performed *by* the text – that is more complex than either affirmation or negation [*pas*]: "Ay, no; no, ay; for I must nothing be. / Therefore no 'no', for I resign to thee" (IV.i.201–2). It is in the deposition scene proper that Richard's rhetorical strategy implicitly turns upon a meditation on the Derridean logic of the gift:[40]

Bolingbroke Part of your cares you give me with your crown.
Richard Your cares set up do not pluck my cares down.
My care is loss of care, by old care done;
Your care is gain of care, by new care won.
The cares I give, I have, though given away,
They 'tend the crown, yet still with me they stay.
Bolingbroke Are you contented to resign the crown?
Richard Ay, no; no, ay; for I must nothing be.
Therefore no 'no', for I resign to thee.

(IV.i.194–202)

What we find in this vertiginous circuit of negation is not so much an oppositional logic of presence and absence as an exigency of profit and loss, proximity and distance that confounds the very logic of 'position' as such. De-position here is inextricably tied to a problematic of giving and taking precisely in so far as language carries within itself (counting and discounting) the process of its own erasure, while at the same time marking what "remains" of this erasure:

I give this heavy weight from off my head,
And this unwieldy sceptre from my hand,
The pride of kingly sway from out my heart,
With mine own tears I wash away my balm,
With mine own hands I give away my crown,
With mine own tongue deny my sacred state,

> With mine own breath release all duteous oaths;
> [...]
> What more remains?
>
> (IV.i.204–10; 222)

This entire speech is so characterised by an immanent radical textual instability that the word 'resign', as Jonathan Goldberg has wryly observed, is used as though "it meant both to give away and to write again",[41] something that is again uncannily evoked in Richard's exhortation to "*mark* me how I will *undo* myself" (IV.i.203). The much remarked upon solar metaphors in the text are not unrelated to this enigma.[42] As both Derrida and Bataille argue, the sun is, pre-eminently, that which both gives and takes in the same gesture: as the aneconomic, self-consuming figure par excellence, the sun constitutively eats away at the scene of its own inheritance: "The very opposition of appearing and disappearing, the entire lexicon of the *phainesthai*, of *aletheia*, etc., of day and night, of the visible and the invisible, of giving and taking, of the present and the absent – all this is possible only under the sun."[43] Richard's well-known moniker as the 'Sun King' is strangely appropriate then for a character who demonstrates considerable expertise at this level of hyper-phenomenology, as one who will "undo myself".

It is precisely this constitutive tension between identity and obliteration throughout the play, this paradox of something that is "disfigured clean" (III.i.8), which also announces a 'general economy' of writing as a (non) place where production stands in a necessary relation to the energy of its erasure.[44] Richard's exhortation to "*mark* me how I will undo myself" (IV.i.203) hints perhaps most persuasively at how every erasure is contingent upon the expedient of a 'mark' in the more recognisably Derridean sense: an exigent that, paradoxically, must insinuate itself minimally in the place of an absence in order to make it legible. That is to say, the very assumption of identity occupies a necessary relation to the ignominy of being "Mark'd with a blot" (IV.i.236) precisely in so far as every identity constitutively inheres in this accession to the period of its own erasure. In this respect, Richard's confrontation with the mirror brings the text into closest proximity to that moment where, according to Derrida, mimesis cannot repress its kinship to writing: "it is nothing other than the staging, the theatre, the visibility of nothing or the self. It is a dramatisation which illustrates nothing, which illustrates the nothing, lights up a space, re-marks a spacing as a nothing, a blank [...]."[45] Ultimately, these speculations should alert us to the significance of the so-called 'deposition scene' in a way that has hitherto largely been ignored in criticism of the play. While, classically, the term 'position' announces a form of constitution whereby something comes to be what it is through its relation to something other, according to Rodolphe Gasche, deconstruction (and *Richard II* it seems) announces "a (non) relation to an alterity that is itself the ground of possibility of positing itself".[46]

If Richard finds himself in the bizarre predicament of, in Marjorie Garber's words, "deposing at his own deposition",[47] we might also say that the text repeatedly imposes the necessity of de-position as something that both gives rise to and is caught, irreducibly, in the paradoxes of the 'postal principle'. Like its tragic protagonist, the text can never successfully "ravel out / [its] weaved up follies" (IV.i.228–9) perhaps because the text itself can arrive at itself, can destine itself only at the limit of a strange power of folding which, ultimately, cannot be unfolded. In so far as critical speculations about the subversive import of *Richard II* perennially return to the occasion of Queen Elizabeth's exchange with William Lambarde, we might end here (where we began) with Lambarde's particularly resonant description of how this discussion of *Richard II* with the Queen was in fact initiated. Previously hidden from view at the "back" of a door, the Queen chanced upon this file bearing the name of Richard II in the "Pandecta of all her rolls, bundells, membranes and parcells that be reposed in the Tower".[48]

In a text that finds such difficulty in constituting a relationship to an exterior that is revealed never to be completely outside, this "pandecta" of "rolls, bundells, membranes and parcells" recalls, irresistibly, the Derridean (non) figure of the 'hymen'. For Derrida, the hymen is the place of writing, troubling every threshold or limit between the sign and referent that is of such paradigmatic significance to classical accounts of mimesis: the 'hymen', that is, as the membranous and porous border that "eliminates the exteriority or anteriority, the independence, of the imitated, the signified, or the thing".[49] According to Derrida the hymen is not a place so much as the figure for a radical and ongoing displacement: "Through the re-marking of its semantic void, it in fact begins to signify. Its semantic void signifies, but it signifies spacing and articulation; it has as its meaning the possibility of syntax; it orders the play of meaning. Neither purely syntactic nor purely semantic, it marks the articulated opening of that opposition."[50] It is strangely appropriate then that, at the very moment when *Richard II* might be said to open on to the very contexts of its own historical possibility, the intangibility of an edge once more becomes a problem. Perhaps the meaning of Richard's tragedy is that which, as Bushy so astutely observes, is always still to come.

Chapter Two

1. John Nichols (ed.), *The Progresses and Public Processions of Queen Elizabeth*, vol. 3 (London, 1823), p. 552.
2. Much of the controversy extends back to the exchanges between E.M. Albright, 'Shakespeare's *Richard II* and the Essex Conspiracy', *PMLA* 42 (1927), pp. 686–728; and Ray Heffner, 'Shakespeare, Hayward and Essex', *PMLA* 45 (1930), pp. 745–80. An overview of subsequent developments in this debate is provided by Leeds Barroll, 'A New History for Shakespeare and his Time', *Shakespeare Quarterly* 34 (1988), pp. 441–64.
3. Stephen J. Greenblatt, *The Power of Forms in the English Renaissance* (Oklahoma: Pilgrim Books, 1982), p. 4.
4. Jonathan Dollimore and Alan Sinfield (eds), *Political Shakespeares: Essays in Cultural Materialism*, 2nd edn (Manchester: Manchester University Press, 1994), p. 8.
5. Quoted in Marion Hobson, *Jacques Derrida: Opening Lines* (London: Routledge, 1998), p. 181.
6. Quoted in Timothy Clark, *Derrida, Heidegger, Blanchot: Sources of Derrida's Notion and Practice of Literature* (Cambridge: Cambridge University Press, 1992), p. 134. Perhaps it is here that we find a suggestive context for Elizabeth's anxious recollection that Shakespeare's play was performed, specifically, in "*open* streets and houses". Dollimore argues that "what made Elizabeth I so anxious was not so much a retrospectively and clearly ascertained effect of the staging of *Richard II* [...] but the fact of the play having been appropriated – been given significance for a particular cause and in certain 'open' contexts". Dollimore, *Political Shakespeares*, p. 9.
7. Jacques Lacan, *The Four Fundamental Concepts of Psychoanalysis*, trans. Alan Sheridan (London: Penguin, 1994), p. 92.
8. Jacques Derrida, 'The First Session', in *Jacques Derrida: Acts of Literature*, ed. Derek Attridge (London: Routledge, 1992), pp. 127–81, p. 156.
9. In so far as the Queen's ruminations here can be called prophetic, her exchange with Bushy also reveals how prophecy, which "returns to itself from the future of its own to-come", renders any 'position' of enunciation deeply problematic. See Jacques Derrida, 'Telepathy', in *Oxford Literary Review* 10 (1988), pp. 3–43, p. 4.
10. Derrida, 'First Session', p. 157.
11. Jacques Derrida, *The Post Card: From Socrates to Freud and Beyond*, trans. Alan Bass (Chicago: University of Chicago Press, 1987), p. 303.
12. James Calderwood, *Shakespearian Metadrama* (Minneapolis: University of Minnesota Press, 1971), p. 84.
13. This still widely held view was first put forward by David Bergeron, 'The Deposition Scene in *Richard II*', *Renaissance Papers* (1974), pp. 31–7, p. 35.
14. John Jones, *Shakespeare at Work* (Oxford: Clarendon Press, 1999), p. 41.

15. Jacques Derrida, *Of Grammatology*, trans. Gayatri Chakravorti Spivak (Baltimore, MD and London: Johns Hopkins University Press, 1980), p. 304. In a pithy essay that also reconsiders the relationship between the Shakespearean text and the question of source, Jonathan Goldberg maintains that "there is no [...] source of the text except through a relay of mediations [...] even the supposed ultimate source – the author – must be considered within a heterogeneous dispersal". Goldberg, 'Speculations: *Macbeth* and Source', in *Shakespeare Reproduced: The Text in History and Ideology*, ed. Jean E. Howard and Marion O'Connor (London: Methuen, 1990), pp. 242–64, p. 242.
16. Jean-Luc Nancy, *The Inoperative Community* (Stanford, CA: Stanford University Press, 1996), p. 43.
17. Geoffrey Bennington, *Legislations: The Politics of Deconstruction* (London: Verso, 1994), p. 246.
18. Derrida, *Post Card*, p. 261.
19. Derrida, *Of Grammatology*, p. 37.
20. Jonathan Goldberg, 'Rebel Letters: Postal Effects from *Richard II* to *Henry IV*', *Renaissance Drama* 19 (1988), pp. 3–29, p. 6.
21. Derrida, *Post Card*, p. 222.
22. Harry Berger Jr., 'Psychoanalyzing the Shakespeare Text: The First Three Scenes of the Henriad', in *Shakespeare and the Question of Theory*, ed. Patricia Parker and Geoffrey Hartman (London: Routledge, 1985), pp. 210–30, p. 221.
23. Jacques Derrida, 'Plato's Pharmacy', in *A Derrida Reader: Between The Blinds*, ed. Peggy Kamuf (New York: Columbia University Press, 1991) pp. 112–42, p. 117.
24. Derrida, *Post Card*, p. 324.
25. *King Henry IV Part 1*, ed. A.R. Humphrieys (London: Routledge, 1978), p. 103, n. 60ff.
26. Derrida, *Post Card*, p. 268.
27. Quoted in Mikkel Borch-Jacobsen, *Lacan: The Absolute Master*, trans. Douglas Brick (Stanford, CA: Stanford University Press, 1994), p. 60.
28. Jacques Derrida, 'Restitutions of the Truth in Painting [*peinture*]', in *The Truth in Painting*, ed. Geoffrey Bennington and Ian McLeod (Chicago and London: University of Chicago Press, 1987), pp. 257–382, p. 286.
29. *King Richard II*, ed. Peter Ure (London: Routledge, 1996), p. 14, n. 170.
30. Derrida, *The Truth in Pointing*, p. 284.
31. Ibid., p. 305.
32. Derrida, *Post Card*, p. 380.
33. I am referring here to Maurice Blanchot's essay entitled *The Step Not Beyond*, trans. Lycette Nelson (Albany, NY: State University of New York Press, 1992). Both here and elsewhere in his later work Blanchot never ceased to interrogate the scene of writing as that which at once traces and effaces, where the *pas* is at once prohibition and transgression. For Blanchot this *pas* must be read simultaneously as negation and the trace or movement of an advance. We might risk a summation of Blanchot's concerns in the suggestion that the step (*pas*) beyond is never completed, or, if it is completed, is never really beyond. Transgression never really transgresses, but only calls for another limit.
34. Derrida, *Post Card*, p. 48.
35. Nicholas Royle, 'Back', *Oxford Literary Review* 18 (1996), pp. 145–58, p. 147.
36. *King Richard II*, ed. Ure, p. 33, nn. 206–7.
37. Derrida, *Post Card*, p. 284.
38. Joseph A. Porter, *The Drama of Speech Acts: Shakespeare's Lancastrian Tetralogy*

(Berkeley, CA and London: University of California Press, 1979), p. 32. In a comment that also provides a useful gloss on the text's problems with destinations, Porter avers that the play "distinctively tends toward the unmarked non-specific direction of address", p. 40.

39. E.M.W. Tillyard, *Shakespeare's History Plays* (London: Penguin, 1991), p. 251.
40. According to Derrida the opposition of to give and to take, of to possess and to be possessed, is a kind of transcendental snare that is an effect of writing. More particularly, it is possible to discern in Richard's resignation speech, both rhetorically and idiomatically, an expression of how "[...] giving-taking in general a priori folds back on language and writing as giving-taking. Giving would come back, come down to taking and taking to giving, but this would also come back to fold itself over not only a language or writing but toward the text in general." Jacques Derrida, *Given Time: I. Counterfeit Money*, trans. Peggy Kamuf (Chicago and London: University of Chicago Press, 1994), p. 81.
41. Goldberg, 'Rebel Letters', p. 5.
42. This strain of imagery in the text has long been the focus of critical discussion. See, for example, Peter Ure's introduction to the play, pp. lxxi-ii. According to Derrida, however, the sun, strictly speaking, is not so much a 'metaphor' as that which announces a certain '*plus de metaphore*': that which betokens, simultaneously, 'more metaphor' and 'no more metaphor'. See Jacques Derrida, 'White Mythology', in *Margins of Philosophy*, trans. Alan Bass (Brighton: Harvester Press, 1982), pp. 207–71.
43. Ibid., p. 251.
44. For a now classic dialogue between Derrida and Bataille on the question of expenditure, see Jacques Derrida, 'From Restricted to General Economy: A Hegelianism without Reserve', in *Writing and Difference*, trans. Alan Bass (London: Routledge & Kegan Paul, 1978), pp. 251–77. I have been similarly concerned in this chapter to analyse those ways in which *Richard II* might be said to conform to the 'general economy' of writing, that is, those ways that it takes into account the non-reserve, of how, paradoxically, the text appears always to keep in reserve this non-reserve.
45. Derrida, 'First Session', p. 160.
46. Rodolphe Gasche, *The Tain of the Mirror: Derrida and the Philosophy of Reflection* (Cambridge, MA and London: Harvard University Press, 1986), p. 158. For Derrida, crucially, 'position' is not simply something addressed by discourse but is a dissimulation produced *by* discourse. To rethink position is therefore to rethink discourse: "As you know, deconstruction means, among other things, the questioning of what synthesis is, what thesis is, what a position is, what composition is, not only in terms of rhetoric, but what *position*, what *positing* means. Deconstruction questions the thesis, the theme, the *positionality* of everything [...]." Jacques Derrida, 'Jacques Derrida on Rhetoric and Composition: A Conversation', *Journal of Advanced Composition* 19 (1990), pp. 1–21, p. 8.
47. Marjorie Garber, *Shakespeare's Ghost Writers: Literature as Uncanny Causality* (London: Methuen, 1987), p. 8.
48. Nichols, *Progresses and Public Processions of Queen Elizabeth*, pp. 552–3.
49. Derrida, 'First Session', p. 174.
50. Ibid., p. 176.

CHAPTER THREE

Platonism and bathos in Shakespeare and other early modern drama

Gabriel Egan

Imitations: play, repertory, venue

IT HAS LONG BEEN noticed that the events of Shakespeare's play *Romeo and Juliet* and those of the play of Pyramis and Thisbe in his *A Midsummer Night's Dream* are alike, and that the former treats seriously what is farcical in the latter. Roger Prior showed that a single source, either George Gascoigne's *The Poesies*[1] or his *Whole Works*,[2] was used for both plays, and in particular the description of a masque to celebrate the marriage in 1572 of two children of Anthony Browne, 1st Viscount Montague.[3] As well as verbal parallels there are collocations of ideas and images, such as strangers daring to enter a feast (as in *Romeo and Juliet* I.v) and phrases about the anticipation of the wedding (as used by Theseus and Hippolyta in *A Midsummer Night's Dream* I.i). Shakespeare then appears to have moved to a poem called 'The Refusal' on the facing page of Gascoigne's *The Poesies* and mined it for the rivalry of Demetrius and Lysander (I.i) and of Hermia and Helena (III.ii). The Gascoigne link gives us additional reason to consider *Romeo and Juliet* and *A Midsummer Night's Dream* as paired plays and to attend to Shakespeare's telling of one story two ways, one tragical and one comical.

The story of Pyramis and Thisbe comes from the Roman poet Ovid's *Metamorphoses* that Shakespeare read in Arthur Golding's English translation that went through seven editions between 1567 and 1612 (STC 18956–62), and it is not surprising that such a well-known Ovidian contemporary as Gascoigne should be amongst Shakespeare's simultaneous reading as he wrote *A Midsummer Night's Dream*. Of course, Shakespeare did not need Golding's translation of Ovid, for he read the Latin text for himself[4] and probably kept both versions open in front of him as he wrote *A Midsummer Night's Dream*. The evidence for this is that Golding's phrases occur in the Hermia/Helena story and yet the "Ninny's tomb" (III.i.91) gag seems to come directly from Ovid's Latin: "ad busta Nini".[5] Moreover, the Hermia/Helena phrases come from the Pyramis and Thisbe material in Golding, so for Shakespeare the high and low characters within *A Midsummer Night's Dream* are related; indeed the farcical lovers and the serious ones share a common language.[6] The two books open in front of Shakespeare were also the same story in different forms, one the language of his Stratford grammar school education and serious art and scholarship, the other the demotic language in which he wrote for the London stage. Enemies of the new theatre industry complained that it reduced elevated themes to mundanity, and as the industry developed in the 1580s this falling off, it seemed to them, accelerated with a new generation of writers. When Shakespeare came to London in the late 1580s or early 1590s the chief dramatists were university-educated men: John Lyly, Christopher Marlowe, Robert Greene, George Peele, Thomas Nashe and Thomas Lodge. Shakespeare, by comparison, was less thoroughly educated, and some of the university men thought they could detect a whiff of intellectual decay across the theatre industry.

A sense that modern versions fail to meet the perfection of the ancient originals pervades early modern drama's engagements with classical culture, but *A Midsummer Night's Dream* playfully locates that anxiety in the classical world itself: a bad impersonation of Pyramis is given at the Athenian court of mythical Theseus by an actor who believes himself capable of playing Hercules (I.ii.24–5). The prologue's explanation of the bad luck governing Romeo and Juliet's love invokes a cosmological and providential model of the world which the play renders unnecessary by showing the mere stupidity which occasions the disaster. In a modern production the degree to which the cosmological cause is suppressed in favour of quotidian causes is often an index of the director's attitude towards the materialist trend in Shakespeare studies. It is possible to make Platonic sense of the over-abundance of causal explanations in the play: the local mistakes (the withheld letter, the compressed time-scheme) are instances of the essential cosmological flaw. Informing the drama of the period's imitations of classical ideals, and especially its uses of bathos, is a response to Philip Sidney's self-conscious reversal of the Platonist model, a reversal which makes the 'beautiful lie' more true than reality.

The entire plot of *Pyramus and Thisbe*, as it occurs in *A Midsummer Night's Dream*, is a bathetic version of the story of the Athenian lovers and, much more closely, of the Veronese lovers in Arthur Brooke's *Romeus and Juliet*.[7] Yet the power relations that structured the occasion of the mechanicals' performance, it has been claimed by James H. Kavanagh, were essentially the same as those that structured the outer play too. The problem faced by the mechanicals is that faced by Shakespeare's fellows as they said to themselves:

> … for *us* to assert an effective ability to manipulate *their* sense of reality, for *us* to disrupt *their* lived relation to the real, would be an unacceptable usurpation of ideological power, possibly punishable by death; we must temper out dramatic practice, restrain its effect, and inscribe in it the marks of our own submission.[8]

In this reading, the fact that the nobles laugh at these fears only confirms the actual ideological conditions that forced the mechanicals to lay bare the constructedness of their entertainment. If this seems like a back-to-front argument – surely the laughter signals that the fears are groundless, that the nobles are willing to suspend disbelief freely and that the artisans' failure to realise this is comic – it is probably supposed to be: Kavanagh's essay is about ideology in Shakespeare and is called 'Shakespeare in Ideology'.

In *The Genius of Shakespeare* Jonathan Bate argued for the effect of Christopher Marlowe in particular upon the early career of Shakespeare, and that Shakespeare dealt with his admiration first by imitating Marlowe's characters and style, then parodying them and finally writing his own versions of them that in effect gave Marlowe an after-life.[9] For Bate these stages occurred successively, but, as this essay will argue, imitation and parody ran through the entire culture of early modern theatre in which Shakespeare worked. The new London theatre industry that emerged in the second half of the sixteenth century built for itself new performance venues unlike any other buildings of the time: wooden open-air amphitheatres in the Roman style. Before the construction of the first permanent theatre spaces in London in the 1560s and 1570s, the large yards of the inns of the city of London were used for dramatic performance. The yards, designed for the unloading of wagons, were enclosed on three or four sides and had galleries around their edges that provided access to the upper rooms available for nightly rental. With the addition of a portable stage, an inn-yard made an effective theatre with space for spectators standing around the stage and under or within the galleries. The first recorded performances were at the Saracen's Head, Islington and the Boar's Head, Aldgate in 1557.[10] E.K. Chambers thought that the Red Lion was such an inn-playhouse, but new evidence shows that, despite the unlikely-sounding name, this was a farm converted to a playhouse in 1567.[11] The stage and galleries were constructed in the garden of the farm by John Brayne, James Burbage's brother-in-law. The galleries were a single storey and the stage was 40 feet by 30 feet by 5 feet high with an attached turret – purpose unknown – reaching some 30 feet above the ground. The entire structure was cheap (under £20 compared to the Theatre's £700), rested on the ground without foundations, and there is no evidence that it lasted beyond the summer of 1567; the contract with the carpenter was to end with the successful conclusion of the first performance of "the play which is called the story of Sampson".[12]

The familial connection between Brayne and Burbage makes it tempting to consider the Red Lion as a prototype for the first substantial open-air playhouse, the Theatre built in 1576 by Burbage in the Shoreditch district just north-east of the city and hence beyond the jurisdiction of the city authorities. A typical corollary to this has been 'and hence beyond the reach of anti-theatricalists', but the early-twentieth-century theatrical history model of a puritan city harrying the players and a fun-loving court protecting them has recently been revised. Margot Heinemann showed that puritans were not simply anti-theatrical and many anti-theatricalists were not puritans.[13] Scott McMillin and Sally-Beth MacLean showed that we can no longer imagine that theatre companies were merely a representative component of humanism's break from religious ideology; the Queen's men formation, for example, was a result of motives "not so much humanist as royalist and Protestant".[14] The relationship between court and city regarding the theatre industry is better understood as a dialectic than a mere struggle, and one largely responsible for the rapid growth of the joint-stock playing companies, at least until Charles I's succession in 1625, whereafter the players were increasingly aligned solely with the court. The Theatre was the model for the open-air playhouses of the new industry that Shakespeare entered, and it was essentially copied in Philip Henslowe's Rose theatre (1587) and Francis Langley's Swan (1595), and its particularities were effectively reborn when it was transplanted to Bankside to form the Globe in 1599 and again when a second Globe was built on the foundations of the first after a fire in 1613.

In 1596 a Dutch humanist scholar, Johannes De Witt, visited the Swan and drew a picture of it that his friend and fellow classicist Aernout van Buchell copied; this copy is extant. De Witt's sketch is the only surviving interior view of an open-air playhouse of the period and it shows a virtually round amphitheatre of between sixteen and twenty-four sides with a stage projecting into the yard surmounted by a stage cover supported on two pillars. External views of the Swan also appear in a number of pictures of London, including a 1627 map of the Paris Garden Manor which appears to show the Swan having a single exterior staircase.[15] None of the external views of the Swan is a reliable guide to its dimensions, but the Hope playhouse contract specified that it should be "of suche large compass, fforme, widenes, and height as the Plaie house called the Swan".[16] Wenceslaus Hollar's sketch of the second Globe shows the Hope to be about 100 feet across, and we may assume the Swan was about the same.[17] De Witt described the Swan as the largest of the London playhouses of its day and wrote that it was made out of an aggregate of flint stones ("ex coacervato lapide pyrritide"), a detail we must doubt given the construction practices of the day.[18] The large wooden columns supporting the stage cover were painted like marble so cleverly as "to deceive the most inquiring eye", and perhaps the external rendering too was deceptive. The described interior marbleisation, the circular shape and the use of classical columns with ornate bases and capitals put the Swan in a neo-classicist tradition of design emerging at the end of the sixteenth century, despite the apparent Tudor bareness of the sketch.

Only one more open-air amphitheatre was erected before the general theatre closure of 1642, the Hope of 1613–14 on the site of the old Bear Garden that the builder Gilbert Katherens was instructed by Henslowe to first demolish. As well as the construction contract for the Hope, several pictures of it survive in the form of preliminary sketches and a final engraving by Wenceslaus Hollar made in 1641. Famously, the engraving has two of its labels reversed, so the the Hope is labelled the Globe and the Globe is labelled "the bearbaiting h[ouse]".[19] The open-air amphitheatres were the only round (or virtually round) buildings in London, and were the first purpose-built theatres for a thousand years. Their antecedent was not the Greek amphitheatre, which had a shallow bowl shape and one tier of seating sweeping upwards, but the Roman amphitheatre as exemplified in the Colosseum, which stacked one deck of galleries on top of another. James Burbage named his playhouse of 1576 the Theatre presumably to make explicit its dependence on the classical model, as its round shape and stacked galleries implied. Foreign visitors got the point and repeatedly referred to the London theatres looking like Roman amphitheatres[20] and were impressed by the faux-marble interior decoration. Eyewitness Johannes De Witt described the painted wooden interior of the Swan as cunningly deceptive and, as C. Walter Hodges pointed out, De Witt's evidence shows that the London amphitheatre was essentially a Renaissance rather than a Tudor design.[21] De Witt's description of the stage posts' "marmoreum colorem" (coating of marble colouring), their entasis, and their ornate bases and capitals all point to classical and Continental influence upon the indigenous building tradition. But De Witt's description of the Swan as made out of flint stones is in conflict with our knowledge that playhouses were timber-framed buildings, although it is possible that an in-fill of flint was used between the timbers. Possibly De Witt was misled into thinking the building was made of flint because its exterior was plastered over and painted to look like stone. The contract for the Fortune theatre specifies that "all the saide fframe and the Stairecases thereof to be sufficyently enclosed wthoute wth lathe lyme & haire"[22] and, to judge from the sketches and engraving of Hollar, the second Globe had such a coating too.

The theatrical venues, then, were of themselves a harking back to a lost European culture that might be revived but which would exist again in synthesis with native Tudor materials and practices. To that extent, we should not be too wary of the term 'Renaissance', which begs no fewer questions than the historians' preferred term 'early modern', which, Douglas Bruster observed, is really "its structural equivalent". Indeed the apparently even more fuddy-duddy alternative 'The Age of Shakespeare' has at least the advantage of "signalling who pays the piper of our academic tune" in the sense of identifying the man without whose work the period would be much less studied.[23] But were the theatres a falling-off from the high standards of the past? Some university men wrote as though they were, or at least they would be if other, lesser writers with lower standards were permitted to debase them. This is the thrust of

Greene's Groatsworth of Wit, with its account of the player who has "terribly thundred on the Stage, and plaid the Scenes of the Deuill in the High way to heauen", who "was a countrey Author … and for seuen yeers space was absolute Interpreter to the puppets".[24] If the company of such men can bring down the university-educated poet Roberto of the story, what disasters must befall the theatre when "an vpstart Crow, beautified with our feathers", a mere player, "supposes he is as well to bombast out a blanke verse" as the best poets? Such a Jack-of-all-trades ("Iohannes fac totum") could not be a gentleman, as Bate observed.[25]

The single most powerful connection between the world of university learning and the new theatre industry is Marlowe himself, whose early plays popularised the dramatic use of blank verse, the "mighty line" according to Jonson when praising Shakespeare's improvement upon it.[26] The thoroughly "lugubrious" *Greene's Groatsworth of Wit*, as Constance Brown Kuriyama put it,[27] alludes to Marlowe as the "famous gracer of Tragedians" who, despite "excellent wit", foolishly "hath said … There is no God" because misled by "pestilent Machivilian pollicy".[28] In his *Alphonsus, King of Aragon*[29] Greene unsuccessfully imitated Marlowe's *Tamburlaine*, and Kuriyama saw Greene's *Friar Bacon and Friar Bungay* as "a transparent comic rejoinder to Marlowe's *Tragical History of Doctor Faustus*".[30] The important point is not that Greene imitated – they all did – but that he failed. As Roslyn Lander Knutson showed, imitation was usual:

> … similarities [between companies' repertories] arose from a principle of duplication. Companies repeated the subjects and formulas that had been successful in their own offerings and in the repertories of their competitors. This principle accounts for the proliferation of offerings on a popular hero; the growth of species of plays within the framework of each genre; the multiplication of a play into two, three, or even four parts; and the emergence of a minor character from one play to become the star in a sequel.[31]

'Imitation' is the usual translation of Aristotle's word 'mimesis', and in relation to classical works its full range of meanings is notoriously difficult to define although clearly copying of some sort comes into it.[32] In *The Republic*, Plato used 'mimesis' in the sense of representation in his famous attack on visual and poetic art in which he claimed that because any real-world object, say a bed, is only an imitation of a perfect Idea or Form of 'bed-ness', a painting of, or a poem about, a bed necessarily is only an imitation of an imitation.[33] Aristotelian and Platonic notions of, and differences of opinion over, the meaning of mimesis in relation to representation suffused literary and dramatic theory in the early modern period, and are central to Philip Sidney's landmark 'refiguring' of the terms of the debate, his *Defence of Poetry*, as we shall see. But it is worth noting at this point that simple copying of another's company's repertory – their plays' heroes, themes and titles – was the standard practice of an early modern playing company.

Greene's *Friar Bacon and Friar Bungay* certainly has something in common with Marlowe's *Doctor Faustus*, but (*pace* Kuriyama) the direction of the copying is not clear. Although it has always been recognised that Shakespeare borrowed widely to make his plays this knowledge has strangely been suppressed in scholarly exploration of particular parallels between the works of Shakespeare and those of his contemporaries. If there is a parallel, it has been assumed, then Shakespeare must be the donor not the borrower. Thus Baldwin Maxwell argued that the anonymous *Thomas Lord Cromwell* must be later than Shakespeare's *Henry V* because it too has "crude and awkward" choruses reminiscent of the Shakespearean model and because of the incident in which "... Bedford's messenger brings Cromwell the note of warning and unsuccessfully urges him to read it at once as 'it doth concerne you neare,' a situation which closely parallels and may perhaps have been suggested by Artemidorus' proffered and rejected schedule in *Julius Caesar*, III, i".[34] That Artemidorus's rejected schedule might be the echo not the original apparently did not occur to Maxwell. Similarly Maxwell found what he took to be an echo of Capulet's "alack, my child is dead, / And with my child my joys are buried" (*Romeo and Juliet*, IV.iv.90–1) in the anonymous play *The London Prodigal*: "shee is dead and in her graue, my cares are buried".[35] R.A. Foakes tried to date Thomas Middleton's *The Revenger's Tragedy* from its similarities with Middleton's *A Mad World, my Masters*; *The Phoenix*; and *Blurt, Master Constable*, Marston's *Antonio's Revenge* and *The Fawn*, and Shakespeare's *Hamlet* and *King Lear*,[36] a necessarily hopeless task since none can reveal the direction of the debt.

Notions of private property in relation to speech and writing have changed fundamentally since the early modern period, and, as Margreta De Grazia observed, quotations marks came to be used not to record *sententiae* – important sayings that anyone might repeat – but combinations of words that belonged to the person who uttered them, which is a notion of ownership of one's labour derived from John Locke.[37] Such reversals in meaning grow out of the contradictory senses of words concerning mimesis in the early modern period, such as 'copy' being "The original writing, work of art, etc., from which a copy is made" (*OED*, copy *n.* 8a), and 'original' being "The fact of arising or being derived from something" (*OED*, original *n.* 1a) and at the same time "The thing (or person) from which something else arises or proceeds" (*OED*, original *n.* 2a). The Stationers' Company that regulated the early modern printing industry of London maintained a register of 'copy' to establish precedence in publishing rights, but without our modern sense of 'copyright': a book might be prevented because it dealt with the same subject as one already registered although written by a different author.[38] Thus the publisher of Shakespeare's *King Lear*[39] must have come to terms with the owner of the anonymous *King Leir* already in print.[40] Entry in the Stationers' Register defended not a writer's ownership of his words but a publisher's right of precedence to exploit a particular topic, so the early moderns would not have shared our surprise to find a writer copying another's phrases. The degree to which Shakespeare did this was shown by Stanley Wells[41] with an example from the account in *Henry V* of the French crown's descent by the female line:

> Hugh Capet also – who usurped the crown
> Of Charles the Duke of Lorraine, sole heir male
> Of the true line and stock of Charles the Great –
> To fine his title with some shows of truth,
> Though in pure truth it was corrupt and naught,
> Conveyed himself as heir to th' Lady Lingard,
> Daughter to Charlemain, who was the son
> To Louis the Emperor, and Louis the son Of Charles the Great.
>
> (I.ii.69–77)

It is clear that Shakespeare had open in front of him the third volume of the 1587 edition of Holinshed's *Chronicles* and more or less copied the following:

> Hugh Capet also, who usurped the crowne vpon Charles duke of Loraine, the sole heire male of the line and stocke of Charles the great, to make his title seeme true, and appeare good, though in deed it was starke naught, conueied himselfe as heire to the ladie Lingard, daughter to king

> Charlemaine, sonne to Lewes the emperour, that was son to Charles the great.[42]

To a modern mind used to the idea that Shakespeare took his plots from elsewhere but cloaked them in his own words, this shows little of the renowned Shakespearean invention, but that word 'invention' itself allowed for discovery not creation: "The action of coming upon or finding" (*OED*, invention *n.* 1). In classical rhetoric, invention in this sense of discovery and not "making up out of nothing"[43] was the essential step in composition.

Copying, then, was built into the theatre industry's venues (copies of Roman archetypes) and its companies' repertories (imitating one another's successes) and what Andrew Gurr called its "software",[44] the playscripts themselves that borrowed stories and their forms of expression. As a rhetorical term for the descent from the elevated to the commonplace, bathos was coined by Alexander Pope in the eighteenth century (*OED*, bathos *n.* 2), but in the imitative culture of early modern theatre it was all around in examples of the classical brought down to the Tudor. For Robert Greene, it existed in the very fact that university men were reduced to writing for the London stages. His *Friar Bacon and Friar Bungay* was performed at the Rose on Bankside on 19 February 1592,[45] and in it Edward III's fool Rafe Simnel imitates the Prince of Wales and bursts into the University of Cambridge Senate House where three learned doctors are making plans for the king's visit. They are not fooled by Rafe's imitation of the prince:

> *Raphe* Doctors whose doting nightcaps are not capable of my ingenious dignitie, know that I am Edward Plantagenet, whom if you displease, will make a shippe that shall hold all your colleges, and so carrie away the Niniuersitie with a fayre wind, to the Bankside in Southwarke, how sayst thou Ned Warraine, shall I not do it?[46]

Rafe's threat is absurd and the doctors have him carried away to prison. But the colleges *had* come to Bankside in the metaphorical sense of university men such as Greene writing this material; this bathos precedes and illuminates the main plot's concern with the prince's descent into love with a keeper of Fressingfield's daughter.

Early modern literary theory and performance

The doubleness of meaning available in early modern conceptions of 'original', 'invention' and 'copy' were put to theoretical use in Sir Philip Sidney's *Defence of Poetry*, which in its crucial section directly attacks Plato's sense of poetry as a copy of a copy. No "Art deliuered vnto mankind", not astronomy, geometry, arithmetic, music, philosophy, law, historiography, grammar, rhetoric, logic or medicine, "hath not the workes of nature for his principall object"[47] with one exception:

> Only the Poet disdeining to be tied to any such subjectio<n>, lifted vp with the vigor of his own inuention, doth grow in effect into an other nature: in making things either better than nature bringeth foorth, or quite a new, formes such as neuer were in nature: as the *Heroes*, *Demigods*, *Cyclops*, *Chymeras*, *Furies*, and such like; so as he goeth hand in hand with nature, not enclosed within the narrow warrant of her gifts, but freely raunging within the Zodiack of his owne wit. Nature neuer set foorth the earth in so rich Tapistry as diuerse Poets haue done, neither with pleasaunt riuers, fruitfull trees, sweete smelling flowers, nor whatsoeuer els may make the too much loued earth more louely: her world is brasen, the Poets only deliuer a golden.[48]

The poet bypasses the quotidian copies of Ideas that are all around us in Nature and connects with the Ideas themselves, and in the case of *Psalms of David* the work is "heauenlie poesie, wherin almost he sheweth himselfe a passionate louer of that vnspeakable and euerlasting bewtie, to be seene by the eyes of the mind, onely cleared by faith?"[49]

Why "almost"? Perhaps because the *Psalms* are still poetry, still representation not the thing itself. Or because Sidney feels that his argument is pulling towards the assertion that man's creativity is like God's, a claim that might sound profane. Having asserted that poets deliver a golden world, Sidney abruptly breaks off ("But let those things alone and goe to man …"), but his argument still draws him to compare human creativity to divine creativity (renamed Nature). Rather than liken the two kinds of creativity, he performs a manoeuvre that we should recognise as deconstructing the difference between them:

> Neither let this be iestingly co<n>ceiued, bicause the works of the one [Nature] be essenciall, the other [man] in imitation or fiction: for euerie vnderstanding, knoweth the skill of ech Artificer standeth in that *Idea*, or

> fore conceit of the worke, and not in the worke itselfe. And that the Poet hath that *Idea*, is manifest, by deliuering them foorth in such excellencie as he had imagined them: which deliuering foorth, also is not wholly imaginatiue, as we are wont to say by the<m> that build Castles in the aire: but so farre substancially it worketh, not onely to make a *Cyrus*, which had bene but a particular excellency as nature might haue done, but to bestow a *Cyrus* vpon the world to make many *Cyrusses*, if they will learne aright, why and how that maker made him.[50]

Sidney accepts that poetry is "an Art of *Imitation* … mimhsis [mimesis], that is to say, a representing, counterfeiting, or figuring forth to speake Metaphorically"[51] but rather than construct a lineage of descending, decreasing authenticity (Plato's Idea –> Instance –> Poetic-Copy) Sidney insists that representation is already present in the relationship between Idea and Instance, between the divine maker and the world he has created. Man's poetic creations stand to man, created in the divine maker's likeness, as God's creations stand to God. By inserting mimesis into the relationship between Platonic Idea and its manifestation, Sidney disables the objection that poets are only copiers with the insistence that reality is only a copy and hence poets are makers of reality.

Sidney's poetics can be fruitfully explicated in relation to the deconstructive project of Jacques Derrida. The key text is this regard is 'Section 4: From/Of the Supplement to the Source: The Theory of Writing', in *Of Grammatology*[52] in which Derrida situated his ideas within the context of Jean-Jacques Rousseau's and William Warburton's views on language. In Warburton's account, the language of speech derived from the gestural language of action, the latter being primary, while Jean-Jacques Rousseau saw two different sources: mere 'need' produced gestural signifying while passion "wrung forth the first words".[53] For Rousseau, signification itself was corrupted at source because figurative language preceded literal language. This counter-intuitive claim needs explanation, and Derrida offered the example of an early human coming across another human and in her terror seeing the potential enemy as someone much larger than herself, for which she invented the signifier 'giant'. Once this had happened enough times the fear wore off and the early human invented the literal 'human' for any other individual and reserved the earlier, fear-laden, term 'giant' for metaphorical use. While still fearful of others, 'giant' represented not what was seen (which was just another human) but the feeling of fear about what was seen, the passion inherent in the signified. But this signified itself was not singular: it represented not only the thing seen but the passionate feeling about the thing seen, so metaphoricity had already entered into the sign at the level of the signified, which was itself a signifier of the passion. The idea 'giant' literally represented the representer of the passion, but only metaphorically represented the 'human' and only metaphorically represented the feeling: "it is the sign of a sign ... It represents the affect literally only through representing a false representer"; a speaker or writer "can reproduce and calculate this operation" and so produce figurative speech or writing.[54] Thus metaphoricity exists at the heart of the sign so there are no literals: "*Il n'y a pas de hors-texte*";[55] the text has no 'outside' because the inside/outside distinction is false. In the popular modern phrasing, metaphor is always already at work and there can be no pure representation free of it.

When an actor-in-character stepped on to the early modern stage, he represented someone who formerly existed or who was invented by the dramatist. He ought not to represent someone alive, and certainly not someone important. As Andrew Gurr observed, the King's men miscalculated disastrously in performing in December 1604 a play about the Gower conspiracy of 1600 against James VI of Scotland (as he was then), for as John Chamberlain wrote the point was not so much "whether the matter or manner be not well handled" but that being represented at all should not happen to "princes ... in theyre life time".[56] It did not require a dramatist to bathetically mock his character, for the very act of representation was a debasement that important people had to be protected from. Ordinary people had no such protection, of course, and the poor women of Pendle who were accused of witchcraft in 1634 had more to fear from dramatic representation than mere humiliation: while they were still in jail awaiting a final verdict, the King's men performed at the Globe a dramatisation of their case, *The Witches of Lancashire*, that 'exposed' the foolishness of anyone who doubted their guilt.[57] In this class distinction we can see the power relations of early modern theatre, and it is instructive that, in his account of the destruction of the Globe by fire during a performance of Shakespeare's *All is True* (*Henry VIII*) in 1613, Henry Wotton worries that the greater the verisimilitude, the greater the harm:

> The King's players had a new play ... which was set forth with many extraordinary circumstances of pomp and majesty, even to the matting of the stage; the Knights of the Order with their Georges and garters, the

> Guards with their embroidered coats, and the like: sufficient in truth within a while to make greatness very familiar, if not ridiculous.[58]

It should be pointed out, in fairness, that the claim that representation was itself debasing was not confined to theatrical performance. In 1616 Jonson stopped writing plays after the failure of his *The Devil Is an Ass*, and he did not resume until 1625. During this period he devoted himself to writing court masques for which Inigo Jones provided the spectacle. It was a partnership that ended acrimoniously in 1631 with a semi-public war of words, and Jonson made a withering attack upon his former friend's work on the visual element of the court masque. "Mythology … painted on slit deal" and "ye mere perspectiue of an Inch board" were among the terms with which Jonson's 'Expostulacion w^t^h Inigo Jones' deflated the desire to represent grand themes in wood and canvas.[59]

The humiliating descent, then, was that of representation itself and when dramatists used bathos they gilded the lily. In *Bartholomew Fair* Jonson presented a puppet show based on Marlowe's translation of *Hero and Leander* that begins:

> ON *Hellespont* guiltie of True-loues blood
> In view and opposit two citties stood,
> Seaborders disioin'd by *Neptunes* might:
> The one *Abydos*, the other *Sestos* hight.[60]

To make it clear that it is Marlowe's version in particular, and not the Ovidian source, that is to be mocked, Jonson has the presenter of the puppets, Leatherhead (= Lantern), explain that Littlewit has adapted the printed text "to a more familiar straine for our people":

> *Lan[tern]* … that is too learned, and poeticall for our audience; what doe they know what *Hellespont* is? Guilty of true loues blood? or what *Abidos* is? or the other *Sestos* hight?[61]

Like Sidney, Jonson was aware of and wrote about the theoretical limitations of representation, and one of his playful devices for drawing attention to the constructed nature of authorship was the bravura display of meta-theatricality such as occurs in the Induction to *Bartholomew Fair*. An actor pretending to be the stage-keeper confides with the audience:

> But for the whole *Play*, will you ha' the truth on't? (I am looking, lest the *Poet* heare me, or his man, Master *Broome*, behind the Arras) it is like to be a very conceited scuruy one, in plaine English.[62]

Behind the voice that seems to come unscripted from a usually invisible, pre-theatrical, functionary of the venue (whose job is to sweep the stage before the actors enter) is the controlling voice of Jonson, mocking our complacency in assuming that what happens inside a theatre could be anything but a construction.

The building in which this took place, Philip Henslowe's Hope, was a radical break in playhouse design, for it replaced a bear-baiting arena and was specifically designed to accommodate performing animals and humans. It used to be argued that open-air amphitheatre playhouse design evolved from the design of animal-baiting arenas when someone had the bright idea of putting the booth stage of a group of travelling players inside one of Southwark's animal-baiting rings[63] but Oscar Brownstein demolished this theory by showing the unsuitability of an animal-baiting ring for the purposes of theatrical presentation.[64] The Hope was in fact the first dual-purpose arena, and so did not carry the neoclassical associations of the Theatre, Globe, Rose and Swan that so clearly drew on Continental taste. John Stockwood called the Theatre in Shoreditch a "gorgeous Playing place",[65] and scholarship on Elizabethan interior decoration suggests that all the playhouses were beautifully decorated.[66] The animal rings came from another tradition altogether that only merged with the theatrical when the Hope was built to rival the newly resurrected Globe in 1613–14.

Henslowe's site formerly showed only animal torture, but now it could show plays too, so one might argue that the tone of the area was raised by the theatricalists. Certainly, by the second decade of the century players were far from the travelling vagabonds they once were: the leading companies had royal patronage and Edward Alleyn founded the College of God's Gift in Dulwich in 1619 to signal his and his profession's new social status. But for Jonson, the Hope theatre venue for his new play *Bartholomew Fair* was an example of drama being dragged down to the level of bear-pit. Such a bathetic descent, however, could be appropriate if the subject matter were lowered to the same level, and hence the scrivener of his Induction observes that, in a perverse way, a sort of decorum has been observed: the venue is as "durty as *Smithfield* [the place represented], and as stinking euery whit".[67] Jonson's reflections on the world of playmaking are apparent in the puppet play that the anti-theatricalist Zeal-of-the-Land Busy fails to prove is profane: the accusation of cross-dressing does not stick because they have no gender-assigning genitals.

The puppets, then, are free of accusations of immorality that might be cast at human players, and yet curiously Jonson chose to include them in "The Persons of the Play"[68] as though they were human characters, even though Leatherhead claims to be "the mouth of 'hem all".[69] Leatherhead is exactly the kind of "Interpreter to the puppets" that *Greene's Groatsworth of Wit* warned its readers about, and his performance of *Hero and Leander* set on Bankside and enacted on Bankside shows that Jonson – MA'd by Oxford and Cambridge but never their student – could invert such fears to show off the extraordinary breadth of his cultural compass.

Conclusion: beyond Shakespeare

For many readers and theatre-goers at the start of the twenty-first century, Shakespeare, not Jonson, is the epitome of high culture, available to be bathetically reworked in advertising campaigns and in such consciously low-brow debunkings as 'The Compleat Works of Willm Shkspr (abridged)' by the Reduced Shakespeare Company.[70] Shakespeare's rise in cultural status was most obviously meteoric in the century or so between the Restoration of 1660 and David Garrick's Stratford Jubilee of 1769, as Michael Dobson has showed.[71] However, the rise began before the Civil War and is discernible in the monumentalising of Shakespeare in the 1623 Folio edition and in others' responses to his plays. Of the latter, a clear and early example is John Fletcher's play *The Woman's Prize, or the Tamer Tamed* (first performed in 1611) that continues the story of Petruccio from Shakespeare's *The Taming of the Shrew* into his second marriage after Katherine's death.

Drawing upon Aristophanes' story of a sex strike by Grecian women, *Lysistrata*, Fletcher's play moves the action to a recognisable London (from Shakespeare's Padua) and gives its Bianca a vision of feminist utopia as an alternative to mere grudging accommodation between the warring sexes:

> *Ilium* shall burn, and I, as did *Aeneas*,
> will on my back, spite of the Myrmidons,
> Carry this warlike Lady, and through Seas
> Unknown, and unbeleev'd, seek out a Land,
> Were like a race of noble *Amazons*,
> We'le root our selves, and to our endlesse glory
> Live, and despise base men.[72]

This alludes to Virgil's *Aeneid* just as Shakespeare in *The Taming of the Shrew* alluded to Ovid's *Heroides* (*Epistle of the Heroines*), but for Fletcher the descent to the familiar can be a way of turning ideals into practical reality. As Margaret Maurer justly commented, "The land across the water where women can enjoy such independence is England, or perhaps more precisely, an English playhouse".[73]

Fletcher's play does not end on such a separatist note (the epilogue refers to teaching "due equality") but its widely recognised undermining of the politics of Shakespeare's conservative play – typical recent responses are David M. Bergeron's[74] and Fiona McNeill's[75] – suggests that imitation need be no kind of falling off. In a sense Fletcher himself was a repetition: he replaced Shakespeare as the King's men's chief dramatist in the 1610s and 1620s. Yet his career was no mere imitation: unlike his strong precursor he tended to write in collaboration with others (Shakespeare only dabbled in collaboration) and he wrote for companies other than the King's men. The many commendatory poems at the beginning of the 1647 edition of Fletcher's plays (presented, rather inaccurately, as the works of Fletcher and Francis Beaumont) repeatedly described Fletcher as the equal of Shakespeare and Jonson and, in certain respects, the surpasser.[76] Leaving aside the subtle details of Bergeron's and McNeill's fine readings, we can see Fletcher surpassing Shakespeare in how he ends the story of Petruccio and his wife: instead of peace arising from the wife submitting to her husband, Fletcher explores the possibilities for separatism and concludes with sexual equality. As well as Shakespeare's play, Fletcher drew upon Jonson's play *Epicoene* that has the subtitle *The Silent Woman*, which is supposed to be a witty and paradoxical expression of what can never be found, like *A Chaste Maid in Cheapside* and *An Honest Whore* or, more recently in Graham Greene's hands, a *Quiet American*. Fletcher's notion of imitation-as-repetition, however, is not merely bathetic descent but real subversion, and hence his subtitle, *The Tamer Tamed*, indicates a transformation that is, paradoxically for a copy that bathetically mocks its original, also a transcendence.

Chapter Three

1. George Gascoigne, *The Posies*, STC 11636 (London: H. Bynneman for R. Smith, 1575).
2. George Gascoigne, *The Whole Woorkes*, STC 11638 (London: A. Jeffes, 1587).
3. Roger Prior, 'Gascoigne's *Poesies* as a Shakespearian Source', *Notes and Queries* 245 (2000), pp. 444–9.

4. A.B. Taylor, 'Introduction', in *Shakespeare's Ovid: The Metamorphoses in the Plays and Poems*, ed. A.B. Taylor (Cambridge: Cambridge University Press, 2000), pp. 1–4.
5. Niall Rudd, 'Pyramus and Thisbe in Shakespeare and Ovid', in Taylor (ed.), *Shakespeare's Ovid*, p. 116.
6. Ibid., pp. 118–20.
7. Mattheo Bandello, *The Tragicall Historye of Romeus and Juliet Written First in Italian By Bandell, and Nowe in Englishe by Ar[thur] Br[ooke]* (London: In aedibus Richardi Tottelli, cum privilegio, [1562]).
8. James Kavanagh, 'Shakespeare in Ideology', in *Alternative Shakespeares*, ed. John Drakakis (London: Routledge, 1985), p. 154.
9. Jonathan Bate, *The Genius of Shakespeare* (London: Macmillan, 1997), pp. 101–32.
10. Oscar Brownstein, 'The Saracen's Head, Islington: A Pre-Elizabethan Inn Playhouse', *Theatre Notebook* 25 (1971), pp. 68–72; Oscar Brownstein, 'A Record of London Inn-Playhouses from *c.*1565–1590', *Shakespeare Quarterly* 22 (1971), pp. 17–24.
11. Janet S. Loengard, 'An Elizabethan Lawsuit: John Brayne, His Carpenter, and the Building of the Red Lion Theatre', *Shakespeare Quarterly* 34 (1983), pp. 298–310.
12. Herbert Berry, 'The First Public Playhouses, Especially the Red Lion', *Shakespeare Quarterly* 40 (1989), p. 134.
13. Margot Heinemann, *Puritanism and Theatre: Thomas Middleton and Opposition Drama under the Early Stuarts* (Cambridge: Cambridge University Press, 1980).
14. Scott McMillin and Sally-Beth MacLean, *The Queen's Men and their Plays* (Cambridge: Cambridge University Press, 1998), p. 34.
15. R.A. Foakes, *Illustrations of the English Stage 1580–1642* (London: Scolar Press, 1985), pp. 24–5.
16. *Henslowe Papers: Being Documents Supplementary to Henslowe's Diary*, ed. W.W. Greg (London: Bullen, 1907), p. 20.
17. John Orrell, *The Quest for Shakespeare's Globe* (Cambridge: Cambridge University Press, 1983), p. 101.
18. Richard Southern and C. Walter Hodges, 'Colour in the Elizabethan Theatre', *Theatre Notebook* 6 (1952), p. 57.
19. Foakes, *Illustrations of the English Stage 1580–1642*, pp. 29–31, 36–8.
20. John Orrell, *The Human Stage: English Theatre Design, 1567–1640* (Cambridge: Cambridge University Press, 1988), pp. 45, 60, 162.
21. Southern and Hodges, 'Colour in the Elizabethan Theatre'.
22. *Henslowe's Diary, Edited with Supplementary Material, Introduction and Notes*, ed. R.A. Foakes and R.T. Rickert (Cambridge: Cambridge University Press, 1961), p. 308.
23. Douglas Bruster, 'Shakespeare and the End of History: Period as Brand Name', in *Shakespeare and Modernity*, ed. Hugh Grady (London: Routledge, 2000), pp. 184, 186.
24. Robert Greene, *Greenes, Groats-worth of Witte, … Written Before His Death* (London: [J. Wolfe and J. Danter] for W. Wright, 1592), E1r.
25. Greene, *Greenes, Groats-worth of Witte*, F1v; Bate, *Genius of Shakespeare*, p. 15.
26. William Shakespeare, *Mr. William Shakespeares Comedies, Histories, & Tragedies. Published According to the True Originall Copies*, STC 22273 (F1) (London: Isaac Jaggard and Ed. Blount, 1623), piA4r.
27. Constance Brown Kuriyama, *Christopher Marlowe: A Renaissance Life* (Ithaca, NY: Cornell University Press, 2002), p. 113.
28. Greene, *Greenes, Groats-worth of Witte*, E4v-F1r.

29. Robert Greene, *The Comicall Historie of Alphonsus, King of Aragon.* [Init. R. G.], STC 12233 (London: T. Creede, 1599).
30. Kuriyama, *Christopher Marlowe*, p. 113.
31. Roslyn Lander Knutson, *The Repertory of Shakespeare's Company 1594–1613* (Fayetteville, AR: University of Arkansas Press, 1991), p. 40.
32. Aristotle, *Poetics*, Introduction, commentary and appendixes by D.W. Lucas (Oxford: Clarendon Press, 1968), pp. 258–72.
33. Plato, *The Republic*, trans. and ed. Francis Macdonald Cornford (Oxford: Clarendon Press, 1941), 10:595a–608b, pp. 314–32.
34. Baldwin Maxwell, *Studies in the Shakespeare Apocrypha* (New York: Columbia University Press, 1956), p. 103.
35. *The London Prodigall* (London: T. C[reede] for N. Butter, 1605), G1v.
36. Cyril Tourneur, *The Revenger's Tragedy*, ed. R.A. Foakes, The Revels Plays (London: Methuen, 1966), pp. lxvi–lxix.
37. Margreta De Grazia, *Shakespeare Verbatim: The Reproduction of Authenticity and the 1790 Apparatus* (Oxford: Clarendon, 1991), pp. 214–20.
38. Peter W.M. Blayney, 'The Publication of Playbooks', in *A New History of Early English Drama*, ed. John D. Cox and David Scott Kastan (New York: Columbia University Press, 1997), pp. 398–9.
39. William Shakespeare, [*King Lear*] *M. William Shak-speare: His True Chronicle Historie of the Life and Death of King Lear and His Three Daughters*, STC 22292 (Q1) (London: [N. Okes] for Nathaniel Butter, 1608).
40. *The True Chronicle History of King Leir, and His Three Daughters*, STC 15343 (London: Simon Stafford for John Wright, 1605).
41. Stanley Wells, *Shakespeare: For All Time* (London: Macmillan, 2002), pp. 147–8.
42. Raphael Holinshed, *The First and Second Volumes of the Chronicles. (The Third Volume.) Newlie Augmented and Continued By J. Hooker Alias Vowell Gent. and Others.* (A. Fleming; F. Thin [I.e. Thynne; and J. Stow]), STC 13569 variant 2, 3 vols (London: [H. Denham,] (at the expenses of J. Harison, G. Bishop, R. Newberie, H. Denham, and T. Woodcock, 1587), *III: Beginning at Duke William the Norman … Now Newlie Recognised, Augmented, and Continued … to the Yeare 1586*, Ggg1v.
43. Brian Vickers, *Classical Rhetoric in English Poetry* (London: Macmillan, 1970), p. 62.
44. Andrew Gurr, 'The Shakespearian Stage, Forty Years on', *Shakespeare Survey* 41 (1989), p. 1.
45. Foakes and Rickert (eds), *Henslowe's Diary*, p. 16.
46. Robert Greene, *The Honorable Historie of Frier Bacon and Frier Bongay* (London: [A. Islip] for E. White, 1594), D4r.
47. Sir Philip Sidney, *The Defence of Poesie*, STC 22535 (London: [T. Creede] for W. Ponsonby, 1595), B4v.
48. Ibid., B4v-C1r.
49. Ibid., B4r.
50. Ibid., C1r.
51. Ibid., C1v.
52. Jacques Derrida, *Of Grammatology*, trans. Gayatri Chakravorty Spivak (Baltimore, MD and London: Johns Hopkins University Press, 1976), pp. 269–316.
53. Ibid., p. 273.
54. Ibid., p. 277.
55. Ibid., p. 158.

56. Andrew Gurr, *The Shakespearian Playing Companies* (Oxford: Clarendon Press, 1996), p. 290.
57. Richard Brome and Thomas Heywood, *The Witches of Lancashire (The Late Lancashire Witches)*, ed. Gabriel Egan, Globe Quartos (London: Nick Hern, 2002), pp. xiii–xv.
58. E.K. Chambers, *The Elizabethan Stage*, 4 vols (Oxford: Clarendon Press, 1923), 2, p. 419.
59. Ben Jonson, *Works*, ed. C.H. Herford, Percy and Evelyn Simpson, 11 vols (Oxford: Clarendon Press, 1947), VIII: The Prose Works and the Poems, pp. 403–4.
60. Christopher Marlowe, *Hero and Leander*, STC 17413 (London: A. Islip for E. Blount, 1598), A4r.
61. Ben Jonson, [*The Second Volume of the Works.*] *Bartholmew Fayre.* (*The Divell is an Asse. – The Staple of Newes.*), STC 14753.5 (London: J. B[eale] for R. Allot, 1631), L2r.
62. Ibid., A4r.
63. Richard Hosley, 'The Playhouses', in *The Revels History of Drama in English*, ed. Clifford Leech and T.W. Craik (London: Methuen, 1975), III: 1576–1613, pp. 121–8.
64. Oscar Brownstein, 'Why Didn't Burbage Lease the Beargarden? A Conjecture in Comparative Architecture', in *The First Public Playhouse: The Theatre in Shoreditch 1576–1598*, ed. Herbert Berry (Montreal: McGill-Queen's University Press, 1979), pp. 81–96.
65. John Stockwood, *A Sermon Preached at Paules Crosse*, STC 23284 (London: Henry Bynneman for George Byshop, 1578), J7v.
66. John Ronayne, 'Totus Mundus Agit Histrionem [The Whole World Moves the Actor]: The Interior Decorative Scheme of the Bankside Globe', in *Shakespeare's Globe Rebuilt*, ed. J.R. Mulryne, Margaret Shewring and Andrew Gurr (Cambridge: Cambridge University Press, 1997), pp. 121–46.
67. Jonson, [*The Second Volume of the Works.] Bartholmew Fayre. (The Divell is an Asse. – The Staple of Newes.)*, A6r.
68. Ibid., A3v.
69. Ibid., L1v.
70. Douglas Lanier, *Shakespeare and Modern Popular Culture*, Oxford Shakespeare Topics (Oxford: Oxford University Press, 2002), pp. 102–4.
71. Michael Dobson, *The Making of the National Poet: Shakespeare, Adaptation and Authorship, 1660–1769* (Oxford: Clarendon Press, 1992).
72. John Fletcher and Francis Beaumont, *Comedies and Tragedies*, Wing B1581 (London: For Humphrey Robinson, and Humphrey Mosely, 1647), Nnnnn4v.
73. Margaret Maurer, 'Constering Bianca: *The Taming of the Shrew* and *The Woman's Prize, or the Tamer Tamed*', *Medieval and Renaissance Drama in England* 14 (2001), pp. 186–206 (p. 198).
74. David M. Bergeron, 'Fletcher's *The Woman's Prize*, Transgression, and *Querelle des Femmes*', *Medieval and Renaissance Drama in England* 8 (1996), pp. 146–64.
75. Fiona McNeill, 'Gynocentric London Spaces: (Relocating) Masterless Women in Early Stuart Drama', *Renaissance Drama* 28: The Space of the Stage (1999), pp. 195–244.
76. Fletcher and Beaumont, *Comedies and Tragedies*, a1v-g1v.

CHAPTER FOUR

"Pluck but his name out of his heart": a Caesarean cross-section

Paul Innes

AN ALTERNATIVE TITLE for this essay might be '*Julius Caesar*: The Graveyard of Critics'. The play seems to attract waves of attention, perhaps because of its peculiar contemporary cultural status. It is first produced at the self-conscious end of a century, and the expectation of the end of a reign. The moment is also that of a new beginning, the erection of the Globe theatre.[1] The play negotiates a late Elizabethan 're-presentation' of a crucial period in Roman history.[2] Furthermore, critical reception has been patchy, varied and at times downright hostile, both to the play and to other critics.

These intersecting and conflicting sets of issues constitute the terrain over which representations are played out. Disentangling them would be impossible, even if such a project were considered desirable. Cross-fertilisation has nourished Renaissance studies for years now. It has entailed a negotiation between our own concerns and those of the plays, by means of the terrain of performance and reading. Even so, some attempt should be made at this particular juncture to undo the complexities of the play and its reception. The beginning of a new millennium for the various cultures that reproduce notions of 'Shakespeare' would seem like a good point of reflection. But the variety of reactions to Shakespeare's plays lays bare the grounds on which those reactions are themselves constructed. The high culture with which Shakespeare has become associated can be seen, positively or negatively, to be under threat. As a writer whose works of popular culture have been promoted to the status of classics, Shakespeare could be seen to be threatened by the rise of a new complex of popular cultures hell bent on forgetting him. In this context, the question arises: what is it about *Julius Caesar* that has caused another wave of critical interest over the last twenty years or so?

Re-presenting the critics

We are not exactly short of overviews of criticism of this play, both of the tradition in general and of newer works.[3] However, scrutiny of the ways in which criticism has moved on from the kind of hostility briefly referred to above to an engagement with issues of politics and representation does have a purpose. There has to be a reason for this movement, and it can be traced to the earlier critics' dissatisfaction with both the structure of the play and its characterisation of Rome's upper classes. Alan Sinfield describes a five-part process here.[4] Overall, his discussion falls into three broad categories. Firstly, he narrates the earliest responses in terms of a rejection of the structural imbalances perceived to make the play faulty, including the removal of scenes that seem to these interpreters to be superfluous, including the death of Cinna the Poet. This is then followed by a more modern emphasis on character psychology. And, finally, he argues for a more cogently politicised awareness of the various contexts surrounding the play, both in its own times and later. Interestingly for my present purposes, he focuses upon the killing of Cinna the Poet in a way that deliberately challenges its earlier excision. Sinfield's analysis is more subtle than this schematic description suggests, but his problematising of the two categories of structure and character is worth noting.

One would expect Sinfield not to be alone in reacting against previous generations of commentators, and this is indeed the case. Steve Sohmer provides a detailed reading of the figure of Brutus that suggests he may not be the good hero-figure familiar from earlier critics. Sohmer refers to Cicero in order to trace an intertextual analysis that underpins Shakespeare's representation of Brutus. This comes in the context of the argument between Brutus and Cassius at IV.iii:

> Readers of Cicero would know that Shakespeare's Brutus is lying. The historical Brutus was not above usury. In 50 BC Brutus had used his influence to exempt from the usury laws a loan made to the people of Salamis at the confiscatory interest rate of 48 per cent. Brutus also notoriously concealed the fact that he himself was the lender. In letters to Atticus, Cicero roundly deplored Brutus's behaviour on both counts.[5]

Sohmer's assumption that such a learned reference is relevant bears some watching, since the implication is that someone in Shakespeare's theatre would have been well educated enough to make the connection. Sohmer continues: "The argument over money between Brutus and Cassius is entirely Shakespeare's invention. It reveals Brutus as a hypocrite, and prepares his hypocrisy in the so-called 'double-report of Portia's death'."[6] This discussion needs to be further glossed with a caveat: the incident reveals Brutus as a hypocrite to *at least some* of Shakespeare's audience. There is the possibility of multiple, even contradictory, responses to Brutus at this point in the play, and the basis on which a response will be made depends on the extent of one's prior knowledge of other texts from Roman history.

In fact, Sohmer takes his argument to its logical conclusion. He quotes Ernest Schanzer's summing-up of critical responses to the play from 1955 in order to foreground his own reaction against the assumptions of prior critics.[7] Despite his incredibly detailed descriptions of calendrical and liturgical issues in the play, however, Sohmer's own position comes into the second of the two groupings suggested by Sinfield when it comes to overall critical analysis. This is understandable, given the extreme difficulty of generalising on the basis of micro-textual information, but some of his conclusions could be questioned. For example, one might not agree with his assertion that "Beginning with *Julius Caesar*, the plays seem to cast transcendental shadows which elude interpretation."[8] Even so, the recognition that character-based criticism can be challenged is an important one.

Other critics have of course noticed the same sets of problems as Sinfield and Sohmer. Richard Wilson has summed up the more recent reactions to the play: "And, as the essays in this volume show, this meant attending, above all, to the ways in which *Julius Caesar* processes the Roman past through the Elizabethan present, with an eye always to future audiences."[9] His formulation is therefore very similar to that which begins the present essay. But his comment comes as part of the Introduction to a collection of essays that deliberately respond to a perceived lack of awareness on the part of the earlier critics. In other words, a critical shift is being enacted upon *Julius Caesar*, and it is one that finds an emphasis only on structural or character problems to be reductive of the possible meanings that can be generated by this play.

The problems inherent in such a project have been very precisely delineated by Margreta De Grazia. Many recent critics are extremely self-reflexive in a way that once again marks them off as reacting against a received tradition, and De Grazia analyses the issues at stake:

> The question is, then: in our eagerness to make the Renaissance relevant to the Modern, have we not been precipitous in identifying it as the onset of the Modern? This is not to say that nascent individualism and capitalism cannot be found in Shakespeare's time. Yet it is to ask, does it make sense to make the nascent dominant before history does?[10]

Coming in the context of a discussion of *King Lear*, De Grazia's question strikes at the very heart of much of our contemporary Shakespeare criticism. The implication is that a criticism that seeks to pay attention to historicity needs a particularly rigorous awareness of the very specificity of the period under inquiry. In other words, it is not enough to see the Renaissance as early modern or proto-Modern or some such formulation. Nor is it enough to describe it as a period of transition somehow sandwiched between the Medieval and the Modern. It is indeed all of these, but it is something more as well, and it would be the task of a materialist criticism to investigate exactly what that means. This kind of criticism has of course been emerging for quite some time, but it has a different trajectory from a broadly historicist wish to interrogate and make sense of the past. It should be possible to note areas of unintelligibility as well, moments at which a modern or even postmodern sensibility seems inadequate to apprehend a Renaissance text.[11]

What is important here is the often overlooked fact that all of the critics discussed in this necessarily brief excursion agree on one thing: that *Julius Caesar* disrupts easy categories of structure and character. The earlier critics deplore the play because of this; later ones take it as their cue for a whole series of movements away from a criticism centred upon either of these two elements. There are various ways in which this is accomplished, but the focus returns constantly to the very issues of representation with which this essay began. Where Wayne Rebhorn sees the necessity of analysing the Elizabeth re-presentation of Rome, Richard Wilson discerns a need for an informed awareness of the carnival culture that underpins the discourse of Renaissance public performance. Wilson goes so far as to suggest that there is in this period a "collision of codes and voices" rather than a unity.[12] How the Shakespearean play-text manages the multiplicity of competing discourses has become the subject of critics such as Wilson. John Drakakis focuses more exactly on representation in political terms, seeking "that liminal area where ideology and subjectivity intertwine".[13] The title of Drakakis's article refers to theatrical representation, a sign, perhaps, of a perceived need to integrate performance issues: '*Julius Caesar* and the Politics of Theatrical Representation'.

Wayne Rebhorn also sees the play as dealing with a series of problems that have much wider social ramifications than an emphasis on character alone would allow. He identifies similarities between Caesar and Brutus that could be interpreted in purely psychological terms, especially their inability to take heed of others' opinions. But he sees this kind of analysis as crucially limited:

> Such similarities have been used to qualify Brutus' status as the hero of the play, to identify moral failings in him that constitute his 'tragic flaw'. I would argue that the play not only undermines – without cancelling – the differences between Brutus and Caesar, but, more important, as it links the pair together, it stresses their resemblances to all the other aristocrats as well and identifies emulation as the common denominator of the entire group.[14]

Rebhorn reminds us that these stage characters operate within a whole network of social competition that indeed defines their identity – the implication, of course, being that they are not purely discrete individuals. This early 'New Historicist' essay accomplishes a great deal more, however. Rebhorn also positions the play in relation to the culture for which it was produced:

> Such a concern with aristocratic self-definition was of vital interest in Elizabethan culture and was in good measure the result of the dislocations caused by social mobility and the ontological insecurity that mobility produced for Englishmen used to living in a seemingly immutable, intensely hierarchical society.[15]

A two-part process is at work here: the play is not simply 'about' Romans; it reproduces them in inevitably changed form so that they can be recognised by Elizabethan contemporaries.[16] Such a productive interplay of meanings would simply be stifled by an emphasis on character alone. Indeed, Rebhorn goes on to make an analogy that would have had immense significance for a contemporary Elizabethan: "Caesar can thus be read as Essex if both are taken as representative types, illustrations of aristocratic emulation and factionalism that were played out to their logical, tragic conclusions."[17] Rebhorn's analysis demonstrates that there are many social reverberations around tragic action and its consequences, and also serves as a fine example of a movement in some critical circles in a new direction.

In a similar manner, a writer who seeks to return to the play's initial context while remaining aware of the emergence of modern meanings is Naomi Liebler. In her book *Shakespeare's Festive Tragedy*, she shares some of the same concerns as Richard Wilson, with her recovering of the popular culture of public performance.[18] But she accomplishes much more than this by undoing the very basis of character criticism. She moves away from an insistence on the individual, which she sees as basically anachronistic, to a discussion of the social nature of this play and others.[19] But she also returns us to Aristotle's very definition of tragedy. For Liebler, following Aristotle, *hamartia* is an impossible choice, or rather a choice that cannot be made without violating one or other of the fundamental codes at stake in the tragic action:

> The fact that the tragic heroes' chosen actions 'miss the mark' (the literal meaning of Aristotle's *hamartia*) does not make those actions or those heroes failures. The precise circumstances of tragedy involve situations in which the task to be done is itself impossible. Tragedy does not represent the failure to do noble, difficult, necessary things; it represents the attempt to do them in a context that will not permit them to be done.[20]

Thus, for example, Orestes does not have some kind of character flaw that allows the tragedy to be centred upon him as an individual. Rather, the divinely sanctioned laws that govern his society force him into a no-win situation. He absolutely must avenge his father's death by killing his murderers, and yet he cannot do so because one of them is his mother, and there is an equally absolute prohibition against matricide. The tragic problem is a dilemma, not a character flaw. Liebler's understanding of tragedy as a fundamentally social form enables its revaluation, and this includes Shakespeare's plays. It opens up the possibility of recovering at least some of the "multiple resonances"[21] that have been occluded by the insistence of later cultures on the primacy of individual experience.

When she turns her attention to *Julius Caesar*, Liebler takes on the double problem of structure and character by analysing the figure of Brutus. Her approach here is different from that of Sohmer, with his intertextual re-reading of Brutus's hypocrisy. Liebler is much more interested in how this figure functions: "Brutus' *hamartia* is his inability to preserve the Republic, to predict the outcome of the history in which he himself participates".[22] Thus *hamartia* is indelibly linked with choice in action, not some internal psychological individuality.

Liebler's perspective demonstrates that the play's critical reception has shifted a great deal. An awareness of fundamental issues raised by criticism in the recent past surely has some resonance for this essay. The difficulty now is how to develop these Roman and Elizabethan social indices in a way that makes sense for a contemporary twenty-first-century reader or audience.

Names

When Cassius tempts Brutus in I.ii.25ff., he does so in terms not only of friendship or philosophy, but of lineage. He uses terms such as "best respect" (l. 59) and "noble" (l. 62), even before the populace acclaims Caesar off-stage for the first time. Cassius has two long speeches after the first acclamation (ll. 90ff.), and after the second (ll. 135ff.). Brutus's reaction to the off-stage noises punctuates Cassius's rhetorical onslaught. The first of these speeches includes Cassius's famous denigration of the physical man called Caesar, while the second emblematises the relative worth of the name of Brutus. The great deeds of Brutus's ancestor who overthrew the Etruscan rulers and established the early Republic become the touchstone for present needs. In his film of the play, Mankiewicz uses pillared busts of past Romans to emphasise just these issues; to a Renaissance audience, the play on homonyms of nobility, name and lineage would be very apparent:

> Brutus and Caesar: what should be in that 'Caesar'?
> Why should that name be sounded more than yours?
> Write them together, yours is as fair a name;
> Sound them, it doth become the mouth as well;
> Weigh them, it is as heavy; conjure with 'em,
> 'Brutus' will start a spirit as soon as 'Caesar'.
> Now in the names of all the gods at once,
> Upon what meat does this our Caesar feed
> That he is grown so great? Age, thou art sham'd!
> Rome, thou hast lost the breed of noble bloods!
>
> (I.ii.142–51)

What this speech does is focus the action in upon naming as crucial, and not only in purely personal terms – compare Richmond's question in the aftermath of Bosworth Field: "What men of name are slain on either side?" (*Richard III*, V.v.12). The collocations here are worked by Cassius, and they are central to the problem of Caesar's pre-eminence.

This may help shed some light on an incident in the play that has puzzled and attracted commentators in equal measure, the seemingly senseless lynching of Cinna the Poet:

3. Plebeian	Your name, sir, truly.
Cinna	Truly, my name is Cinna.
1. Plebeian	Tear him to pieces, he's a conspirator.
Cinna	I am Cinna the poet, I am Cinna the poet.
4. Plebeian	Tear him for his bad verses, tear him for his bad verses.
Cinna	I am not Cinna the conspirator.
4. Plebeian	It is no matter, his name's Cinna. Pluck but his name out of his heart, and turn him going.

(III.iii.26–34)[23]

Given the discussion above of the importance of moving away from character to a more socially aware engagement with representation, it would seem important to try to deal with this extremely difficult incident. The scene is perhaps the most problematic in the play for any observer to deal with fully and effectively. Perhaps the simplest way to do so is simply to cut it as not making any sense. However, the scene is the Shakespearean play's elaboration of a short section from Plutarch.[24] There is a debate occurring here in Shakespeare's play that needs to be contextualised in terms of the relationship between poetry and politics.[25] The raising of this issue in a scene that is extended and refined from Plutarch would seem to be a convincing counter simply to removing it altogether. After all, if a critic believes in coherence, then surely this example of Shakespeare's imagination at work absolutely must be retained.

Dennis Kezar makes an important assertion in his essay '*Julius Caesar* and the Properties of Shakespeare's Globe' when he sees it as emblematic of the ways in which the play as a whole tackles representation: "In this scene Shakespeare schematizes the fate of all communication in the play."[26] Richard Wilson similarly picks up on the problem of meaning, but he also explicitly politicises it: "The fact that this formalism is propagated in a play put on at the popular playhouse only betrays the bad faith, of course, of the notion that literature has no ideology."[27] What these various discussions reveal is that the scene represents something other than itself, which for these critics manifests itself as an instance of the relationship between violence and representation.

But might not such a conclusion seem too abstract for a play that represents violence so directly? Although Cinna the Poet is murdered offstage, the implication that he is torn apart by the mob is quite open. The extreme nature of the violence must surely point to something more than a debate about art and politics. It might be possible further to interrogate this scene by reference to the critical issues highlighted in the previous section of this essay. The focus here will be upon the function of names in *Julius Caesar*, the very denoting of the inviolable status of the individual so beloved of so many, and picking up on Cassius's insistence on the importance of names in I.ii.

To return to Cinna's murder, and the title of this essay, the comment by the Fourth Plebeian recognises that one's name is so much a part of one that it nests in that crucial internal organ, the heart. This could be glossed by a recognition that one's name is so closely a part of one that it inheres in the heart of the matter. Even so, it can also be ripped out like the heart itself, or "pluck'd" out as the rioter would have it. This does not only enact violence on the individual, it recognises that the name is open to a social engagement, albeit in this case an incredibly vicious one. An assertion that the name has a wider social function should not come as a great surprise, given the Elizabethan anxiety about name, inheritance, lineage and family, and at this point one would remember Wayne Rebhorn's insistence on the social competitiveness of both the Romans and the Elizabethans, or at least their upper classes. To impose a later culture's view of the name as purely 'private' would therefore be anachronistic, to put it mildly.

The rioters simply do not care that they have the wrong man in this scene, but they do take his name as being a good enough excuse to kill Cinna. The emblematic status of the scene needs to be investigated. Kezar, Taylor and Wilson are all correct when they sense that the scene is doing something in addition to its bare violence; I would add that the scene emblematises a very serious concern throughout the play with representations of the multiple social meanings of names. This makes the play non-realistic in the Brechtian sense, but it also places it very precisely at the moment of its construction.

The primary name, of course, is that of Julius Caesar, the aspiring man of the play's own title. But 'Caesar' is itself a title. It ceases simply to be an element of the name, or *nomen*, of a Roman individual. It refers to the ruling dynasty of the early Roman Principate and Empire. It then carries on through the later Empire as the secondary co-ruler of the Augustus of each half of the Empire after Diocletian. From there it becomes a title continued in what is known in the West as the Byzantine Empire, leading to the Czar of Russia. It is also the Kaiser of Germany (which is, incidentally, how the Roman contemporaries of Gaius Julius Caesar would have pronounced it). 'Caesar' is not just the name of an individual; it is the name of political power. If this is so, then the tragedy of Julius Caesar is, in social terms, intelligible in a way that the tragedy of the individual Julius Caesar has never been: his name haunts the text (literally, for Brutus at least) after his death, such that the second half of the play works out the tragic trajectory of who will inherit the name of Caesar and, thus, his power.

In a different context, infused with anthropology and rites of passage, Marjorie Garber has also analysed the significance of names in *Julius Caesar*, picking up specifically the importance of the *nomen*:

> Of all Shakespearean *nomen-omen* instances, however, none is more striking than the episode of Cinna the poet in *Julius Caesar*. (The Roman plays, with their natural interest in the cognomen, seem to take 'name' as a thematic element with some consistency.) On his way to Caesar's funeral, Cinna is halted by a gang of plebians who challenge his loyalty and ask his name. Unluckily, he bears the name of one of the conspirators, and the plebians, taking the name for the thing, fall upon him and beat him [...] The scene is a vivid emblem of the confusion which has fallen upon Rome after the murder of its ruler.[28]

Although Garber's discussion comes in a wider context of how Shakespearean plays deal with the transition between various stages of life, her vocabulary is most suggestive. The way she uses the term 'emblem' is especially significant given the comments made above. Garber goes on very carefully to connect the name of 'Caesar' with Octavius's coming of age, symbolised by his assumption of the family name of Caesar which will very soon become the patronym of a dynasty.[29] She does so via the struggle not only between the conspirators and the 'Caesareans', but by means of the almost submerged conflict between Antony and Octavius. Shakespeare does not give any details at all of the massive military campaign fought out between Antony and Octavius that raged across Italy after the conspirators fled to Greece to raise troops there.[30] In this war, Octavius proved successful, partly through a superior generalship which is conventionally absent from his portrayal in both *Julius Caesar* and *Antony and Cleopatra*, and partly because Caesar's veteran legions fought for Octavius as Caesar's named successor. It is crucial in this context that Octavius is not recognised as Caesar until Act V, as Garber notes, and here both Antony and Brutus refer to him as such. At least some of Shakespeare's audience would have known the history of the Italian conflict between Octavius and Antony that led to the recognition of the former as Caesar's real heir.

In Roman history, these two were not the only possible inheritors of what psychoanalysis might call the name of the father. Brutus was a third:

Decius Here lies the east; doth not the day break here?
Cinna O, pardon, sir, it doth; and yon grey lines
That fret the cloud are messengers of day.
Casca You shall confess that you are both deceiv'd.
Here, as I point my sword, the sun arises,
Which is a great way growing on the south,
Weighing the youthful season of the year.

(II.i.101–8)

Here Casca makes emblematic use of the conventional Renaissance pun on sun/son to point out Brutus, who is at a different point on the stage conversing separately with Cassius.[31] The royal associations of the sun come together with a very precise intertextual reference to Brutus as illegitimate son of Caesar.[32] Again, some of Shakespeare's audience would have been aware of this possibility, adding to the whole atmosphere not only of plotting Caesar's death, but of who will succeed him as well. Will it really be a new version of the old Republic with so much at stake?

There is even more to the name of Caesar. Gaius Julius was also *pontifex maximus*, the very title, as Steve Sohmer reminds us, inherited by the Popes.[33] Sohmer inevitably sees this as a negative association, due to the Protestant hatred of what they saw as Antichrist. But for Renaissance England the self-conscious growth of an Empire links the Caesars with

Henry VIII, who not only proclaimed English suzerainty over the whole British Isles, but most famously united the royal power with the religious – just like the Julius to whom he is compared in Wyatt's famous sonnet. And it cannot go unremarked here that James of Scotland is the most likely candidate to succeed to Elizabeth's throne, thus uniting the Scottish and English crowns, just as this play is being produced. James's relationship to Henry is almost exactly that of Octavius to Julius; James is one generation further away, but the correspondence can only be echoed in the play's fraught problematising of succession, in a manner so similar to exactly that which occupied the minds of so many English at the turn of the seventeenth century.

If the death of Cinna the Poet were the only instance of names and their importance, then all of the associations just charted could be construed as a misreading. But it is followed by another short scene in which names are central: the proscription scene. Here, the Second Triumvirate carves up the spoils:

Antony These many then shall die, their names are prick'd.
Octavius Your brother too must die; consent you, Lepidus?
Lepidus I do consent –
Octavius Prick him down, Antony.
Lepidus Upon condition Publius shall not live,
Who is your sister's son, Mark Antony.
Antony He shall not live; look, with a spot I damn him.

(IV.i.1–6)

The generative language masks political horse-trading of the most cynical kind. A brother and a nephew are both consigned to death in another scene that is emblematic of the play's insistent concern with relative rank and political power. I would argue that it is no accident that the two scenes of Cinna's death and the proscription come together. They constitute the aftermath of Caesar's death and precede the destruction of the conspirators.[34] This placement is pivotal, condensing the play's concerns in a way that moves the tragedy of Caesar towards its inevitable and logical conclusion with the deaths of the conspirators.

Julius Caesar therefore does not have a double structure at all. It plays out the progression of a tragedy that cannot be reduced only to some notion of character psychology. The lexical item that is the phrase 'Julius

Caesar' has much more linguistic force than this: it is a multiple metonymy, a link to many discourses of inheritance and power that can easily be missed because of an a-historical assumption that tragedy lies in the singular personage. This assumption, as Naomi Liebler reminds us, is itself based on a misreading of Aristotle, which seems fitting enough given the play's constant rehearsing of mistakes and misunderstandings, manipulated as they are by and through language and performance. And one final mistake needs to be corrected: Caesar was not born by section, as his name suggests; it was his father. The Elizabethans got that wrong, and this should serve as a reminder to those of us who would seek to unscramble the codes and associations of this play.[35]

Given the forces associated with names in the play, with their writing, powers of inheritance and so on, Caesar's own use of his name stands out:

> *Soothsayer* Caesar!
> *Caesar* Ha? Who Calls?
> *Casca* Bid every noise be still; peace yet again!
> *Caesar* Who is it in the press that calls on me?
> I hear a tongue shriller than all the music
> Cry 'Caesar'! Speak, Caesar is turn'd to hear
>
> (I.ii.12–17)

Caesar's slippage from first to third person here takes place just before the soothsayer delivers his first warning, and many other examples could be adduced. This could be taken to be just one more example of Caesar's pompous nature at work. However, there is again an intertextual echo. In the case of Caesar's pronouncements about himself, a double representation is in operation. He is linguistically divided from his own sense of self at these moments, but also this is a secondary use of the narrative technique Caesar used in his published work on the Gallic Wars – and the technique is so well known that the Asterix books caricature him for it.

It is not the first time that intertextuality has been noted in this discussion. It is now time to work through the implications, because if some but not all of the audience will understand these allusions, what does this technique say of the production of meanings in the play as a whole? To recall the earlier references to multiple discourses noted from critics such as Richard Wilson, John Drakakis and Naomi Liebler, what we are beginning to discern here is a multiplicity of simultaneous representations. Not all of the meanings will be available to all of the audience members, but all of them are active at least to some extent, such that different, even contradictory, meanings are produced at exactly the same time. This is almost like an extension of Shakespeare's wordplay, but because of its intertextual roots it cannot be defined purely in terms of Shakespeare's own creative consciousness. It is more like a kind of logic, a set of conditions within which Renaissance stage representations are constructed and played out, at least in plays that purport to be dealing with some historical material.

Renaissance performance

How might such a logic be grasped? If representation of historical events and characters takes place on different levels at the same time, then there is an inevitable issue about how far the play of meanings extends. It could be so radically dispersed that it constitutes a kind of postmodernism before its time. But the movement does not have to be either all fragmented or indeed all united in a single tragic figure. It is now time to turn to the knowledge we already have of the conditions of Renaissance performance to try to begin, at least, to untangle how this operation might have worked on the stage.

In a sense, our concept of the 'audience' gets in the way. The multiple meanings possible in a play such as *Julius Caesar* need to be related to a more dynamic idea of how Renaissance audiences responded to the plays they saw and heard. Thus, there is not a single audience at all – and work has already been done by Andrew Gurr on the heterogeneous social composition of the London play-going public that would back up such a claim.[36] He has, in collaboration with Mariko Ichikawa, more recently expanded on his work on the sociology of the theatres by speculating upon what would have happened in performance itself: "But three-dimensional acting makes it wrong to think of any 'normal' direction to look in. Acting in the round requires a non-linear positioning, facing in whatever direction the action requires."[37] This is a direct result of the very architecture of these theatres, and we are only beginning to scratch the surface of what this might mean in practice. The plays are radically dynamic in a way that cannot physically take place on a proscenium stage. The two authors refer to Robert Weimann's ground-breaking work on the zonal nature of such staging[38] and indeed they go on to try to work out, following Weimann's commentary, how *Hamlet* might have been staged.[39]

Part of the problem for my own chapter is that these are only preliminary steps. Weimann's work needs more fruitful development, if only because much performance study still seems marked by an unfortunate critical focus on character-based analysis, as mentioned previously in relation to Alan Sinfield's work. Character psychology is one example, here drawn from the work of John Russell Brown: "Stanislavski's concept is particularly appropriate for Shakespeare's plays which for centuries have held audiences' attention by truth of utterance, and by reality and depth of characterization."[40] The critical position of this book shows its age (it was first published in 1966), and it would be a simple matter to follow on from my earlier comments on character psychology. Truth, reality and characterisation are all herded together in defence of a performance tradition that is somehow identical over the span of centuries. The seventeenth- to eighteenth-century period is glossed over, and Stanislavski is somehow correct for Shakespeare (Chekhov would definitely not agree!). These are familiar assertions, and, despite the value of such books in reminding us of the debt to theatre and performance, the overall commentary can be seen to be extremely problematic indeed in relation to the kinds of representations of *Julius Caesar* now under discussion. It could be argued that this is not entirely fair, since of course this kind of critical vocabulary was unavailable to John Russell Brown at that time, which would be a reasonable enough point to make. However, performance study still holds on to these kinds of character-based notions:

> When an actor finds what is useable for himself or herself, the result is a new interpretation. But this does not imply that Shakespeare was weak or uncertain in purpose as he wrote. Such a variety is possible because his mind focused on the inner beings of his characters, rather than on their outwardly visible physique or their past history.[41]

In this later book, Brown continues to insist on recognisably Stanislavskian acting techniques even as he tries to update his earlier work. The assumptions that underpin the insistence on performance can be seen to undermine their usefulness as a caveat to the excesses of the text-based literary critical tradition.

There are more extreme examples, such as can be found in the Preface to Ralph Berry's book *Shakespeare in Performance*: "The taming of the audience is the central challenge to all playwrights."[42] As a massive over-generalisation this one is hard to beat – one could just imagine, say, Brecht's response. "Taming" them implies that there is a hierarchical privilege accorded to the playwright who does the taming, but whether this is adequate to explain the popular culture of Shakespeare's stage is a moot point. The difficulty lies in how to take such generalised writing about performance and taking something useful from it that can be related specifically to the Renaissance staging of the plays. But of course there are other options, and some of them have been explored much more helpfully:

> In a culture in which those who would oppose theatrical representation continued to insist upon the power that inheres in the theatrical image itself, *Julius Caesar* is not so much a celebration of theatre as an unmasking of the politics of representation per se. The play does not *express* meaning; rather, in its readings of Roman history it *produces* meanings.[43]

The emphasis John Drakakis places here on the politics of representation depends upon a self-reflexive awareness that infuses the Renaissance stage, and it is of course a critical commonplace that Shakespeare's plays are well aware of their artificiality.

But to return to a scene that has already been discussed, it might be possible to suggest the kinds of representational practices that can be enacted on this kind of stage. I have already referred to the way in which Casca points towards Brutus in the conspiratorial gathering in Brutus's house (II.i). Sohmer is interested in the astronomical exactitude of this scene, possibly played with Casca pointing towards the Tower of London, traditionally said to have been founded by Caesar during one of his British excursions.[44] But if Brutus and Cassius are separated from the rest of the group as the stage directions indicate, then what is seen in action is a convention of the zonal stage. One pair of characters is in a separate stage location from the others, and the larger group forces attention upon the smaller pairing. The dramatic effect of this could be intensified if the Casca group is in the central downstage position, effectively right in the middle of the round and, hence, the audience. In effect, the majority of the audience is drawn into possible collusion by means of Casca's gesture. And others with a different point of view will see this operation being enacted upon both Brutus and other parts of the audience itself.

But all of this takes place in the midst of the multiple productions of meaning traced out earlier in this essay. How does this multiplicity relate to the kinds of movements and moments possible on the contemporary Elizabethan stage? Sohmer interprets the issue as a doubling of effect: "Shakespeare wrote for two audiences, which is why his occasional *Julius Caesar* still stands today."[45] Sohmer's interest is in what he sees as the two kinds of audience member who attended one of these plays: the majority, and the educated.[46] But if the audience is split by multiple viewing positions, multiple levels of education and multiple social ranks, surely much more is happening than a mere doubling of meaning?

Representations

Simultaneous different possibilities are produced by and through *Julius Caesar*. The identification of the major critical issues of character and structure is in itself nothing new, but it has cleared the way for an investigation of the play's interrogation of names, intertextual reference and, ultimately, Renaissance playing. Much work of this kind still needs to be done on this play alone, never mind the whole bloated corpus of the plays and their critics. But the various representations that have been touched upon – and produced – by this essay constitute the terrain over which meanings are enacted. This is only to be expected in a volume concerned with representations, published at this particular historical juncture. Perhaps the play haunts recent criticism because of the way it continues to evade a full elaboration, and perhaps this is because of the vertiginous gulf that separates the Renaissance from the twenty-first century.

It has been the contention of this essay that *Julius Caesar* is not in any simplistic way 'about' Julius Caesar. The play has been taken as a test case for an attempt to produce an analysis that is aware of other criticism, the play of language and Renaissance performance, something of a tall order for a short essay. Pinning down multiple meanings is never easy in such circumstances, especially when total fragmentation is being avoided. Hence this attempt could be seen to be as sceptical of an easy dizziness of meaning as it is of monolithic constructs. 'Shakespeare' is one of those constructs, but at least the critical tradition that has helped to put this edifice together can be unpicked because of its uneasiness about *Julius Caesar*, not to mention other plays. The tracing out of multiple meanings necessarily entails a deep suspicion of any straightforward reduction of the play of meaning by reference to a single point. What is needed is more materialist criticism and performance issues will necessarily be a part of it. But this area in particular needs further exploration. By linking it to a more conventional reading process, it should be possible to locate these plays more precisely within the moment of their initial production than has been managed until recently. Such a project has an agenda, of course, but then all criticism does. Shakespeare has always been appropriated by someone or other; we need to pay more attention to the performance of that appropriation. *Julius Caesar* is a site of contestation, reworking and representation. It remains to be seen what new resonances will emerge.

Chapter Four

1. For a detailed discussion of *Julius Caesar* and the opening of the new Globe, see Steve Sohmer, *Shakespeare's Mystery Play: The Opening of the Globe Theatre 1599* (Manchester: Manchester University Press, 1999).
2. Wayne Rebhorn, 'The Crisis of the Aristocracy in *Julius Caesar*', in *Julius Caesar: Contemporary Critical Essays*, ed. Richard Wilson (Hampshire and New York: Palgrave, 2002), p. 32.
3. See, for example: Robert S. Miola, 'Shakespeare and his Sources: Observations on the Critical History of *Julius Caesar*', *Shakespeare Survey* 40 (1987); John Ripley, *Julius Caesar on Stage* (Cambridge: Cambridge University Press, 1980), especially the Introduction, pp. 1–8; and the Introduction to Wilson, *Julius Caesar*.
4. Alan Sinfield, *Faultlines: Cultural Materialism and the Politics of Dissident Reading* (Oxford: Clarendon Press, 1992) pp. 10ff.
5. Sohmer, *Shakespeare's Mystery Play*, p. 157.
6. Ibid.
7. "There is widespread disagreement among critics about who is the play's principal character or whether it has a principal character, on whether it is a tragedy and if so whose, on whether Shakespeare wants us to consider the assassination as damnable or praiseworthy, while of all of the chief characters in the play violently contradictory interpretations have been offered." Ernest Schanzer, 'The Problem of *Julius Caesar*', *Shakespeare Quarterly* 6 (1955). Quoted in Sohmer, *Shakespeare's Mystery Play*, p. 184.
8. Sohmer, *Shakespeare's Mystery Play*, p. 185.
9. Wilson, *Julius Caesar*, p. 2.
10. Margreta De Grazia, 'The Ideology of Superfluous Things', in *Subject and Object in Renaissance Culture*, ed. Margreta De Grazia, Maureen Quilligan and Peter Stallybrass (Cambridge: Cambridge University Press, 1996), pp. 20–1.
11. For a much more detailed discussion of these issues than is possible here, see Francis Barker, *The Culture of Violence: Essays on Tragedy and History* (Manchester: Manchester University Press, 1993) pp. 195ff. As a British Cultural Materialist critic, Barker is well aware of the constant conflation of British critics such as himself with the project associated with the American New Historicists. This is something he deplores for political reasons and for reasons of critical clarity and rigour; his differentiation between historicism and materialism is produced within this context.
12. Richard Wilson, *Will Power: Essays on Shakespearean Authority* (Hertfordshire:

Harvester Wheatsheaf, 1993) p. 45.

13. John Drakakis, '*Julius Caesar* and the Politics of Theatrical Representation', in *Shakespeare: The Roman Plays*, ed. Graham Holderness, Bryan Loughrey and Andrew Murphy (New York: Longman, 1996) p. 39.
14. Rebhorn, 'The Crisis of the Aristocracy' in Wilson (ed.), *Julius Caesar*, p. 30.
15. Ibid., p. 31.
16. See also Gary B.Miles, 'How Roman Are Shakespeare's "Romans"?', *Shakespeare Quarterly* 40 (1989).
17. Rebhorn, 'The Crisis of the Aristocracy', p. 48.
18. Naomi Conn Liebler, *Shakespeare's Festive Tragedy: The Ritual Foundations of Genre* (London and New York: Routledge, 1995).
19. Ibid., p. 13.
20. Ibid., p. 20.
21. Ibid., p. 37.
22. Ibid., p. 106.
23. All references to the play are taken from the second edition of *The Riverside Shakespeare* (Boston, MA: Houghton Mifflin, 1997).
24. See Dennis Kezar, '*Julius Caesar* and the Properties of Shakespeare's Globe', in *English Literary Renaissance* 28 (1998), p. 25.
25. Kezar refers to Gary Taylor's essay 'Bardicide', in *Shakespeare and Cultural Traditions: The Selected Proceedings of the International Shakespeare Association World Congress, Tokyo 1991*, ed. Tetsuo Kishi, Roger Pringle and Stanley Wells (Newark, NJ: University of Delaware Press and London: Associated University Presses, 1991). He takes issue with Taylor's position that in the abstract Shakespeare is opposing poetry to politics.
26. Kezar, '*Julius Caesar* and the Properties', p. 44.
27. Wilson, '*Julius Caesar*', p. 21.
28. Marjorie Garber, *Coming of Age in Shakespeare* (New York and London: Routledge, 1997), p. 59.
29. Ibid., p. 61.
30. For a discussion of the politics and military history of these campaigns, see John Warry, *Warfare in the Classical World: War and the Ancient Civilisations of Greece and Rome* (London: Salamander Books, 1998), pp. 234ff.
31. I am grateful for this point to Dr Grzegorzewska of Warsaw University.
32. See Sohmer, *Shakespeare's Mystery Play*, pp. 83ff. for full details and bibliographical references.
33. Ibid., p. 37.
34. Cf. Kezar, '*Julius Caesar* and the Properties', p. 43, for the confluence of writing and bloodshed in the play.
35. See Sohmer, *Shakespeare's Mystery Play*, p. 177.
36. See the work of Andrew Gurr, in particular *The Shakespearean Stage 1574–1642*, 3rd edn (Cambridge: Cambridge University Press, 1995), and *Playgoing in Shakespeare's London*, 2nd edn (Cambridge: Cambridge University Press, 1996).
37. Andrew Gurr and Mariko Ichikawa, *Staging in Shakespeare's Theatres* (Oxford: Oxford University Press, 2000) p. 10.
38. Robert Weimann, *Shakespeare and the Popular Tradition in the Theater* (Baltimore, MD: Johns Hopkins University Press, 1978). See especially pp. 208ff.
39. Gurr and Ichikawa, *Staging in Shakespeare's Theatres*, pp. 121ff.
40. John Russell Brown, *Shakespeare's Plays in Performance*, Updated and revised edn

(New York and Kent: Applause Theatre Books, 1993), p. 45.
41. John Russell Brown, *William Shakespeare: Writing for Performance* (Houndmills, Hants.: Macmillan, 1996), pp. 41–2.
42. Ralph Berry, *Shakespeare in Performance* (Houndmills, Hants.: Macmillan, 1993), p. vii.
43. Drakakis, '*Julius Caesar* and the Politics', p. 41.
44. Sohmer, *Shakespeare's Mystery Play*, p. 90 and p. 94.
45. Ibid., p. 138.
46. For a Lacanian view of doubling in Shakespeare, see Philip Armstrong, 'Watching Hamlet Watching: Lacan, Shakespeare and the Mirror/Stage', in *Alternative Shakespeares*, vol. 2, ed. Terence Hawkes (London and New York: Routledge, 1996).

CHAPTER FIVE

"Bananas on a mango tree": colonial mimesis, hybridity and modern Indian theatre

Poonam Trivedi

I

IF THE IMPACT of the Western encounter on Indian society and culture were to be encapsulated in one word, it would have to be 'imitation' or, shall we say, 'mimesis'. Not just in politics and governance but in the arts too, and particularly in literature, the engagement with the West began with the imitation of Western forms. Imperial hegemony and coercion notwithstanding, a large number of elite Indians voluntarily and eagerly took up the engagement with the new. The form of the novel, especially, was speedily emulated, poetry took on new dimensions and exposure to Western drama became a turning point. What was the attraction and power of this Western 'baggage' which came, first with mercantile trade, and then with colonial rule? Why did it induce a kind of cultural amnesia and seduce Indians into importing an alien culture and traditions? And what were the consequences, immediate and long-term, of this kind of identification in the creative sphere? Many reasons have been adduced for this adoption of Western practices: new education, the formation of a new middle class and the growth of urbanisation are those that are usually accepted. This essay aims to extend this understanding by exploring these issues with regard to Indian theatre, going back to the moment of initial contact with the West to try to recover some of the fascination, the first sense of shock and frisson which is attendant on all such encounters with a startling newness. This is because the essay argues that a major part of the power of these new cultural forms, including those of the theatre, which contributed to their 'imitation', was their inherent realistic mimeticism, and that, while this encounter with late-eighteenth- and nineteenth-century realism triggered a renaissance of the arts in India, the developments and implications thereof continue to be debated till today. For the effect was fundamental: it resulted in a paradigm shift, akin to the discovery of perspective in the European Renaissance. Ways of viewing changed; the traditional theatre forms lost their audiences and declined.[1]

This analysis of the colonising and controlling dimension of realistic mimeticism negotiates a range of the semantic and theoretical positions elucidated by Günter Gebauer and Christoph Wulf in their historical reconstruction of the development of the concept of mimesis. It begins by seeing 'mimesis' in its primary sense of a "direct re-creation of the actions and utterances of people", a "do-as-if".[2] This elevated into the Aristotelian aesthetic principle of close correspondence with observed reality generating both pleasure and profit becomes central to our understanding of the enchantment cast by English literature. Hence, as in the European Renaissance, the imitation of Western forms in India served not so much as a model of mimetic subordination but as an intercultural interaction, which created for itself "a margin of freedom", a "self consciousness",[3] of the possibility of the new. The bourgeois realism of much of nineteenth-century English literature fed the need of the growing middle class to position itself as symbolic capital. Indian imitation was rarely a slavish copy; rather it was a re-making of something different. Inherited codes and past traditions infiltrated, and Western realism was hybridised. From the post-colonial perspective, there was subversion through imitation. In the evolution of modern Indian theatre, colonising mimesis, which began as a copying, soon turned into 'mimicry' where the very act of doubling displaced the authority of the original.

Indian theatre on the eve of colonisation, around the 1700s, existed in a popular but amorphous form. The classical and formal Sanskrit theatre which had its heyday during the fourth to fifth centuries AD had died out by the eighth century with the emergence of the regional languages. Its place was taken by the development of the several regional 'folk' or popular forms which some believe to have pre-dated the classical Sanskrit theatre, but which now flowered in the genres recognisable today. While Sanskrit drama was literary and courtly, the 'folk' forms were improvisatory and communitarian; while Sanskrit plays were largely confined to aristocratic themes of amorous or political intrigue, the popular theatre consisted mainly of a retelling of the mythological tales from the epics and the *puranas*; but while Sanskrit drama was more poetic and sophisticated and the popular drama more informal and celebratory, they both, nevertheless, shared the same aesthetic code laid down by the *Natyashastra* (2 BC–AD 2), the equivalent of Aristotles' *Poetics*. The *Natyashastra* held representation, *anukaran*, to be a recreation, not an 'imitation' holding a 'mirror to nature'. Art or *anukriti* was to be judged in its own terms, the aim of which was to configure the essence of the emotive life, *rasa*, for the aesthetic delectation of the spectator. In practice, this view resulted in a heightened poetic stylisation in performance where a blend of the mimetic and symbolic through the gestural, aural (music) and kinetic (dance) was the norm. Both the seemingly opposed streams of Indian theatre operated on the principles of non-illusionism and presentationalism: their principle of development was not action or *agon*, but contrast and elaboration, not conflict and denouement but accretion and iteration; their conclusion was neither tragic nor comic but reunifying and harmonising. To the Indian viewer, *natya* or drama was not a mimetic impersonation but a re-enactment (Sanskrit *abhinaya* = acting, literally means to "carry forward") of well-known stories where the pleasure lay in perception of a new finesse, in the improvisatory juxtaposition of the sacred with the secular, in the combination of the devotional with the entertaining.[4]

With such a performative aesthetic, plays could be performed anywhere, in the temple or the courtyard or at the crossroads. They used no scripts or scenery, and a rough-and-ready stage – often four bamboo poles and a cover-sheet – would be rigged up to demarcate the performative space. Properties were a bare minimum, for the setting would be established with the actor's body and speech. No front curtain was used; instead, some forms used a handheld half-curtain to heighten entrances and exits making them revelatory and mysterious. Scenes flowed one from another, demarcated by choric singing and dancing. Space and time were both construed in a non-realistic mode. Characters, too, were archetypes and costumes, therefore, typified. Acting was characterised by engagement and disengagement, both being in the part and stepping out of it. Virtuosity was what was valued – a set part learnt to such perfection that improvised innovations and 'playing around' with it were expected to be instinct. Performances were commissioned for festivals, for example in the harvesting season; the audience was the whole village and the sponsor the local landowner. Plays would start late in the evening and often last through the night. Music, singing, dancing and a recitative chanting were the backbone of the show. The occasion would be simultaneously religious and secular, ritualistic and festive.[5]

A rare surviving description of one such play which was put together by Vishnu Das Bhave, known as the father of Marathi drama, in 1843, called *Sita Swayamvara* (The Choosing of the Bridegroom by Sita), also considered the first Marathi play, is vividly evocative of the semiotics of these pre-colonial performative codes in action:

> The stage setting of the play was very simple. It consisted of a piece of red cloth hung at the back and a few wooden properties. The Sutradhara (Impresario) was present with his chorus of singers and musical accompanists throughout the play. They occupied a corner on the right side of the actors in front of the back curtain.
>
> The play opened with benedictory songs in honour of the presiding deities. The first player to enter was the clown, or Vidushaka, dressed like a jungle creature with green leaves tied to his head dress. The Sutradhara entered into a humorous repartee with the clown and enlisted his help in the performance. The God Ganapathi then entered and assured the Sutradhara that the performance would be a success.
>
> The Goddess of Learning, Saraswati, then entered dancing on a wooden peacock. Ganapathi and Saraswati were entertained to dance and music by the Gandharvas and Kinnaras ... The play started, after the departure of Ganapathi and Saraswati, with a short description of the plot by the Sutradhara.
>
> At the beginning of every scene, the same procedure of giving a resume was followed. The Sutradhara sang a song giving in outline the events to be acted and the players spoke the dialogue, which was not written but roughly decided beforehand. A few leading actors including the clown were allowed more liberty to depart from the set lines.
>
> The actors were subject to the direct and vigilant control of the Sutradhara who prompted them in dialogue as well as movements. All the characters, except the demons, sang songs appropriate to the mood of the scene. The Sutradhara and the members of the chorus not only provided instrumental music but often joined in the singing. The entries of the demons were a noisy and spectacular affair. The red painted faces of the inhuman [sc. non-human] characters looked fierce when lit up by naked torches.[6]

It is more than evident that this performative schema was the complete opposite of the broad realistic mimeticism with which the English theatre came to India.

The earliest modern theatres in India were built by the British *c.*1770s[7] in the colonially founded cities of Calcutta, Bombay and, later, Madras. These were proscenium theatres built like the eighteenth-century English box stage. An epistolary novel on the earliest period of Anglo-India, *Hartley House* (1789), affords an acute description of the Calcutta Theatre (1774) – set up with the help of David Garrick, who sent scripts, scenery and stage machinery – in the words of its narrator Sophia Goldborne:

> It consists only of pit and boxes to be admitted to the first of which you pay eight rupees (20 shillings), to the last a gold mohor (40 shillings). It is therefore no wonder that the house is about the size of the Bath Theatre and consists of Pit and boxes only, [the] first an area in the centre, the second a range of commodious enclosed or rather separated, seats around it, from one corner of the stage to the other. No expense has been spared to gratify either the eye or the ear; a very pleasing band of music saluted the present Governor on his entrance and the pit was crowded with spectators. It is lighted upon the English plan with lamps at the bottom of the stage and girandoles at proper distances with wax candles covered with glass shades as in the Verandahs to prevent their extinction.[8]

Another visitor, Mrs Eliza Fay, who has left an account of her visit to Calcutta from 1780 to 1784, refers to the Calcutta Theatre as being "very neatly fitted up, and the scenery and decorations quite equal to … and the characters supported in a manner that would not disgrace any European stage".[9] Sophia Goldborne was more completely transported by her experience of the Calcutta Theatre: "as for myself, my attention was so engaged by the piece that my heart several times asked if it could be possible I was at the distance of 4000 miles from the British metropolis".[10]

It would not be hard to imagine the dislocating novelty such a quintessentially Western and English staging practice constituted for Indians. Scholar-critic S.K. Das sees this impact in terms of a "blinding glare".[11] There is evidence, contrary to popular belief, that many Indians did find their way to the English theatre. As early as 1789, Sophia Goldborne notes the presence of "country-born ladies … of dark complexions"[12] in the boxes, and later, with the spread of English education, English theatre became a cultivated practice among the Indians. Emily Eden, sister of the Governor-General, Baron Auckland, recounts in her journal a production of *Macbeth* in Calcutta more memorable for its audience members:

> Thursday, November 11, 1841: We went last night to see *Macbeth* – a bold attempt ... The house was over-full, and it must be a wonderful change to people who remember India ten years ago to see quantities of baboos [Indian clerks], who could not get seats, standing on their benches reading their Shakespeares, and then looking off at the stage, and then applauding on the backs of their books. The native generation who have been brought up at Hindu College are perfectly mad about Shakespeare. What a triumph it is for him, dear creature! Plays that he wrote nearly 300 years ago acted to a race that were hardly known in his time, and who yet see the truth of his writing just as much as the courtiers of Queen Elizabeth did.[13]

It was in the schools and colleges that Indians were first inducted into Western performative modes, with Shakespeare as the high point of every performative endeavour. Recitation and playing of scenes from Shakespeare by amateur students began as early as 1824 to showcase the mastery of the English language and, more crucially, their imitation of the speech and elocutionary manners of the English. Collegiate dramatic societies sprang up in the 1860s in Bombay and Calcutta and, although the challenge of playing Shakespeare in English was immense, the enthusiasm was unbounded. A review in the *Bombay Gazette*, 6 November 1871, comments on the obstacles that the local youth had to face in sustaining this new-found love for drama:

> They surmount difficulties which would stagger many a European. Language has to be acquired; histories of habits totally different from those they meet in their own society have to be gathered or guessed at; properties and the necessary paraphernalia of the stage have to be procured – not an easy thing, by any means in India; and we are not sure that difficulties of a social kind have not to be encountered and overcome. So great is the difference ... that probably an Englishman present at a Parsee representation of a European play may look on with similar feelings to those which might be expected from Aeschylus if he could ... come back and witness our revival of a Grecian play, and the attempts of the moderns to ape the life of the ancients.

A whole spectrum of 'aping' was required, the very body language of performance was changed, and the illusionist stage, artificial lighting, realistic make-up and costuming, alien to indigenous practice, needed to be imported.

At the most immediate level, it was the spatial dimensions and the material practice accompanying the bourgeois realism of the Western theatre which impressed Indians. Bhave, who also staged his *Sita Swayamvara*, the first traditional play, in a Western playhouse, the Grant Road Theatre (1846–60) in Bombay, has recorded that he was primarily attracted to it by its orderliness – the seating plan, the curtains, scenery, props, lighting and the ticketing process, features which were totally absent in the Indian staging practice. But more pervasively, it was the introduction to Western perspectivism and realism which created a fundamental shift: the illusionist box-stage was packaged with its own kind of script, setting and acting methodology. The concept of a scripted play on secular themes, with realistic make-up, costuming and acting, within a recognisable *mise en scène*, where performance was a pretence, a make-believe slice of life in imitation of the world around you, was a path-breaking revelation for Indians.

The first original Indian plays written on the Western model which appeared in the mid-nineteenth century (*Kulina Kula Sarbasva* (All in All Noble One, Bengali, 1854, staged 1857) and *Thorle Madhavrao Peshwe* (Marathi, 1857, staged 1860)) began to be termed 'bookish plays' in Marathi, not signifying pejoratively an academic quality, but rather highlighting the fact that they were for the first time written and published in book form and therefore available for anyone who cared to read or perform them and no longer the exclusive property of a particular caste sanctioned by custom to perform them. They were also written in prose, the language of everyday 'real' discourse, until then not considered suitable for literary and artistic creation. The logo-centricism of Western literature took over Indian theatre, for until then most of the folk plays had passed down orally through generations, with only a few folk forms preserving a token script, e.g. the 'attakathas' or play stories of *Kudiattam*, which were in effect a kind of director/player's manual of interpretations and instructions.

The challenge posed by this new aesthetic with fixed roles based on a given/immutable text went beyond the book, as it were, and on to the stage. It was most acutely felt in the acting sphere, for the actors, who were earlier free to improvise according to their own proclivities, were now forced to memorise other people's words. Audiences, too, began to expect something more, and productions are known to have advertised themselves as those in which "the actors will generally speak according to the book".[14] An entire new body language and culture had to be adopted, and for plays in translation a double adaptation needed to be effected. An essay by V.V. Shirwadkar, a well-known Marathi playwright who has translated Shakespeare, recalls such a moment of tension in one of the earliest stagings of *Othello*, translated into Marathi by Mahadevshastri Kolhatkar in 1867:

> We can find descriptions of how the old actors in the habit of extempore speeches and acting used to get bewildered while rehearsing the 'bookish' plays … as for example in Ichalkaranjikar Mandali's presentation of *Othello* … Performing the mythological plays the senior actors, though illiterate, would show their oratory keeping the story in mind. The 'prose-based' plays changed that style entirely. Since there were different types of language, styles of enacting, appropriate gestures etc. in them, the Mandali was burdened with remembering these plays word-for-word. Obviously, then, criticism of it started, indirectly in the beginning, sometimes by dilly-dallying and sometimes by criticizing it directly: "Whoever memorizes the speech of Sumer Singh in Narayanrao's farce? How many have memorized their roles in Damaji? Then why do we need to memorize only these books? It should be enough that we do not miss the meaning." This kind of debate started. When they took up *Othello* for staging the Mandali believed that the person who acted as jester (in mythological plays) could easily play the role of Iago; all that was needed was to give him some directions. But I told the Mandali that in 'prose-based' plays speeches will not come out well without matching actions.

Shirwadkar also underlines how much of a 'helping hand' Shakespeare gave in the development of Marathi theatre, a fillip that is not often acknowledged in the traditional histories:

> Plays of Sanskrit poets were set in the repertoires of the Ichalkaranjikars and others. But since the subjects of these plays were known to all and there were familiar characters in them like the jester etc., there was some scope for going beyond the written text while staging them. This facility was not there in Shakespeare's plays. In them, it was necessary to remain faithful to the words of the poet and the character he has created, the storyline and the *rasa-pari-poshan* [complete development of the *rasa*]. In the next period of 15 years, after staging *Othello*, they brought some more translations of Shakespeare onstage. These plays accomplished the important task of firmly establishing literary language on the Marathi stage: or at least expedited it.[15]

A generation later, another rare record by Pammal Sambanda Mudaliar, recognised as the father of modern Tamil theatre, who translated, directed and acted in five Shakespeare plays, is to found in his memoir, recently translated into English. This documents in detail not just the meticulous care with which he set about translating *Hamlet*, but also the changed attitudes towards role playing and the adoption of rigorous Western methods of preparation to direct and perform the role of Hamlet in 1906. Sambanda laboured over the translation for six years, and, while the names were Tamilised (Hamlet became Amaladityan – the Pure One), the story remained faithful to the original. His fascination for the role, he says, stems from the fact that "this character casts such a spell on the minds of all actors … [it] abounds in possibilities for an actor … It is only in the character of Hamlet that one sees many splendid opportunities to express all the *rasas* (moods/emotions)." Aware of the complexity of the part, he was not content to just match word and gesture but tried to delve into the inner reaches of the character. He read, he says, "almost all the books that were available on this play … in the libraries in Chennai … in particular … all the critical works written on this character, Hamlet … and what eminent actors had written about how they played this role". He mentions he studied how Edmund Kean, Kemble, Beerbohm Tree, Edwin Booth, Forbes Robertson, Frank Benson and others played Hamlet. Confessing that he was left "thoroughly confused" he tried to find his own way relying on his actor's instincts. "It is the performer's part that is tough. For those who do scholarly studies would see the validity of both schools in the debate and step aside contented that they had done their work. But the actor has to believe in one or the other [view] and perform accordingly."[16] The challenge of the individuation of character and of enacting a psychological realism was now more comprehensible and was being better negotiated by Indian actors and directors, significantly, by using traditional categories of *rasa* to 'place' a foreign text that would then be worked upon with Western methods.

The 'en-gendering' of roles, not just texts, created further challenges. Realistic mimeticism demanded that women enact their own body language and that women, not boy actors, perform their own selves. In Calcutta, Girish Chandra Ghose, actor, director and playwright, who is seen as the maker of modern Bengali theatre, was one of the first to spend considerable energy in training women to perform on stage. Until almost 1872 female parts had been performed by male actors in most parts of the country, but in Calcutta, due to the greater exposure to English amateur theatre and the shows of the travelling companies who employed actresses, Indian women were accepted earlier on-stage. Binodini Dasi, the best known of the Bengali actresses of the nineteenth century, reveals in her autobiography, *Amar Jiban* (My Life) (1912), the intricate processes of imbibing theatrical mimeticism and even a cultural osmosis:

> Girish babu would instruct me with great care in my roles. His was a wonderful teaching method: first, he would explain the *bhava* (essence) of the role in question, then he asked me to memorise the lines. After this was done, he would, at his convenience, come to our home and … talk to us about numerous English actresses and the works of famous English poets such as Shakespeare, Byron, Milton and Pope. He discussed their works in the form of stories and sometimes he read out sections from the text to explain them the better. He taught us a range of behavior, discussing every aspect separately.

Realism, imitation, identification to emulation, the familiar trajectory of an annexing mimesis, is to be found in the story of the early Indian stage. All the early acting, even in the case of women, a craft which gave them a legitimacy (Binodini came from the red-light area) and status, was consciously honed by the English model. As Binodini admits,

> I would be anxious to see the performance of any famous British actor or actress who happened to come to the city … I liked very much the stories narrated by Girish babu about famous British actors and actresses and whatever else he read out to us from books: he explained to us the various kinds of critical opinions expressed about Mrs. Siddons … about the kind of costume that Ellen Terry always wore; how Bandmann dressed in his role as Hamlet; how Ophelia always wore a dress made of flowers.[17]

The praxis of psychological realism was not confined to an individuation of roles; it went beyond to demand a larger 'byplay', an ensemble-like interaction amongst the actors on-stage. This was a convention lacking in traditional Indian theatre, with typified characters and well-known stories. The very first public performance of *Othello* in English, by an Indian, Baishav Charan Auddy, opposite a white Desdemona, in Calcutta in 1848, although lauded for "enlisting the audiences' feelings on his side" was mainly criticised for the actor's restrictive lack of byplay.[18] Half a century later, Pammal Sambanda is more aware of the essential place of responsive byplay in the Western performative practice. His memoir narrates how he would not only read out the play to his cast but also parts of critical works, explaining the finer points and nuances of acting. Further, he would by personal demonstration show how they should play their parts and the stage-business, something he found them particularly deficient in: "they stand chewing beaten rice", quips he. As he underlined, "if this is not done, no enactment can come alive".[19]

From text and character to setting, the structure of performance changed. While the traditional theatre had a minimal setting, now stages were being architecturally designed with proscenium arches painted with scrolls for the complete picture frame effect. They were fitted with cycloramas, flats and rolling curtains, perspectivally painted to give an illusion of depth. As theatre historian A.V. Kulkarni has noted:

> The drop curtain in the old mythological plays used to bear crudely drawn, gaudily coloured representations of the deities – Ganapati, Maruti or Shankar-Parvati. But when 'bookish' plays were performed, an attempt was made to convey to the audience the exact location of the scenes, such as roads, temples, gardens, palaces, hills, jungles, or rivers by means of curtains depicting them as faithfully as possible. Since some of these plays dealt with contemporary subjects and since, meanwhile, education in the new English techniques of painting had become available, skills in curtain painting improved ... the greatest change was visible in the settings. Earlier a garden used to be represented by means of a few branches stuck on the stage; but now, in addition to the gardens painted on the curtains, real trees, potted shrubs and plants would be placed on the stage to complete the illusion of the real.[20]

II

Yet the mimetic realism imported into Indian theatre remained half-baked: the power of the indigenous tradition was too strong, old habits were not so easy to jettison and strange hybridities, an amalgam of the symbolic and the realist, came into being – like putting bananas on a mango tree. (This phrase derives from the title of a collection of essays in Kannada on the development of Kannada theatre by K.V. Akshara in which he analyses the hybrid nature of his regional theatre.[21]) Vishnu Das Bhave performed his *Sita Swayamvara* within the boxlike confines of the

Grant Road Theatre, quite unperturbed by the dislocating hybridities which were, however, not lost on the reviewer from the *Bombay Times*, 11 March 1853: "The Gods and Goddesses of wisdom seemed quite at home ... while sitting on chairs and couches, and the combat between Luxman and Indrajit was carried on (the weapons being bows and the combatants dancing fiercely round each other) in an English-looking parlour." Plays in translation were invariably adapted and localised. Not only were Indian names and locales used but Indian songs, music and dances too were interspersed. Many of the early Shakespeare plays performed in Indian languages were changed into *sangeet natakas* (musical dramas) with conventions of the classical tradition like a *nandi* (prologue) and *sutradhara* (impresario) added. Since the *Natyashastra* does not permit the depiction of death on stage, tragedies like *Lear* and *Romeo and Juliet* were given a happy ending. Even when the intention was to perform Shakespeare faithfully, songs as a concession to indigenous taste were nearly always conceded. Girish Ghose's faithful translation of *Macbeth* (1893) was a test case: painstakingly put up in a Scottish style, with scenery by English painters, it was praised by the critics but failed at the box office, even although it had interpolated many songs.[22]

A hybridity of forms and presentation became the popular norm: it was defined by a broad realism unconcerned with a rooting verisimilitude, by a mimeticism jostling with an expressionism, with the everyday juxtaposed with the marvellous and prose interspersed with poetry. The main credit or discredit for consolidating this type of hybridity is attributed to the Parsi theatre, the first modern commercial theatre in India, which consciously developed a hybrid style as its signature. Its Shakespeare, for instance, did not stop at broad adaptations into the local milieu, with song and dance, but telescoped several plays into one. One of its most popular adaptations that was played over several years and in all parts of the country, *Saubhagya Sundari*, was an amalgam of *Othello*, *Cymbeline*, *As You Like It* and *Twelfth Night*. Parsi theatre borrowed unashamedly from the West: it copied the Victorian vogue for spectacular illusionism and specialised in special effects staging, with rapid changes of the drop curtain, and 'trick scenes' showing flying gods or terrifying demons, and disasters like fires, shipwrecks, collapsing bridges and crashing trains. It cashed in on the fashion for the Gaiety girls and introduced the choric dance in Indian plays blending, in the process, Indian folk and classical music with the Western. Popularity of the melodrama fed into its own scripts giving native emotionalism a fillip and dovetailing the sensational into the marvellous. Its acting styles were declamatory and histrionic. This eclectic hybridity of performance – and self-imaging – of the Parsi theatre was not welcomed by all: serious writers and critics lambasted it as crude and inauthentic. It was not incidental that the driving force behind this theatre, in both economic and ideational terms, was the Parsis (Zoroastrians), a rootless immigrant community with no stake in the local cultures. They modelled their theatre on the European travelling companies and toured the length and breadth of the sub-continent. Their shows were hugely popular and spawned a host of similar *natak* (play) companies wherever they visited. The Parsi theatre companies and the company *nataks* generated an 'alchemy', a transformative wave which unified theatre practice, creating a pan-Indian 'national' identity for the theatre. From the 1870s to the 1930s the eclectic hybridity of the Parsi theatre set the trend all over India.[23]

III

It is often argued that realism in India was a failure because it was imported without the necessary sociological development. Without the requisite presence of an individualising bourgeoisie springing up on the back of an industrial revolution, no true realism was possible. This may be so in some contexts, but a major, historically documented, local factor was the promulgation of the Dramatic Performances Act in 1876, a draconian piece of legislation designed to crush the mushrooming of satire against the government. Indian theatre had begun in the modern period under discussion with plays in the realistic mode; the earliest written plays were historical or social problem plays. Almost all were critical of the British government, indirectly, if not openly. Performances of *Nil Darpan* (Indigo Mirror, 1860), a play of stark realism depicting the exploitation of the indigo farmers by the British planters, had started a furore, but it was a later farce, *The Police of Pig and Sheep* (1875), lampooning the local officials, Hogg and Lamb, which provided the ultimate provocation. After this Act, which required all plays to be cleared by a censor before performance or publication, writers had to resort to allegory to voice their dissatisfactions; mythological and historical plays became popular, but the initial drive towards a direct, and often biting, realism had been deflected.

Another reason as to why realism did not prosper in Indian theatre derives from the very nature of mimesis. Gebauer and Wulf point out how the primary meaning of the act of imitation produces identification, leaving the performer in a condition of equivalence and sameness with the Other. "Such an act of complementary seeing produces a correspondence between people",[24] they assert, which goes a long way in explaining why, in the earliest stages, Indian attempts to perform English plays were greeted with hostile fulminations in the Anglo-Indian press. When the first private theatre in Bengal, Prasanna Kumar's Hindu Theatre, opened in 1831 with scenes from *Julius Caesar*, under the direction of H.H. Wilson, Sanskrit scholar and Company servant, the newspaper *East Indian* remarked:

> We hear that the performances are to be in the English language. Who advised this strange proceeding we know not, but it is surely worth reconsidering. What can be worse than to have the best dramatic compositions in the English language murdered outright, night after night, foreign manners misrepresented and instead of holding the mirror up to nature caricaturing everything human? We recommend our Hindu patriots and philanthropists to instruct their countrymen by means of school [education] and when they are fitted to appreciate the dramatic compositions of refined nations, it will be quite time enough [*sic*] to erect theatre ... A theatre among the Hindus with the degree of knowledge they at present posses will be like building a palace in the waste.

(*Asiatic Journal*, January–April 1832)

The social space of the theatre was not without its political charge; its mimeticism was perceived as transgressive. Role playing became social climbing; the slave pretended to become the master. No wonder that realism of the Western variety did not or could not take root in Indian theatre.

"The story of Indian drama is extremely tortuous and more dramatic than that of any literary genre", says S.K. Das in his *History of Indian Literature*.[25] Drama took longer to react to the Western impact; it was more hesitant, in comparison with the novel or poetry which succumbed to a more immediate mimicry of the Western forms. Drama being a performative medium was lumbered with its own body of languages, its material bases that could never be fully overturned. It absorbed the new impulses, but reflected them back in an appropriatory manner, in its own indigenous terms. Yet this evolutionary process of borrowing, assimilating and transforming, of presentation and re-presentation, was not without friction. It posed challenges in practical terms as seen in the accounts of the actors and directors; it forced writers to change and experiment with new genres and, most critically, it exposed political issues of identity and authenticity. If 'imitation' was to be the way forward, were the old and the traditional to be rejected? If the new was modern, how relevant remained the traditional? All through the colonial period, English and Western literature, imposed by government dictate, was held as an inspirational model, not as a mechanical one for mimicry, particularly in drama. "The ideal of our theatre will always be Shakespeare"[26] was the belief of Rabindranath Tagore, although in practice he wrote plays that strove for a synthesis between a Western rationalism and realism and an Indian humanism and symbolism. Yet this high estimation of Western art was a contested and debated one. As early as 1930, the Kannada dramatist V. Raghavan sounded a caveat, which was not heeded by many:

> Dramatic renaissance in India today will not be truly Indian if it is only going to create an imitation in India of European theatre; an organic and truly Indian theatre has to be raised, and in this task, the theoretical Sanskrit literature on 'Natya' dance and drama, the example of Sanskrit dramatists like Kalidasa and Shudraka, and the many vernacular survivals in the various provinces in the form of dances and dance-dramas have got to play a great part … It must be preserved from modern contamination and slander.[27]

The one permanent effect of the colonial experience, particularly with regard to drama, was to drive a wide and sharp wedge between tradition and modernity. While earlier there were two parallel streams of the Sanskritic and the folk or popular which borrowed and interacted with each other, now there are three mutually antagonistic streams – of the urban modern Indian theatre inspired directly by Western models, the rural folk theatre which continues albeit in many modified or degenerated forms, and a museumised classical Sanskrit theatre. And fifty-five years after independence we do not seem to be any closer to bridging these divides, at least not in a comprehensible manner. Although many attempts have been made, for example the 'back to the roots movement' which received official sanction in the 1970s and 1980s, and there is considerable experimentation and discussion about the need to evolve a common idiom, the schism between the urban/rural remains. Girish Karnad, contemporary award-winning dramatist, candidly voices the dilemmas of writing today: "there [is] no other (beyond the Western) urban tradition to look to ... what are we, basically city dwellers, to do with this stream [of traditional theatre]? What did the entire paraphernalia of theatrical devices, half curtains, masks, improvisation, music, and mime mean?"[28]

In such a situation there is reason to wonder whether there is something inimical to realism in the Indian social, creative psyche? Or is it a fact that an alternative kind of mimetic realism, more of a *vraisemblance extraordinaire*, best seen in the evergreen popularity of Bollywood's Hindi cinema, has been forged which interposes the ideal with the empirical, the fabulous and the possible with the observed and the determined, and which may be a more acute mirror of the inner needs of a vast community of viewers? Bollywood cinema, which rose on the ashes of the Parsi theatre, inherited its hybrid praxis, an eclectic mix of Eastern and Western forms, and has achieved a similar pan-Indian appeal and success. Now when Bollywood's lush musicality and emotionalism have acquired a global reach thanks to the Indian diaspora and even a global recognition and acceptability, is it not the moment to re-examine the given notions of the 'real', the 'pleasurable' and the 'poetic'? And may not this eclectic and hybrid mimeticism, the bedrock of Indian theatre and film, be seen as another version of a 'magic realism' which has evolved in resistance to, and to keep at bay, first a colonising aesthetic and now a globalising imperative? And further, may it not be that this hybrid mimeticism, intertwined with the issues of identity and nationality, is part of the decolonising process and not of surrender, and therefore may it not be admitted into the expanding meanings of mimesis?

Chapter Five

1. For the history of Indian theatre see Adya Rangacharya, *The Indian Theatre* (New Delhi: National Book Trust, 1971); R.K. Yajnik, *The Indian Theatre: Its Origins and its Later Developments under European Influence* (London: Allen & Unwin, 1933); and Hemendra Nath Das Gupta, *The Indian Stage*, 1st edn 1944–46, rpt (New Delhi: Munshiram Manoharlal, 2002).
2. Günter Gebauer and Christoph Wulf, *Mimesis: Culture, Art, Society*, trans. Don Renaeu (Berkeley, CA: University of California Press, 1992), pp. 310, 311.
3. Ibid., p. 311.
4. For Indian poetics, see Manmohan Ghose, *Natyashastra*, in English translation (Calcutta: Royal Asiatic Society, Bengal, 1950).

5. For traditional Indian theatre see Kapila Vatsyayan, *Traditional Indian Theatre: Multiple Streams* (New Delhi: National Book Trust, 1980); M.L. Varadpande, *History of Indian Theatre: Lok Ranga, Panorama of Indian Folk Theatre* (New Delhi: Abhinav Publications, 1992); and Farley P. Richmond, Darius L. Swann and Phillip B. Zarilli, *Indian Theatre: Traditions of Performance* (Delhi: Motilal Banarsidas, 1993).
6. *The Marathi Theatre 1843–1960* (Bombay: Popular Book Depot, 1961), pp. 3–4.
7. The first English theatre in Calcutta is dated 1753 but survived only for a year or so.
8. *Hartley House: A Novel of the Days of Warren Hastings* (London: J. Dodsley, 1789, rpt Calcutta: Thacker, Spink, 1908), p. 202.
9. Eliza Fay, *Original Letters from India*, ed. Rev. Walter Kelly Firminger (Calcutta: Calcutta Historical Society, Thacker Spink, 1908), anthologised in *Calcutta in the Eighteenth Century: Impressions of Travellers*, ed. P. Thankappan (Nair, Calcutta: Firma KLM, 1984), pp. 199–200.
10. *Hartley House*, p. 207.
11. S.K. Das, *Indian Ode to the West Wind: Studies in Literary Encounters* (New Delhi: Pencraft International, 2002), p. 19.
12. *Hartley House*, p. 207.
13. Emily Eden, in Thankappan (ed.), *Calcutta in the Eighteenth Century*, p. 748.
14. Shanta Gokhale, *Playwright at the Centre: Marathi Drama from 1843 to the Present* (Calcutta: Seagull Books, 2000), p. 16.
15. V.V. Shirwadkar, 'Shakespeare in Marathi Theatre', in *Roopakam*, Shakespeare Volume (Quarter Centenary Commemoration Volume), ed. G.M. Watve (Poona: Marathi Natya Parishad, 1965), pp. 27–8, 32–3, trans. Harish Thakkar. For the place of Shakespeare in India, see Poonam Trivedi and Dennis Bartholomeusz (eds), *India's Shakespeare: Translation, Interpretation and Performance* (Newark, DE: University of Delaware Press, 2004); and John Gillies, Ryuta Minami, Ruru Li and Poonam Trivedi, 'Shakespeare on the Stages of Asia', in *Cambridge Companion to Shakespeare on Stage* (Cambridge: Cambridge University Press, 2002).
16. Pammal Sambanda Mudaliar, *Nataka Medai Ninaivuhal*, subtitled in English *Over Forty Years before the Footlights*, trans. Venkat Swaminathan, *Sangeet Natak* 123, Jan.–Mar. 1997, pp. 27–8, 32–3. For a detailed account of the performance of *Hamlet* in India, see my own 'Play[ing]'s the thing': *Hamlet* on the Indian Stage', in *Hamlet Studies* 24 (2002).
17. Binodini Dasi, *My Life and My Life as an Actress*, ed. and trans. Rimli Bhattacharya (Delhi: Kali for Women, 1998), pp. 78, 80.
18. See review in the *Bengal Harkaru and India Gazette*, 1 and 19 August 1848. For a discussion of this production see my own, 'Re-locating Shakespeare: Acting and Reacting to *Othello* in India', in *Shakespeare in China: Perspectives and Performances: A Collection of Theses* (Shanghai: Shanghai Theatre Academy, 1999).
19. Pammal Sambanda Mudaliar, *Nataka Medai Ninaivuhal*, p. 31.
20. A.V. Kulkarni, *Marathi Rangbhoomi* (Marathi Theatre) (Pune: Venus Book Stall, 1961), 2nd edn, pp. 64–5, trans. Shanta Gokhale, *Playwright at the Centre*, p. 16.
21. K.V. Akshara, *Maavina Maradalli Baaleya Hannu* (Banana on a Mango Tree) (Heggodu: Akshara Prakashoina, 1998). One of the essays in English translation, 'The Dreams of Kannada Theatre: A Turn-of-the-Century Narrative', was published in *Theatre India* 2, November 1999.
22. On the performance of Shakespeare in traditional folk forms, see my own 'Folk Shakespeare', in Trivedi and Bartholomeusz (eds), *India's Shakespeare*.

23. For the history of Parsi theatre see Somnath Gupt, *Parsi Thiyetar: Udbhav Aur Vikas* (The Parsi Theatre: Origins and Development) (Allahabad: Lok Bharati, 1981), parts of which in English translation by Kathryn Hansen have been published in *Sangeet Natak* 36: 1, 2, 3–4.
24. Gebauer and Wulf, *Mimesis: Culture, Art, Society*, p. 5.
25. S.K. Das, *A History of Indian Literature, 1800–1910, Western Impact: Indian Response*, vol. VIII (New Delhi: Sahitya Akademi, 1991), p. 117.
26. Rabindranath Tagore, Introduction to *Malini* (1896), in *The Collected Works of Tagore*, vol. 5 (Calcutta: Government of West Bengal, 1961), p. 485.
27. V. Raghavan, *Rangasthala* (Playing Space), trans. K.V. Akshara (Mangalore: Polali Shastry Smaraka Samiti, 1980), p. 55.
28. Girish Karnad, Introduction to *Three Plays* (New Delhi: Oxford University Press), pp. 7, 12.

CHAPTER SIX

Court masque and the (re)production of aristocratic identity

Monika Smialkowska

THE COURT MASQUE occupies a somewhat paradoxical position in recent criticism of Renaissance literature and culture. Despite the genre being frequently used in interrogations of the workings of power and ideology, the masque tends to be viewed as a reflection or expression of the ruling elite's world views. The corollary of such analysis is a rather monolithic account of the masque, in which the genre's internal inconsistencies are explained as reflecting the "sustaining contradictions" of the royal power or factional divisions within the social elite.[1] This chapter proposes to shift the critical attention away from treating the genre as an expression of the dominant social group's values towards accounting for the processes whereby the elite's self-image is constructed and projected in the masque. To this end, I shall first examine the reasons why the current criticism of the masque tends towards the former model, and then outline an alternative theoretical position – one in which the masque is constructively involved in the production of the elite's identity. My contention is that the key area for this cultural production lies in the masque's constant efforts to establish a clear-cut opposition between the 'high culture' of the elite and the 'low culture' of the non-elite. The masque's mimesis, therefore, is not a simple reflection of the reality existing outside the textual domain, but a dynamic operation of establishing and reinforcing social differences. Such an interpretation opens up new possibilities for accounting for the masque's generic fractures and inconsistencies, treating them as the symptoms of the internal contradictions and the lack of completion characterising the masque's ideological operations.

As is well known, theoretical developments in the 1980s and 1990s put in doubt an earlier assumption that Renaissance art was a reflection of a unified and harmonious "Elizabethan world picture".[2] Early modern dramatic genres in particular have come to be understood as not simply mirroring, but rather actively participating in the construction of social reality in the period. Moreover, they have frequently been seen as interrogating and subverting the period's dominant ideology, a position best captured by the title of Jonathan Dollimore's influential book, *Radical Tragedy*.[3] The court masque, however, remains to a large extent immune from those radical conclusions which have refigured our understanding of early modern literature and culture. The genre still tends to be analysed as an expression of dominant ideology and a reflection of the ruling elite's concepts of the world. Paradoxically, the persistence of this opinion is partly due to the fact that the masque served as a testing ground for New Historicist analysis. New Historicism, together with Michel Foucault's theories, has paved the way for a radical rethinking of the relationship between history and literature: one in which both historical 'facts' and literary works began to be considered as textual constructions, involved with the workings of power and ideology. At the same time, however, New Historicism, especially in its early phases, has tended to understand power as all-encompassing and totalising. In this type of account, literary and artistic works usually become hopelessly entangled in producing and perpetuating dominant ideology, whose subversion is all but impossible.[4]

New Historicist analyses of the masque owe much to the pioneering work of Stephen Orgel. In his early accounts of the masque, he argues that the genre offers an idealist mimesis of dominant world order: "The end toward which the masque moved was to destroy any sense of theatre and to include the whole court in the mimesis – in a sense, what the spectator watched he ultimately became."[5] The masque is analysed as a genre through which "a deep truth about the monarchy was realized and embodied in action", an expression of "the strongest Renaissance beliefs about the nature of kingship".[6] Such analysis presents the world of the court entertainments as one in which the boundaries of reality and fiction dissolve: the masque conflates its literary idealisations and the reality of the court. Consequently, the genre becomes a monolithic statement of its central idea, which coincides with official court propaganda. There is little room for subversion in this scheme, since even the unruliness of the antimasque is there only in order to be contained and incorporated into the overall unity.[7]

Martin Butler points out that such an "understanding of the masques as theatres of power" is "broadly congruent with other current paradigms in which the past is encountered less as a process than as geography: the carnival, the prison, the landscape tour, the great aristocratic household", which have been advocated by New Historicists.[8] These paradigms present power as circulatory and history as a structure rather than as "a sequence of events and motives". As Butler argues, a major drawback of New Historicist analysis is that it "make[s] every masque seem to do more or less the same thing – legitimate the monarch".[9] The masque becomes a political monolith, in which even a seeming subversion of royal power is always already incorporated into its perpetuation. And the consequence for the theoretical understanding of the masque's representational premises is, in Lloyd Davis's words, that "the masque is conceived as 'super-mimetic' … [A]s text and event it seems to efface the 're' in representation and to reveal meaning as historical presence and action."[10]

How difficult it has become to question the notion that the masque affirms the existing order by means of Neo-Platonic idealist mimesis is indicated by the treatment of the genre in Dollimore's *Radical Tragedy*, a book explicitly concerned with demonstrating subversive elements of Renaissance drama. Dollimore poses a question as to whether the antimasque's misrule subverted dominant order or rather reinforced it by acting as a safety valve. His socio-historical answer is that "it could be either depending on occasion and context".[11] However, he does not provide an example of the subversive use of the masque in its most typical, that is courtly, context. Instead, he focuses on subversive applications of the masque within revenge tragedy. He reasserts that the masque, when appearing on its own, as a court performance, "was clearly an ideological legitimation of the power structure, as was the preliminary antimasque".[12]

This function of the masque has recently been disputed in the light of revisionist historians' analyses of the period. Revisionism attempts to dispense with the 'Whiggish' notion that the early Stuarts' policies separated the English nation into two opposed camps (the country and the city; the Roundheads and the Cavaliers), which, as that rift progressively deepened, caused the inevitable cataclysm of the civil war.[13] Instead, revisionists advocate a view of the early-seventeenth-century society as a group of individuals and factions, each with its own interests, constantly vying for power, gathered around the sovereign's court. This shift in historical analysis brought about corresponding changes in masque criticism. Most importantly, critics of revisionist orientation, such as Kevin Sharpe or Martin Butler, argue that the masques contain both praise and criticism of the king, and that those conflicting messages originate in the factional divisions of the court itself.[14] Instead of being an expression of the royal will, the masque becomes a site of negotiation of multiple voices and conflicting points of view.

The limitation of this approach, however, is that it still encourages a view of the masque as reflecting the ideology of the elite, albeit an elite which is factionally divided. The masque is assumed to speak the elite's language, while inconsistencies in particular entertainments are explained as resulting from different opinions within that elite, rather than from ideological fractures inherent in the genre. In this way, revisionist criticism, while in one sense moving away from the monolithic view of the masque, ends up constructing another monolith – that of the ruling elite, engaged in internal power negotiations, but largely immune from external pressures from the subordinate classes. Moreover, it moves away from an account of the masque (and literature in general) as participating in the production of ideological structures towards one which sees it as a reflection of the purposes of certain individuals and factions. The focus shifts from macro- to micro-politics, from ideology to local issues of the day and political transactions conducted chiefly within the privileged social groups.

Both New Historicism and revisionist criticism make important contributions to the exploration of mimesis in the masque, the former by drawing attention to the masque's active role in perpetuating courtly ideology, and the latter by putting in doubt the assumption that that ideology is completely unified and identical with that of the monarch. However, neither New Historicism nor revisionist criticism fully accounts for the irresolvable tensions and contradictions at the heart of the masque as a genre. In fact, both critical approaches to some extent encourage the view of the masque as "super-mimetic": New Historicist analysis tends to conclude with the genre staging the monarch's omnipotent presence, while in revisionist accounts the opinions voiced in the masque can be traced back to their origin in individuals or groups at the court. In other words, the masque seems to reproduce a traceable original meaning which can be recovered and closed down, rather than participating in a construction of ideology which is self-contradictory and never fully complete.

By combining some of the insights of New Historicism and revisionist criticism this chapter proposes to shift attention from assuming that the masque imitates courtly reality (be it ideal and unified or factional) to the examination of the processes whereby the elite's self-image is constructed and projected. This type of analysis is aided and encouraged by recent feminist explorations of the masque, in which the genre emerges as an arena of large-scale ideological struggle, rather than purely topical negotiation. Yumna Siddiqi and Kim Hall, amongst others, uncover inconsistencies produced by the masque's combination of contemporary discourses intended to achieve a unified ideological stance, such as those of gender and race.[15] Meanwhile, Clare McManus in her recent book demonstrates how significant ideological fractures emerge as a result of the masque's bringing together of tropes such as female submission, bodily display, and verbal silence of both male and female aristocratic performers.[16] These types of analysis demonstrate that the dominant ideology is not naturally given or self-contained, but constructed in relation to other discourses, which that ideology attempts to subordinate, but without which it cannot function.

Such a relational model can be applied to the examination of popular and high culture in the masque, an area highly constitutive of the masque's form and meaning, but relatively little explored in the light of modern critical theory.[17] It is striking how prevalent the presence of 'low' culture is in the masque, despite the genre's exclusive and elitist character. The antimasque sections frequently include lowlife characters, who disrupt courtly decorum with their irreverent speech and behaviour. My contention is that those characters are introduced in order to construct aristocratic identity by repeatedly staging a clear-cut opposition between the high culture of the elite and the low culture of the non-elite, through a simple formula: 'We are what we are because we are not what they are.' However, elite ideology constructed in such a relational manner (by contrasting the elite to the plebeians) is fraught with internal contradictions and instabilities. Ideological rifts and anxieties surface in many masques, especially in the way in which the genre is frequently unable to control the popular elements which it introduces: lowlife characters tend to be difficult to silence, subdue or banish. Moreover, the masque encourages questions about the manner of the imitation (or, rather, simulacrum) of reality which it offers, by self-consciously foregrounding its role in the construction of ideological stratification of culture.[18]

One of the masques in which these processes are particularly visible is Ben Jonson's *Neptune's Triumph for the Return of Albion.*[19] Stephen Orgel interprets this entertainment, written for Twelfth Night 1624, but never performed, as "a serene extension of the royal will", while Martin Butler's revisionist analysis explains the masque's contradictions in the light of the rift between the policies of James I and his son Charles, concerning the negotiations for Charles's marriage to the Spanish Infanta.[20] However, an examination of the interaction between popular and high culture adds another dimension to the understanding of this masque: one in which the entertainment does not unproblematically reflect dominant ideology and in which what is at stake is not only the topical matters of the day, but also broader issues connected with the construction of aristocratic identity.

Neptune's Triumph begins with a dialogue in which the Poet explains to the Cook the "device" of the imminent masque. It is going to present Neptune's reception of his son, Albion, and his loyal servant, Hippius, coming back from a dangerous overseas voyage. This allegory represents the return of Prince Charles and the Duke of Buckingham from their expedition to the Continent to negotiate for Charles's marriage with the Spanish Infanta. Those events, however, took place some three months before the masque's scheduled date. No wonder, then, that the Cook asks: "But why not this, till now?" (l. 115). The historical reasons for the delay might have been twofold: firstly, the prince returned in October, which was not the masquing season; and secondly, his return was not an unequivocally happy occasion, since the plans for the Spanish marriage came to nothing. This was a cause for rejoicing for the majority of English Protestants, but not for King James, who had long cherished hopes for an alliance with Spain.[21] The Poet, though, answers the Cook's question with a different explanation: "It was not time / To mix this music with the vulgar's chime" (ll. 115–16). Instead of dwelling overtly on the entertainment's immediate political circumstances, the Poet moves the discussion to the realm of aesthetics, launching into a tirade which distinguishes the masque from the popular celebrations which greeted Charles's return:

Stay, till th'abortive and extemporal din
Of balladry was understood a sin,
Minerva cried; that what tumultuous verse
Or prose could make, or steal, they might rehearse,
And every songster had sung out his fit;
That all the country and the city wit
Of bells and bonfires and good cheer was spent,
And Neptune's guard had drunk all that they meant;
That all the tales and stories now were old
Of the sea monster Archy, or grown cold;
The muses then might venture undeterred,
For they love then to sing, when they are heard.

(ll. 117–28)

As David Lindley points out, "this ingenious justification turns scorn for popular celebrations into good reason for delay".[22] Apart from this practical application, however, the speech plays another ideological role: it constructs a definition of popular culture, which is to serve as a negative in opposition to which aristocratic culture is defined. The vulgar pastimes – balladry, bells and bonfires, drinking and tale-telling – are presented as noisy and disorderly. They have an almost manic intensity, as the pun on 'fits' suggests: the popular songsters sing 'fits', that is sections of songs, but they also seem to have singing fits (l. 121). Above all, those pastimes are derided in moral terms. They are sinful and "abortive" outbursts of no lasting value: after a while the stories grow old and the noisy celebration dies out.

The aristocratic masque is set in sharp opposition to this picture of indulgence and disorder.[23] It is connected with poets rather than songsters, and it is placed under the patronage of classical deities of wisdom and creativity: Minerva and the Muses. The masque, as the Poet says earlier on, is concerned with "certainties" (l. 12) and by implication it is an important and permanent form of art rather than a fleeting outburst of mad jollity. This, however, turns out to be rather an illusory impression. As it becomes clear throughout *Neptune's Triumph*, the masque is indeed very much tied to the contingencies of time and circumstance. The Poet himself admits bitterly that he is "A kind of a Christmas engine, one that is used at least once a year for a trifling instrument of wit, or so" (ll. 20–2), which points to the mechanical as well as seasonal nature of the masque, a fact which the Neo-Platonic and allegorical explanations tend to obscure. The Poet is a servant of time in another sense as well, as the Cook reminds him: "you are to know the palate of the times, study the several tastes, what every nation … can expect from you" (ll. 29–32). The masque, far from being a transcendent carrier of eternal truths, is in fact subject to the changing tastes and requirements of its audiences. Moreover, the genre emerges not as a natural mirror of ideal courtly reality, but rather an 'instrument' for constructing that reality.

All this suggests that the masque, just like the vulgar entertainments, is not above the contingencies of time and politics. The Cook's and the Poet's exchange, however, carries an even more disturbing hint that, in fact, popular and high culture are not as hermetically sealed off from each other as the aristocracy might wish them to be. The Poet's statement "It was not time / To mix this music with the vulgar's chime" does imply that at some other time such mixing, however undesirable, might be possible. This may come as a surprise, considering the efforts of the court elite to keep the masque free from contamination by the unelevated crowd. It might seem that there could be no *time* for mixing the elite with the vulgar, because the two were supposed to occupy distinct *spaces*: the streets and theatres for the vulgar and the Banqueting House for the elite.[24] Even more surprisingly, it is the masque that finally makes concessions: the courtly celebrations have to be postponed until the vulgar have "sung out their fit". The music of the court is in danger of getting drowned out by the popular noise, and the Muses have to wait with their song until they can be heard. Paradoxically, the expression of the allegedly superior culture of the aristocracy becomes dependent on and subject to the whims of the vulgar.

A further question is why the elite should bother with the "vulgar's chime". Surely the aristocrats would not be distracted from the true music by the ringing of the bells and from the gloriously lit scene at Whitehall by the underlings' bonfires? One answer to this question is that perhaps the vulgar were not as insignificant as the elite wanted them to be. Their subscription to the official order was essential to its upholding, and their refusal to internalise dominant ideology, manifested either in an outright refusal to act out their roles (such as the radical Protestants' unwillingness to participate in popular pastimes) or by aspiring to encroach upon high culture (for example, by appropriating elements of chivalric romances for black-letter publications), was becoming a serious threat to the ruling elite.[25]

Another explanation lies in the court's need to consolidate its position when faced with the political crisis of 1623–4. As Martin Butler demonstrates, both Prince Charles and Buckingham, by breaking the Spanish marriage negotiations, dissented from James's politics and became associated with more radical Protestant groups.[26] Many courtiers shared the crowds' rejoicing at the Spanish fiasco, and were not deaf to their joyful noise. *Neptune's Triumph*, however, does not wish to acknowledge the possibility of internal divisions within the court, blaming only the "vulgar's chime" for the delay of the masque's presentation. In this way, the masque displaces the feelings and reactions which were no doubt also felt by some of the elite exclusively on to the vulgar, in order to belittle the sentiments which were not in accord with the king's policies: as Butler argues, "popular acclamations" are "incorporate[d] [in the antimasque] in order that they might be disparaged".[27] Butler analyses this move in terms of the precise historical moment: factional divisions of the court, and especially "the competition over power between ruler and heir".[28] In addition to this, however, there is also a broader ideological operation at work here, connected with the elite's self-definition in relation to popular culture. This operation aims to establish a unified court in opposition to the masses outside Whitehall. In order to do so, the grounds of the debate are shifted from political to aesthetic. What defines your position becomes not so much *what* you are saying or singing, but *how* you are saying it: in a harmonious and decorous way or in a disorderly and noisy way. And the masque becomes a forum where social distinctions, in the guise of aesthetic differences, can be defined and rehearsed.

The processes intended to produce the elite's consolidation and self-definition against an easily identifiable 'other' are characterised by conflicting demands: the two cultures have to be kept absolutely separate in order to sustain their difference, but, at the same time, they have to be brought together for the sake of contrast. This creates a paradoxical effect of the elite claiming the natural superiority of their culture, while at the same time depending on popular culture for the construction of this superiority. The same impulse which aims at the total exclusion of the "vulgar's chime" from *Neptune's Triumph* paradoxically grants it a place in the masque: in order to exclude and denigrate, the masque has to mention, and thus include, the masses outside the court. By the very act of asserting its refusal to do so, the masque mixes "this music with the vulgar's chime". The introduction of popular culture for the purposes of defining aristocratic culture in opposition to it brings with it a threat of contamination of the latter by the former.

Moreover, the position of the exchange between the Poet and the Cook within the structure of the entertainment signals that the dreaded mixing and contamination are already happening. The discussion comes in the antimasque section, since it belongs to the preliminary dialogue of the lower-order characters, almost certainly played by professional actors. The section is at times comical, as when the Cook describes his art in lofty terms as the pinnacle and sum total of all other arts. It is full of references to the earthy reality of the life of minor court servants, as well as to the technicalities of the staging of the masque. What is surprising, however, is that the description of the solemn "device" of the entertainment comes in this section as well: the Poet explains his allegory of the highest matters of the state, which is soon to be presented by the choicest courtiers to a mere Cook. One might expect that this would be the signal for the change of tone and subject, and that the main masque would start immediately. Not so: straight after this exposition of the allegory of the masque, the Poet proceeds to describe the vulgar pastimes which delayed the courtly celebrations, and then he keeps on chatting to the Cook. The tone of this conversation is curiously mixed, as the Poet speaks in solemn tone about the imminent main masque, and the Cook brings the discussion back to the kitchen:

> *Cook* How do you present 'em?
> In a fine island, say you?
> *Poet* Yes, a Delos,
> Such as when fair Latona fell in travail
> Great Neptune made emergent.
> *Cook* I conceive you.
> I would have had your isle brought floating in, now,
> In a brave broth, and of a sprightly green,
> Just to the colour of the sea; and then
> Some twenty sirens singing in the kettle [...].
>
> (ll. 130–7)

Finally, the Cook asks about the antimasques prepared for the occasion. The Poet answers that there are none, and explains to the astonished Cook:

None, I assure you, neither do I think them
A worthy part of presentation,
Being things so heterogene, to all device
Mere by-works, and at best outlandish nothings.

(ll. 157–60)

Ironic as this statement may be, coming from a character in the antimasque section of the entertainment, it is in accord with the general ideological structure of the masque: the antimasques are unworthy and "heterogene", which implies their otherness; they are at best outlandish nothings, which suggests their low position outside the 'real' masque.

However, the Cook will have none of this. He chides the Poet: "Make not yourself so ignorantly simple" (l. 163), and he proceeds to present an antimasque: "a metaphorical" "dish out of the kitchen" (ll. 169, 167). The dish is a stew made out of gossip-mongers, which harks back to the "extemporal din" of the vulgar, whose fault was telling stories in prose, verse and ballads, concerning matters beyond their comprehension. In this way, the entertainment presents a series of appropriations: first, the vulgar are criticised for babbling about the affairs of the state, which are supposedly above their reach and understanding; they are usurping what rightfully belongs to the elite. Later, however, this very babbling and its perpetrators become a subject of the elite's amusement. In fact, they turn into a dish which the aristocrats may consume, that is, totally incorporate.

Such a total incorporation and containment of the popular may be the ideological aim of the masque at one level of its meaning. It is, however, debatable how successful this operation is. After all, the vulgar culture – or at least its representation – gets admitted into the aristocratic entertainment, which brings the threat of the contamination of elite culture by its popular counterpart. The rotten ingredients of the Cook's disgusting stew might be vulgar in origin, but they are presented to the cultivated courtiers, and, if you are what you eat, the implications are obvious. Of course, the aristocrats never actually eat the stew; they only watch it. Preserving the distinction between the actual and the symbolic consumption becomes crucial. No matter how much the aristocracy uses the popular forms, these forms must remain clearly separate and subordinate in order to preserve the divisions which are necessary for the construction of the elite's identity.

An attempt at such a separation is made in the court masque by strictly distinguishing the 'vulgar' antimasque from the 'elevated' main masque, and staging a clear progression from the former to the latter, culminating in the triumph of the main masque. In *Neptune's Triumph*, however, this distinction is not fully sustained. As I have mentioned above, the description of the solemn "device" of the masque comes in the antimasque section, between the comic discussion of the importance of the art of cooking and the antimasque of the metaphorical stew. In this way high and low matters mingle and interpenetrate in the antimasque section. They are not even distinguished by a difference in the style of enunciation: although the dialogue begins in prose and then changes to blank verse, this change does not correspond to the beginning of the description of the "device" of the masque. Instead, the shift occurs when the Cook starts his oration about the merits of his art; from that moment on, blank verse persists until the beginning of the revels, and both the solemn "device" and the comic ingredients of the Cook's stew are described in this metre.

Not only are high and low matters mingled in the preliminary section of the entertainment, but the vulgar does not disappear for ever with the appearance of the aristocratic masquers. After the actual revels, the Cook jumps in again with another antimasque, this time of sailors. This second entry of the antimasque suggests that the entertainment is not a neat progression from the antimasque disorder to the main masque order, but rather a curious interchange of the two. Similar themes and images permeate the whole entertainment, both the antimasque and the main masque. Food and eating is one such recurrent trope. The Cook is obviously concerned with these matters, but he also describes the Poet's art in gastronomical terms: just as the Cook has "to know how to please the palates of the guests", the Poet has to "know the palate of the times" (ll. 28–9). The news-mongers in the Cook's stew are presented as consumers who "relish nothing but *di stato*" (the affairs of the state, l. 176), but the aristocrats who will watch the antimasque are implicated in the vocabulary of eating as well, as the "dish" is expected "to take the present palates" (l. 168). Even the main masque itself is not free from this imagery, as the masquers are invited by the Chorus to:

> Bring all the pleasures of the stage,
> And relishes of rhyme;

Add all the softnesses of courts,
The looks, the laughters, and the sports,
And mingle all their sweets and salts [...].

(ll. 293–7)

Elsewhere, Proteus sings about Neptune drowning his cares in nectar at the Ocean's feast (ll. 264–6). This seems distinctly more elevated than the antimasque's noisome stew, until the Cook adapts this vocabulary to present his second show: "a dish of pickled sailors, fine salt sea-boys, shall relish like anchovies or caviar, to draw down a cup of nectar in the skirts of a night" (ll. 346–8).

The entertainment thus mingles the themes and the images of the high and the low, even as it attempts to establish a firm, hierarchical distinction between them. In *Neptune's Triumph* the antimasque/main masque division, intended to establish and sustain the clear separation and superiority of aristocratic culture from the inferiors outside the court, fails to achieve this goal. The very introduction of the representations of 'lower' forms of culture for the purposes of contrast makes the elite culture to a certain extent dependent on them: as soon as a relational model is introduced, it becomes hard to argue that one of its elements is totally self-sufficient. Moreover, the antimasque and the main masque are not always sufficiently clearly separated to contain the tensions introduced by representational practices aimed at defining elite culture in opposition to popular culture.

As the above analysis of *Neptune's Triumph* demonstrates, the masque does not so much represent the elite's culture as rather actively participates in its construction by attempting to establish a firm opposition between the 'high' culture of the aristocracy and the 'low' culture of the plebeians. This process produces tensions and contradictions, since the elite culture inevitably becomes dependent on and entangled with its despised 'other'. *Neptune's Triumph*, like many other masques, reveals those tensions through the mutual interpenetration of the main masque and the antimasque sections.[29] Moreover, the discussion between the Poet and the Cook concerning the functions of their art foregrounds the masque's own role in the production of the elite's ideology. Such self-consciousness and self-referentiality is a feature of many masques, achieved through exposing the mechanics of the courtly shows – their grounding in the precise historical moment and their dependence on the contribution of such non-aristocratic figures as poets, actors, carpenters or costume makers.[30] The masque draws attention to the fact that the genre, far from being a Neo-Platonic reflection of ideal reality, in fact plays an active part in the ideological processes involved in constructing the 'reality' and the self-image of the court.

The rest of the chapter will demonstrate these features, using as an example Inigo Jones's and Aurelian Townshend's masque of 1632, *Albion's Triumph*.[31] This masque includes a lengthy prose exchange between Platonicus and Publius (a Neo-Platonic philosopher and a plebeian) who discuss the status of the entertainment in relation to reality and Platonic ideas. Publius announces that he has seen a triumph of the victorious King Albanactus (Charles I): "Though I have earned it with the sweat of my brow in January, yet I am glad I saw it; for there never was such a sight seen" (ll. 136–8). Publius emphasises the tangible reality of such a triumph – to see it, one has to sweat in the crowd, and endure all kinds of inconveniences: "Some trod on my toes. Some cried; some kept it in; for my part, I confessed all, for fear I should be pressed to death" (ll. 147–50).

Platonicus, in contrast to Publius, claims to have seen the triumph without leaving his own study. Publius reminds him that the study is located "backward", so "one can see nothing but the sky" from it (ll. 159–60). Platonicus, however, insists that he has seen the triumph, "and a true one; thine was but a show" (l. 163). This is a Neo-Platonic argument for the existence of the ideal reality of the triumph, as opposed to its outward, bodily, manifestation. According to this doctrine, the masque is a representation of an ideal truth, which precedes and is independent of its physical actualisation: in Neo-Platonic terms, what Publius saw in the street was just the body of the entertainment, while the truth lies in its soul. Platonicus argues that what Publius saw was empty appearances, suggesting that the Caesar's chariot was made "of wood, perhaps gilt, perhaps gold" (l. 178). He questions the external reality of the courtly shows – the triumphant engines of Caroline ideology are perhaps made of gold, perhaps they are gilt, but most probably they are just wood, like any other theatrical machines.

Platonicus wants Publius to skip the 'insignificant' details and pass to the essentials: that is, to the description of the noble persons involved in the triumph, especially the king. This is, however, the moment of Publius's revenge: "Sir, I saw him not as he was born, naked, but since you affect such brevity, I saw the King and a great deal more, and so I turned my back, and went away" (ll. 181–3). Publius clearly implies that the 'additions' surrounding the king are important, and you cannot get any story or interpretation if you strip them all away. The 'truth' about monarchy only becomes real in its bodily manifestation.

Surprisingly, Platonicus is forced to agree: "Nay, good Publius, now thou art too brief" (l. 184). Then Publius tells the whole story of what he saw: Caesar, captive kings, ladies, wild beasts, giants, dwarfs, lictors, pictors and priests (ll. 190–4). Only now can Platonicus offer an allegorical interpretation of the show:

> For a supplement to thy lame story, know I have seen this brave Albanactus Caesar, seen him with eyes of understanding, viewed all his actions, looked into his mind, which I find armed with so many moral virtues that he daily conquers a world of vices, which are wild beasts indeed. For example, ambition is a lion, cruelty a bear, avarice a wolf; yet he subdues them all. To be short, no vice is so small to scape him, nor so great but he overcomes it, and in that fashion he triumphs over all the kings and queens that went before him. All his passions are his true subjects; and knowledge, judgement, merit, bounty, and the like, are fit commanders for such a general; these triumph with him. And this, Publius, is more than you can find in the street.
>
> (ll. 202–15)

It seems that the patrician Neo-Platonism totally subdues the plebeian ignorance, as Platonicus has the access to the essential truths which are inaccessible to Publius. However, Platonicus's explanation comes only as a "supplement" which cannot even start without Publius's "lame story". Similarly, the external trappings – chariots, giants and pygmies – are necessary for the production of the mysterious meaning of the masque. After all, in the actual performance the masque audience were presented with "the forum of the city of Albipolis, and Albanactus triumphing, attended like a Roman emperor, [...] seen afar off to pass in pomp" (ll. 130–2), not with the empty study-room of a Neo-Platonic philosopher.

The triumph of Neo-Platonic essence over the external, bodily pomp is at best partial in *Albion's Triumph*. Publius's answer to Platonicus's claim that his allegorical explanation is "more than you can find in the street" is "I grant it" (l. 216). However, Publius immediately changes subject: instead of dwelling on the allegory, he asks Platonicus to accompany him to the amphitheatre. From the elevated, spiritual interpretations we are back to the world of vulgar spectacle, as the exasperated Platonicus exclaims:

> Why, beforehand I know there will be gladiators, saltators, and sights to please the people. Wert not thou better stay here and see Caesar present himself to this fair goddess, seeking sweet rest after all his labours?
>
> (ll. 222–5)

Platonicus suggests the viewing of the main masque, rather than of the "sights to please the people". Publius, however, gives a curt and scornful answer: "I should sleep at such a sight" (l. 226). Surprisingly, Platonicus, instead of abandoning or chasing off the incorrigible Publius, agrees to accompany him to the amphitheatre:

> I will go with thee, if it be but to teach thee to read in thy own book. Outsides have insides, shells have kernels in them, and under every fable, nay almost under everything, lies a moral.
>
> (ll. 229–32)

Platonicus, with commendable patience, offers to teach Publius to read the spectacles in a Neo-Platonic way, looking for their true essence and moral. Publius, however, takes the advice literally and picks up a stone to examine what moral lies beneath it: "If there lie not a moral under it, then have you taught me false doctrine" (l. 340). Again, Publius fails to learn Neo-Platonic philosophy, and again he gets away with it. Although he is chastised as "fool", he has his way: Platonicus goes with him to the amphitheatre, and the vulgar shows, consisting of fools, saltators, buffeters, dancing satyrs, giants and pygmies, fencers and morescoes, are presented as the antimasques (ll. 247–54). Moreover, contrary to his earlier promise, Platonicus does not elucidate the 'real' meaning of the shows: the antimasques pass unexplained and straight after them the entertainment proceeds to the main masque. The two characters do not speak again, and their discussion on the merits of Neo-Platonic philosophy for the spectacles of state ends with Platonicus exasperated and Publius uncomprehending.

It is not clear what this lengthy exchange proposed to the aristocratic viewers of the masque. Perhaps they were being advised to strive to understand the masques in a Platonic way: to look for Jonsonian "more removed mysteries" under the façade of the outward show. This would set them apart from the ignorant multitude who, Publius-like, are only able to gaze without understanding. In other words, the masque would establish a firm opposition between the nobles, privy to the real meaning of the masque, and the mob outside Whitehall. This, however, unwittingly places the aristocrats in a position where they depend on the vulgar masses for the construction of their own identity. Platonicus's explanation follows after Publius's description of the outward show; the aristocrats' wisdom can only be appreciated when compared with the commoners' ignorance. Significantly, the final scene of the apotheosis of the court in *Albion's Triumph* takes place in front of the "landscipt in which was a prospect of the King's palace of Whitehall and part of the city of London seen afar off" (ll. 338–40). The epitome of the aristocratic culture cannot be separated from the city culture, to which it is allegedly opposed and superior, but without which it cannot exist.

Like many other masques, *Albion's Triumph* stages a problematic relationship of aristocratic to popular culture. This relationship consists of a mutual construction of high and low culture in a process of constant appropriation, definition and re-definition, and social struggle on the cultural level. Its corollary is that the elite attempts to appropriate elements of popular culture into the masque, in order to construct its own self-definition in opposition to that culture. However, this process is not smooth and unproblematic: it involves tensions, ambiguities and contradictions, and its outcome is not a predetermined success of the elite's manipulations, but rather a fluid situation of constant negotiation and readjustment which, at the very least, exposes the operations of power.

In conclusion, the model that this chapter proposes is one in which the masque's meaning is not fully exhausted by locating its source either in the monolithic royal authority or in the topical issues of the day and the interests of specific courtly factions. Instead, the genre is seen not only as reflecting 'original', extra-textual meanings, but also as participating in the production of that which it celebrates – aristocratic identity – through the constant juxtaposition of representations of popular and high culture. This dynamic process of producing and reproducing the elite's self-definition is never fully complete or flawless, which accounts for the masque's generic fractures and contradictions, such as its often inconsistent tone or the lack of containment of its 'vulgar' elements. Moreover, by frequently offering a self-referential commentary on the ways in which its meaning is produced, the masque foregrounds its role as an ideological instrument. Instead of generating a seamless façade congruent with the elite's purposes, the genre exposes and interrogates the arbitrary and contradictory nature of the processes involved in the construction of dominant culture.

Chapter Six

1. The first model is generally followed by critics associated with the New Historicism, while the second one is favoured by those influenced by revisionist historicism (see later in the chapter for a fuller account). The phrase "sustaining contradictions" is introduced by Jonathan Goldberg in *James I and the Politics of Literature: Jonson, Shakespeare, Donne, and their Contemporaries* (Baltimore, MD: Johns Hopkins University Press, 1983), p. 116.
2. E.M.W. Tillyard, *The Elizabethan World Picture* (London: Chatto & Windus, 1943).
3. Jonathan Dollimore, *Radical Tragedy: Religion, Ideology and Power in the Drama of Shakespeare and his Contemporaries* (New York: Harvester Wheatsheaf, 1984).
4. For a more extensive account of New Historicism, see Jeremy Hawthorn, *Cunning Passages: New Historicism, Cultural Materialism, and Marxism in the Contemporary Literary Debate* (London: Arnold, 1996).
5. Stephen Orgel, *The Jonsonian Masque* (Cambridge, MA: Harvard University Press, 1965), pp. 6–7. Orgel's more recent work modifies his early accounts to include factors disturbing the monolithic order, such as the strains which the requirements of aristocratic females placed on the courtly poet. See 'Marginal Jonson', in *The Politics of the Stuart Court Masque*, ed. David Bevington and Peter Holbrook (Cambridge: Cambridge University Press, 1998), pp. 144–75; and 'Jonson and the Amazons', in *Soliciting Interpretation: Literary Theory and Seventeenth-Century English Poetry*, ed. Elizabeth D. Harvey and Katherine Eisaman Maus (Chicago: University of Chicago Press, 1990), pp. 119–39.
6. Stephen Orgel, *The Illusion of Power: Political Theater in the English Renaissance* (Berkeley, CA: University of California Press, 1975), p. 38.
7. See Orgel, *Jonsonian Masque*, p. 93.
8. Martin Butler, 'Courtly Negotiations', in Bevington and Holbrook (eds), *Politics of the Stuart Court Masque*, pp. 20–40, esp. pp. 20–9.
9. Ibid., p. 23.
10. Lloyd Davis, 'Praise and Presence in Elizabethan and Jacobean Court Drama', *AUMLA* 83 (1995), p. 7.
11. Dollimore, *Radical Tragedy*, pp. 26–7.
12. Ibid., pp. 27–8.
13. Sharpe ascribes this view to such historians as Lawrence Stone, Perez Zagorin, R. Ashton, R. Ollard and Graham Parry. See Kevin Sharpe, *Criticism and Compliment: The Politics of Literature in the England of Charles I* (Cambridge: Cambridge University Press, 1987), pp. 1–6.
14. See Sharpe, *Criticism and Compliment*, esp. pp. 22–9 and pp. 179–264.
15. See Yumna Siddiqi, 'Dark Incontinents: The Discourses of Race and Gender in Three Renaissance Masques', *Renaissance Drama* 23 (1992), pp. 139–63; Kim F. Hall, *Things of Darkness: Economies of Race and Gender in Early Modern England* (Ithaca, NY: Cornell University Press, 1995); Aasand Hardin, 'To Blanch an Ethiop, and Revive a Corse: Queen Anne and the *Masque of Blackness*', *Studies in English Literature* 32 (1992), pp.

271–85; and Stephen Orgel, 'Marginal Jonson', pp. 144–75.

16. Clare McManus, *Women on the Renaissance Stage: Anna of Denmark and Female Masquing in the Stuart Court (1590–1619)* (Manchester: Manchester University Press, 2002).
17. Enid Welsford's 1927 study *The Court Masque: A Study in the Relationship between Poetry and the Revels* (Cambridge: Cambridge University Press, 1927; repr. New York: Russell & Russell, 1962) remains the most extensive exploration of the topic. More recent accounts include Leah Marcus's *The Politics of Mirth: Jonson, Herrick, Milton, Marvell, and the Defense of Old Holiday Pastimes* (Chicago: University of Chicago Press, 1986; repr. 1989). This book (not concerned exclusively with the masque) argues, along New Historicist lines, that popular culture was used by the early Stuarts for the purposes of implementing royal policies. Another angle is offered by Patricia Fumerton, whose analysis (again, not concentrating solely on the masque) reveals aristocratic culture as inherently fragmented and engaged in a constant process of self-definition, involving displacement between history and aesthetics, central and peripheral; see *Cultural Aesthetics: Renaissance Literature and the Practice of Social Ornament* (Chicago: University of Chicago Press, 1991).
18. This analysis is indebted to recent discussions of the mutually constructed nature of popular and high culture by social historians. See, among others, Bob Scribner, 'Is a History of Popular Culture Possible?', *History of European Ideas* 10 (1989), pp. 175–91; Roger Chartier, 'Culture as Appropriation: Popular Cultural Uses in Early Modern France', in *Understanding Popular Culture: Europe from the Middle Ages to the Nineteenth Century*, ed. Steven L. Kaplan (Berlin: Mouton, 1984), pp. 229–53; Tim Harris, 'Problematising Popular Culture', in *Popular Culture in England, c. 1500–1850*, ed. Tim Harris (Basingstoke: Macmillan, 1995), pp. 1–27; and Michel de Certeau, *Heterologies: Discourse on the Other*, trans. Brian Massumi (Minneapolis: University of Minnesota Press, 1986). For a sustained application of this type of analysis to literature, see Peter Stallybrass and Allon White, *The Politics and Poetics of Transgression* (London: Methuen, 1986).
19. In David Lindley (ed.), *Court Masques: Jacobean and Caroline Entertainments, 1605–1640* (Oxford: Oxford University Press, 1995), pp. 136–46.
20. See Orgel, *Illusion of Power*, p. 71; and Butler's 'Courtly Negotiations', esp. pp. 33–6. Patricia Fumerton also analyses *Neptune's Triumph* in the contexts of the Spanish match, but she adds another dimension to the picture by discussing England's foreign trade at the time, and especially the scandal of the English sailors of the East India Company participating, together with pagans, in the sack of the Portuguese/Spanish trading settlement of Ormuz in 1622; see *Cultural Aesthetics*, pp. 169–206.
21. See Orgel's notes in *Ben Johnson: The Complete Masques*, ed. Stephen Orgel (New Haven: Yale University Press, 1969), pp. 504–5; Lindley's notes in *Court Masques*, pp. 255–7; and Butler's 'Courtly Negotiations', p. 35.
22. Lindley, *Court Masques*, p. 257.
23. As Butler argues, "there is an insoluble contradiction between the courtly joys of the main masque and the popular acclamations". 'Courtly Negotiations', p. 35.
24. In relation to this topic, I have profited from hearing Professor Martin Butler's talk 'The Rites of Exclusion' at the Animated Porcelain conference, Keele University, 2000.
25. For the account of the Protestant opposition to the Stuart propagation of popular pastimes (especially the controversy surrounding the *Book of Sports*), see Marcus, *Politics of Mirth*, esp. pp. 106–13. For explorations of the appropriations of chivalric

discourse, see Charles C. Mish, 'Black Letter as a Social Discriminant in the Seventeenth Century', *PMLA* 68 (1953), pp. 627–30; Alice S. Miskimin, 'Ben Jonson and Captain Cox: Elizabethan Gothic Reconsidered', *Renaissance Drama* n.s. 8 (1977), pp. 173–201; and Norman Council, 'Ben Jonson, Inigo Jones, and the Transformation of Tudor Chivalry', *English Literary History* 47 (1980), pp. 259–75.

26. Butler points out that the masque demonstrates "a royal discourse in crisis, in which the usual languages no longer signify because of a now open collision between ruler and heir". 'Courtly Negotiations', p. 33.
27. Ibid., p. 35.
28. Ibid., p. 36.
29. See, for example, Jonson's *The Gypsies Metamorphosed* (1620), Davenant's *Salmacida Spolia* (1640) and Shirley's *The Triumph of Peace* (1632). Jonson's *Christmas His Masque* (1616/17) is an extreme case, in which the main masque fails to occur.
30. See Jonson's *Love Restored* (1612), *The Masque of Augurs* (1622) and *Love's Welcome at Bolsover* (1634), Shirley's *The Triumph of Peace* (1632) and Carew's *Coelum Britannicum* (1634).
31. In Stephen Orgel and Roy Strong (eds), *Inigo Jones: The Theatre of the Stuart Court*, 2 vols (Berkeley, CA: University of California Press; London: Sotheby Parke Bernet, 1973), *Inigo Jones*, II, pp. 453–77.

CHAPTER SEVEN

The distorting mirror: theatrical mimesis on the early modern transvestite stage

Christian Billing

> Be not too tame neither, but let your own discretion be your tutor: suit the action to the word, the word to the action; with this special o'erstep not the modesty of nature: for any thing so overdone is from the purpose of playing, whose end, both at the first and now, was and is, to hold, as 'twere, the mirror up to nature; to show virtue her own feature, scorn her own image, and the very age and body of the time his form and pressure.[1]

I

ON FIRST READING, Hamlet's advice to the players appears to be straightforward enough. He seems to say that the truest (and therefore the best) style of acting is both naturalistic and mimetic.[2] He states that actors should neither be too introverted before their spectators nor rage like barnstorming medieval Herods. Moreover, he asserts that players should endeavour to present the actions and behavioural traits of their time exactly as they are, in such a manner that they create an accurate and objective 'reflection' of their audience on stage. To consolidate this theory, he provides a powerful metaphor – one that aligns theatre with the one true reflective surface that we all understand to give a perfectly accurate image of the subject who chooses to locate him- or herself in front of it: the mirror.

Read on the page, this speech seems to make sense; we note it and move on… the idea that art 'reflects' society has become almost axiomatic. As soon as one considers Hamlet's remarks in practice, however, the metaphor begins rapidly to break down. Thinking about the proxemic and kinaesthetic relationships between actors and audiences (in both early modern and contemporary theatres) one immediately has to concede that the boundary between stage and spectator has to be a much more complex optical device than the conventional mirror for this metaphor to work. If the analogy is to go any distance at all, some kind of two-way apparatus is required; yet even this device would be a strange contraption, given that its surface is required simultaneously to be reflective and transparent so as to allow spectators to observe what takes place on stage (looking through its surface) whilst also permitting them to see their own appearance (reflected back from it). And this duality is an essential part of Hamlet's model, since it is only by conflating the two images of actor and self that spectators can interpret what they see as both a performance and their own likeness – and therefore engage in the self-reflective process of identification, enlightenment and education that lies at the heart of Hamlet's supposed view of theatre.

Tropes of imitation and reflection such as this are to be found in accounts of theatrical representation from Plato's *Republic* onwards – yet I have always found them somewhat dissatisfying. As a way of exorcising my demons with regards to theatrical mimesis I here intend to draw some scientific and historically specific attention to a range of factors that render such an understanding of the nature of acting problematic from an early modern perspective. I will argue that far from acknowledging theatre as a realistic, impartial and socially accurate 'reflection' of society, Hamlet's mirror metaphor taps into a nexus of interpretation that deliberately draws attention to the artificial and socially coercive nature of dramatic representation.

II

Reflected light is one of the most natural phenomena in the world. It is how we see any object that is not in itself incandescent. The absorption and reflection by non-luminous objects of the various frequencies of electromagnetic radiation that are visible to humans within the spectrum of light produced by incandescent objects are what give our world its colour and visual texture. Whilst all surfaces naturally reflect light to some degree, however (with standing water being the most reflective surface occurring in nature and matt black objects the least), the use of manufacturing technology to manipulate reflected light so as to bounce nearly all of it back in rectilinear fashion from an unnaturally smooth vertical surface in order to create a self-conscious reflection of a subject-self is the work of man alone.[3] As with any of the advanced perceptual and representational systems that differentiate the world of human creation from that of nature, reflection has a grammar that must be learnt. Its artificiality necessitates a set of special interpretative rules. As Jonathan Miller has observed:

> In nature there are no vertical surfaces offering deceptive views of a 'virtual' beyond. So the invention of artificially reflective materials complicate[s] the scene considerably, and although human beings have learned to live in a world which now includes mirrored walls and plate-glass windows, it's easy to underestimate the perceptual problems created by surfaces which are reflective enough to provide misleading views. We take it for granted that the 'virtual' view to be seen in a mirror is automatically distinguishable from the 'actual' view seen through a doorway or a window, but the distinction requires cognitive work.[4]

Since the advent of manufactured reflective surfaces, humans have had to learn to understand the signs and signifiers that allow us to make sense of reflection. This process is commonly completed within the first two years of an infant's life; as a result, none of us remember having done it – but anyone who has ever bumped into a sheet of glass or, perhaps more stupidly, a mirror will know the reason why we bother. Artificial reflective surfaces present us with a very practical problem: because they are unnatural they can lead us into danger. The more 'perfect' they are, the more easily we can be duped by them. The better a reflective surface is, the more it ceases to exist (perceptually at least), presenting us instead with a deceptive notion of 'virtual reality' beyond the plane of a two-dimensional surface that has become, to all intents and purposes, invisible.[5]

To save ourselves embarrassment (and injury) we soon learn to spot reflections; we look for surrounding frames (notice, for example, the way that mirrors and vertical reflective surfaces such as glass doors and shop windows almost always have one),[6] or other tell-tale signs of reflection such as the presence of our own form, writing that appears to be backwards, dirt or second reflections on the surface of the glass, optical distortions caused by imperfections in the manufacturing process, a tint in the reflective material, the greenish hue of glass that bleeds into the reflected image…[7] Crucially, all of the ways in which humans tell that they are viewing a reflection centre on their perception of essential difference between what they understand reality to be and the reflections of reality with which they are sometimes presented. One fact is therefore fundamental to my argument: awareness of reflection is based on a prescriptive and codified knowledge of what things *should* look like; we compare reflected images to a normative understanding of the world that we inhabit in order to make sense of them (ironically, of course, it is just this fact that gives rise to the biggest fallacy of all regarding mirrors, the erroneous notion that they reverse the objects they reflect).[8]

One of the most illuminating ways of observing the cognitive processes of differentiation that allow us to spot reflection is to look at artistic depictions of mirrors. This is because artificially produced images of reflection demonstrate to us most graphically the disparity between two two-dimensional forms: (i) the artist's impression of three-dimensional reality and (ii) the artist's impression of surfaces that reflect that reality. In a recent landmark study of reflection in the visual arts, Miller has outlined the ways in which painterly depictions of reflection underscore the artifice of their cultural production (one stunning instance of which is Kulmbach's *Coronation of the Virgin* (1514) – a painting in which God the Father, seated on high, holds a glass orb that contains reflections of some very earthly mullioned windows).[9] The fact that artists' supposedly faithful representations of reflected reality frequently betray their own cultural location in such startling ways is significant to my argument,[10] and I shall return to it below, but more fundamental to my present line of reasoning is the very manner in which we, as viewers, discern that two-dimensional surfaces reflect – or, in the case of art, are supposed to reflect – reality.

In the majority of households in Europe until the middle of the seventeenth century, reflective surfaces were almost always made out of materials other than glass. If households were rich enough to have glass mirrors they were more often than not curved in shape and made from blown glass coated with an amalgam of tin and mercury. This is because the manufacturing process that allowed for the production of sheet glass (a technique that involves pressing molten glass between rollers), an obvious prerequisite for the production of flat mirrors, was not developed in Europe until the mid-sixteenth century – at which time its inventors, the

Venetian glass industry, were keen to keep their secret well under wraps. Hand-blown convex mirrors were expensive in sixteenth-century Europe, and flat ones prohibitively so. From their invention up until the mid-seventeenth century, only the richest households in the areas surrounding Venice and Nürnberg (the two major centres of European glass production) could afford, or indeed had ready access to, substantial plate-glass mirrors. The transportation of such fragile objects was one obvious problem and the sophisticated methods required to produce flat mirrors only became established in the workshops of Paris and London by around the middle of the seventeenth century.[11] When Louis XIV had the Chateau of Versailles built between 1660 and 1685, for example, much of the public astonishment at its magnificence was caused by the lustrous abundance in its staterooms of what were still unusual plate-glass mirrors. The modern technique of mirror making (which involves placing sheet glass in a vacuum and coating the surface with molten silver or aluminium) was not invented by Justus von Liebig until 1835 – and it is only from this point in time that we can truly consider cheap, mass-produced flat mirrors to have come into common circulation.

These historical facts help to explain why most artistic representations of mirrors from the mid-fifteenth until the mid-seventeenth century have some kind of obvious distortion depicted within their reflections.[12] It is a point worthy of note, especially when we consider the ways in which concave or convex mirrors reflect. In the majority of early modern artistic depictions of mirrors, curvilinear depictions of rectilinear objects in reflection indicate to us that the reflecting object is curved in shape because they play upon our understanding of what the reflected objects *should* look like in reality (in the example given above, we understand that God the Father is holding a curved glass orb because the earthly windows that we see in it are distorted).[13] These facts have serious implications for Hamlet's mirror analogy.

To make the point more clearly, let us consider two Renaissance representations of mirrors: those contained in Van Eyck's Arnolfini portrait of 1434 and Parmigianino's self-portrait of 1524.[14] In both paintings the artists have undertaken deliberate deformations of their subjects in order to communicate the fact that their observers are looking into convex mirrors. In the Arnolfini mirror (which Van Eyck deliberately places at the vanishing point of his perspective scene) we read a curved surface because of the marked bowing that is evident in the bed frame, the windows and the ceiling that the mirror purports to reflect. In Parmigianino's self-portrait, a curved ceiling and window again invite us to read the flat surface of the painting as a convex mirror – but here the whole effect is further exaggerated by a grotesquely distorted hand that indicates the closeness of this body part to the mirror's hypothetical curve. Two things are of note in relation to Hamlet's assertions: firstly, these early modern depictions of mirrors do not present accurate and true reflections of their subjects – indeed the very way in which we are invited to interpret these objects as mirrors is dependent upon our appreciation of their distorting properties; and secondly, the subjects represented are clearly not us, the onlookers. Just as with the stage action presented in early modern theatre, we are invited to gaze into a scene and requested to interpret it as a mirror – yet in both art forms we are unable to discern any obvious reflection of ourselves. In both cases, something a lot more distorted and manipulative is going on. What we see is a deformed representation of the world – something rotten in the state of Denmark – and we are invited to contrast this aberrant vision of reality with the normative social and political order that we understand should exist.

Moving back to the paintings, on closer analysis the mirror in the Arnolfini portrait can be said to be doing a significant amount of ideological work. Firstly, it augments the opulence of the scene; this mirror is a manifestation of the early modern fascination with material objects; the very fact that the couple possess one is as significant to the portrait as the austere and yet finely executed nature of their clothes, the painstaking detail in their furnishings or the presence of fresh fruit and a pet. The Arnolfini mirror underscores the status of these newlyweds – a social position that is significantly above average. Secondly, the mirror reveals the skill of a painter who is deliberately manipulating his audience and openly acknowledging the artifice of his medium. Van Eyck is mocking the one advantage that sculpture was said to have over graphic art and doing what two-dimensional painting was not supposed to be able to do: showing the front and the back of its subject at the same time.[15] Such an act would be extremely problematic if we were to consider Van Eyck's art to be in any way naturalistic or mimetic because my final point about this scene is that it requires the artist to *lie* to us. Instead of seeing the true reflection that would have appeared in a real mirror if one had ever existed (i.e. the painter's easel and Van Eyck busily at work) the artist has replaced himself with a fictional pair of visitors who behold the newlyweds and are thereby themselves placed at the very heart of the painting. Far from offering a reflection of reality, this 'mirror' demonstrates the power and significance of Van Eyck as a maker of visual culture (he's got one over on the sculptors) – whilst simultaneously commenting on the central place of reception, observation and interpretation in painterly art. In Parmigianino's self-portrait, the optical distortion that causes his hand to seem so large is likewise an accentuation of the significance of his agency as creator of visual culture. Both 'mirrors' are thus clearly a long way from mimetic or naturalistic representations because they deliberately manipulate their spectators in two fundamental ways: (i) on a literal level they demonstrate limitations of manufacture that meant that very few Renaissance mirrors could show the true dimensions and proportions of their subjects;[16] and (ii) on a metaphorical level they reveal that, when these distorting optical characteristics are used as artistic tropes, early modern mirrors become layered with numerous strands of socially relevant connotation. They function as a site of negotiation in the spectators' understanding of the artifice of cultural production.

It is not only in painterly art that we see the mirror as manipulative tool. A survey of the mirror as literary trope in the sixteenth and early seventeenth centuries likewise reveals it to be a virtual surface in which readers are invited to observe anything but an accurate reflection of their own faces. In pamphlets purporting to act as mirrors the reader-viewers of early modern England are invited to observe anything from moral treatises[17] to political discourses[18] via anti-theatrical tracts,[19] seafaring instruction manuals,[20] exemplary biographies,[21] female conduct books,[22] histories of defeated rebellion and ineffectual kingship[23] and religious diatribes.[24]

The letter to the readers of William Baldwin's *Myrrour for Magistrates* presents us with one typical example of the mirror as literary trope. In the apologia to a volume that contains much of the source material for Shakespeare's history plays we read:

> When the printer had purposed with him[s]elf to print Lidgates translation of Bochas, of the fall of Princes, and had made priuye thereto, many both honourable & worshipfull: he was counsayled by diuers of them to procure to have the storye continued from where as Bochas left unto this present time, chieflye of such as fortune had dalyed with here in this Island: which might be as a myrrour for me[n] of all estates and degrees as

> well as Nobles as other to behold the slipperye deceytes of the wauering Lady, and ye due reward of all kinde of uices.[25]

The *Myrrour for Magistrates* presents the fall of incompetent rulers and defeated rebels as a function of their vice. It is a reflective surface that exhorts men of all degrees not to emulate its characters' divergence from socially accepted norms. Significantly, the author concedes that the work has been produced at the behest of "many both honourable & worshipfull". Through a range of anti-exemplars that includes Richard II, Harry Percy and Edmund Mortimer, the powers that be are using the trope of the mirror to exhort princes to rule effectively and nobles and commoners to know their place. Is such a mirror a true reflective surface? Or is it rather a distorting, prescriptive and manipulative weapon in the literary armoury of the holders of political authority? As the Cultural Materialist School has adeptly demonstrated, one of the primary ruses of power is to present itself as natural. What could be more natural than looking in a mirror and seeing the disastrous results of abandoning one's preordained role in a hierarchical system of governance?

Owing to a combination of their rarity, disfiguring optical properties and use as a metaphor for guided instruction, far from providing unbiased reflections of their subjects early modern mirrors were seen as vehicles for social education – repositories of codified moral and political advice that proclaimed: 'Look here and see what *I* want you to see of the world…' If theatre can be said to hold a mirror up to nature, it is this understanding of the object that I want to keep in mind during my analysis of early modern drama.

III

Twenty years ago Lisa Jardine took issue with the proposition that "Shakespeare's genius enabled him to transcend patriarchal partisanship, and to project on stage a spectrum of female qualities which reflected the burgeoning emancipation of the wives of the London bourgeoisie."[26] Turning to a mirror metaphor she observed:

> Shakespeare takes no position on women, any more than on any other issue according to this view. He simply mirrors in a perfectly reflecting glass the varieties of womanhood in contemporary society, or rather, in that sector of society with which his genius felt most closely attuned

> (London City burghers and their families). Because that sector of society recognised the emancipated woman, female qualities in Shakespeare's plays square conveniently with present day feminist notions of acceptable womanhood.[27]

With regards to the other major feminist approach of the early 1980s, Jardine framed her critique in equally optical terms; she did not agree that Shakespeare's maleness:

> makes it inevitable that his female characters are warped and distorted [...] that [he] did his best to be a true reflecting glass, but that contemporary society's limited understanding of women combined with his own male viewpoint have skewed the resulting picture.[28]

Twenty years after Jardine's study of women in early modern drama, these two approaches to gender-political criticism (that plays passively reflect the proto-feminist ideals of their creators, or their misogyny) are fortunately no longer the primary modes of analysis. As a result of the historicist approach of Jardine and others, play-texts can no longer be considered to serve scant ideological purpose and simply to reflect the social conditions from which they are produced. Rather they are deemed a significant force in the network of influences that helps to shape the culture in which they are fashioned. In the rest of this essay I want to employ the idea of theatrical representation as a coercive ideological tool that comes from my consideration of Hamlet's mirror metaphor in order to emphasise the fact that play-texts are important elements in the creation of gender-political opinion in the early modern period. To do so, I will turn to Middleton and Dekker's *Roaring Girl*, a text that has often been championed as a proto-feminist document. I intend to demonstrate that, far from being a celebration of women who reject patriarchal control and choose to fashion their existence as they see fit, this male-authored text attempts to neutralise and recuperate the disruptive social energies of the unruly women who emerged in London during the early years of the seventeenth century.

Based on the real-life character Mary Frith, the dramatic construct 'Moll Cutpurse' provides a significant opportunity to look into one mirror held up to nature in 1611. The play should make for rich pickings if I am looking for evidence about the gender politics of early modern London: its subject, who was still living at the time of the play's composition and performance, is a feisty woman who moves through geographical terrain that one can easily find on contemporaneous maps of the capital; she buys recognisably fashionable material goods and deals with social issues very much at the fore of the cultural agenda in the early years of the seventeenth century – including cross-dressing and female agency. So what ideological work is being done by this reflection upon feisty femininity?

Jean Howard has recently attempted to argue that (as she puts it, fortunately for her as a contemporary feminist) there is much more to Moll Cutpurse's representation in *The Roaring Girl* than the conservative and recuperative aspects that are to be found in the depiction of most cross-dressed heroines in early modern comedy. She has even maintained that Moll's cross-dressing "destabilises the very essentialist binarisms that the 'corrective' cross-dresser [such as Portia or Rosalind] overtly wishes to uphold."[29] Pinning Moll's radical potentiality on the double position that she occupies as erotic object *and* subject within the play, Howard has asserted that, despite being the most highly eroticised figure in the drama (she is desired by Sebastian, Laxton and Trapdoor), Moll never actually subjugates herself by agreeing to become the mere object of masculine affections.[30] For Howard, it is Moll's subjectivity that is paramount to her figuration as a radical force within the text. Her celibacy, auto-eroticism and what Howard terms the rejection of 'phallus oriented sexuality' allow Moll to critique both social and sexual injustices from a distance as well as to propose possible alternatives to heterosexuality structured along patriarchal lines. Howard points out that, unlike Shakespearean heroines, Moll Cutpurse does not get married at *The Roaring Girl*'s conclusion.[31]

Much of this reading of Moll's assertive subjectivity is summed up for Howard in the scene in which Moll plays her viol da gamba in front of Sebastian Wengrave and Mary Fitzallard (a scene that she sees as one of *The Roaring Girl*'s most erotically charged moments). Howard has claimed that, for her, the most emancipatory moment of the entire play (and, according to the hierarchy of texts that she sets up from Jonson's *Epicoene* through a variety of Shakespearean comedies to *The Roaring Girl*, perhaps in the entire early modern dramatic canon) comes when Moll undertakes what Howard calls an extraordinary musical "masturbation".[32] Commenting on Moll's 'stroking' and 'fingering' of her viol da gamba (in Act IV scene I), Howard has argued that, unlike other staged representations of female musicians:

> Moll Cutpurse is even more transgressive in that her instrument is not the lute, able to be tucked decorously beneath the breast, but the viol, played with legs akimbo. Moreover, she seems to appropriate this instrument not so much to make herself an erotic object, as to express her own erotic subjectivity [...] She has and acknowledges her sexual dreams; she has and acknowledges her 'instrument', that viol with which she is so insistently linked, the fingering of which seems to symbolise her skill at clitoral masturbation, as well as her potential skill at manual stimulation of the male penis [...] on the stage when Moll actually plays her instrument what the spectator actually sees is a woman whose strokes and clever fingering occur in the space between her own legs. Her viol suggests her own sexual instrument and her masturbatory playing of it a final defiance of patriarchal, phallus orientated, sexuality [...][33]

Rather than seeing auto-eroticism, however (in that whatever Moll is doing here she is doing to herself), when I look at this scene, I find that – like so much else surrounding Moll – the stage image that is produced is both phallocentric and pornographic. Rather than a female-authored act of sexual and social liberation, I see a male-authored fantasy that displays Moll as an object of heterosexual masculine desire, a grotesque transvestite satire that openly mocks not just Moll's but all women's supposed autonomy and independence.

As Gustav Ungerer has shown, the viol da gamba was a prominent sexual metaphor in early modern music and literature; in contrast to Howard's reading of the instrument, however, Ungerer reveals it to be a metaphor that was intrinsically linked to male sexuality – where it was uniquely conceived of in relation to acts of phallic penetration.[34] In a wide-ranging and deft analysis, Ungerer has drawn attention to the sexual undercurrents of Christopher Simpson's musical manual *The Division-Viol, or, The Art of Playing Ex tempore upon a Ground. Divided into Three Parts*, in which the early modern author inadvertently draws attention to the penis-like nature of the viol's neck as he instructs: "Let the top of the viol be erected towards your left shoulder; so, as it may rest your posture, though you touch it not with your hand."[35] Ungerer has also pointed out a passage in the section 'The Motion of the Right Arm and Wrist' that advises debutants to avoid fluid arm and wrist actions because:

> I told you before that you must stretch out your Arm streight, in which posture [playing long Notes] you will necessarily move your shoulder Joint; but if you stir that Joint in quick Notes, it will cause the whole body

to shake; which (by all means) must be avoided; as also any other indecent gesture.[36]

What I want to suggest is that the short, jerky wrist actions and arm movements that Simpson feared his students might produce without careful practice of their bowing technique are better suited by far to a comic representation of penile masturbation than to the sort of 'clitoral manipulation' to which Howard refers in her reading of this scene – and therefore that what Moll is actually engaging in here is a sort of two-handed pornographic caress of both the phallic neck of her viol (as she runs her hooked fingers over it) and of the air (with an equally encircling and stroking bow hand). Indeed, Moll herself implies in the scene itself that it is multiple male members in which she has the most profound interest as she observes "it shall ne'er be said that I came into a gentleman's chamber and let his instrument hang by the walls!" (IV.i.85–7) – a comment to which Sebastian replies "Why well said, Moll, I' faith; it had been a shame for that gentleman then, that would have let it hang still and ne'er offered it to thee" (IV.i.89–90).

Sebastian certainly seems to be rather turned on by the time that Moll's dextrous hand[i]work has concluded; he subsequently describes her to his father as "a musician, sir: one of excellent fingering [who …] Has the most delicate stroke" (IV.i.170 and 172). Moreover, in early modern literature the erotic valence of the viol da gamba itself was ubiquitously linked either to manipulation of the penis (prior to anal or vaginal penetration) or to the act of phallic penetration – as the erotic riddles of Giovan Francesco Straparola, or the following sonnet on the viol by Pierre de Larivey, canon of St-Etienne, demonstrate:[37]

Je ne le veux celer, quand je me trouve à point,
Je vas veoir mon amy, je le pren, je l'embrasse,
*Et si souvent son nerf * entre mes doigts je passe*
Que je le fais roidir, ne le voulust il point.

Après, le voyant prest, gaillard et bien en point,
Mes deux cuisses s'ouvrant d'un assez large espace,
Je le mects entre deux, et si bien je le place,
Qu'on ne nous diroit qu'un, tant de près il me joint.

Adonc, d'un maniment frétillard et adextre,
Remuant haut et bas, ore à gauche, ore à dextre,

Entre mille douleurs j'accomply mon désir;
Et si par fois son nerf devient lasche et s'abaisse,
Aveques les deux doigts si bien je le redresse,
Que plus, qu'auparavant j'en tire du plaisir.

(I don't want to hide it , when I find myself in the mood
I go and see my friend, I take him, I hug him,
And if I pass his string/member* between my fingers
So much as to make it stiff, he doesn't mind at all.

After, seeing him ready, lusty and stiffened up,
Opening my two thighs (a big enough amount)
I put him between them, and if I place him so well
As to make us seem one, so close he is to me,

Then, with a dextrous and quivering motion
Moving up and down, left to right
Between a thousand agonies I pull off my desire;
And if sometimes his string/member* goes floppy
[and shrinks]
With my two fingers I straighten it out so well
That I draw even more pleasure from him than before.)

References to viols in Shakespeare, Marston, Jonson and Donne all likewise refer to either homosexual or heterosexual phallic penetration.[39] In addition, while Moll 'masturbates' with her viol she sings two songs, both of which refer to heterosexual sex.

Yet it is not only Moll's songs and viol playing that I consider to rely on male-centred fantasies of female subjugation during erotic contact – and I would now also like to question the degree to which *The Roaring Girl* as a whole undercuts the "*telos* of heterosexual 'companionate' marriage", or contains what Howard has posited to be a "submerged, and sometimes an overt, resistance to heterosexual coupling".[40] Much of the homoerotic dynamic that is argued to be evident in the play is centred on this viol da gamba scene. In it, Sebastian kisses his cross-dressed fiancée, Mary, and, as he does so, famously comments to the other cross-dressed figure who accompanies them:

* the word 'nerf' in sixteenth-century French could be used as a substitute for either 'chord' (string) or 'membre viril' (penis)[38]

> I'd kiss such men to choose, Moll,
> Methinks a woman's lip tastes well in a doublet [...]
> As some have a conceit their drink tastes better
> In an outlandish cup than in our own,
> So methinks every kiss she gives me now
> In this strange form, is worth a pair of two
> (IV.i.46–56)

It is a kiss of which Jean Howard has observed:

> It is not the [transgressive] context that makes the kiss 'worth a pair of two' [this is the lead-up to Moll's viol playing and Sebastian is in his father's chamber with his fiancée at this moment. Sir Alexander has also forbidden a marriage between the two young lovers] but the very fact that Sebastian is kissing what looks, on the outside, like a boy; in sum that his most intense erotic pleasure is what we would now call homoerotic in nature ...[41]

Howard reads Sebastian's kiss as unquestionably homoerotic and has even gone as far as to say:

> Framed in accordance with Galenic notions of biology, it is the potential man within the young woman that constitutes the true object of Sebastian's desire. Indeed, the name Sebastian itself in some quarters carried homoerotic connotations in the Renaissance, largely because of the long iconographic tradition of representing the arrow pierced saint and his intimate relationship with Christ as 'an indirect ideal of homo-erotic love.'[42]

I want to put a different frame around this scene than that of Galenic biology, however, because in contrast to Howard I think that this *is* one of those moments on the Renaissance stage when the transvestism of a boy actor was accepted as verisimilitude and that Sebastian is fully aware of the anatomy of his fiancée at this point (in fact, I believe that there is bawdy wordplay on the sort of mind's-eye decortications of the cross-dressed female body that is not infrequently seen in early modern comedy, combined with a lewd reference to Mary Fitzallard's breasts, in the line "this strange form, is worth a pair of two").[43] Moreover, the eroticism of the scene is, I think, largely due to its transgressive inversions of father-versus-son power relations and because, far from being homoerotic, the heterosexual *telos* of Sebastian and his fiancée Mary's increasingly inevitable marriage fully dictates this scene's erotic dynamics. What is a turn-on for Sebastian (and his audience) in this scene is that he is doubly getting one over on his father; he pretends not to realise that Sir Alexander is aware of the cross-dressed Moll, yet he knows that he really is unaware of his actual cross-dressed lover, Mary. Sebastian (who, let us remind ourselves, is the well-to-do, virile, young and presumably attractive male hero of this play) is thus at the narrative centre of the scene as much as he is at the centre of the Fortune's stage; he controls it; he has stage-managed it, and it is precisely at this moment that every character (including Moll) is doing what he wants them to: Mary is kissing him, Moll is acting as a pandress and a smoke-screen to his father (as well as a piece of distinctly phallocentric pornography capable of satisfying any man who walks into the room) and Sir Alexander is not getting beyond the first layer of any of these deceptions.

As recent historical studies have shown, the disruptive social energy of assertive cross-dressed women in early-seventeenth-century London was a significant factor in the development of proto-feminist thought. The recuperation of such figures into what looks on the surface like sympathetic comedy, however, is often and in many ways a subtle recovery of this rebellious and threatening figure. Returning to the idea of the mirror with which I began this essay, the distortions in a predominantly male public theatre audience's normative understanding of what women *should* do in patriarchal society (an opinion of femininity that subordinates it a priori to masculinity and dictates compliance with their sexual desires) are precisely what allow them to identify 'Mad Moll' as a humorous distraction.

Perhaps the real *hic muliers* of London did call into question the inevitability of heterosexual 'companionate' marriage. Perhaps some had a desire to overthrow patriarchy, for as one literary example put it: "what greater glory can come to the masculine woman (as you terme her) then [*sic*] to overrule her parents and husband?"[44] Dekker and Middleton's Moll, however, ranks her feminist subjectivity as secondary to the overall needs of a narrative closure that actively embraces heterosexual union. Women's eroticisation through the assumption of masculine attire perhaps did stir up 'dangerous' homoerotic lusts in men – but, far from turning them away from the institution of marriage, the evidence in this play suggests that such desires could either be performed by wives who were prepared to 'ingle' (practise sodomy) with their husbands within the institution, or through extra-marital relations with boys or other men.

Whilst the clothing that the real *hic mulier* wore indicated that she had turned her back on a patriarchal *telos* that exploited her as currency in the dynastic marriage market, the fact that she quickly became read in pamphlet literature and in the 'play world' of the theatre as what Mary Beth Rose has described as an object of "free floating sexuality" repeatedly led to her subsumption into semi-pornographic fantasies that relied on her ability to provide polyvalent sexual satisfaction for men.[45]

Whatever the motivations of the real-life women who engaged in the cross-dressing phenomenon – and we cannot know them – one thing is clear: it is evident from the intensity of contemporaneous debate that masculine authority and gender identity were put under considerable strain. Responses to assertive women in poetry, drama and pamphlet literature not only reveal the extent of the crisis but also make obvious male recourse to the cultural media in their attempts to reassert dominion. Mark Breitenberg has recently observed that, since the controversy over cross-dressing that emerged in the 1620s appeared to be well in excess of the actual threat posed by the limited numbers of females who engaged in the phenomenon, women must not have been the source of the problem but were rather "catalytic signs of a set of prior fears and anxieties".[46] He points out that a stable sex and gender system would not have been disturbed by "such an infrequent and obviously theatrical play with gender identification".[47] He misses the point. Theatrical play is dangerous. Why else were costume stores amongst the first sites to be liberated in the Paris uprisings of 1968?[48] Breitenberg's comments reveal a common prejudice against theatricality. To many, theatrical play is ineffectual fantasy.[49] It has little power to change the world in which we live. In contrast to his view, I consider the decision of early modern women to play histrionically with the signifiers of their sex to be hugely significant – and yet we should still ask ourselves two vital questions: (i) who had been doing precisely this for the previous thirty years? and (ii) who still controlled the primary means of theatrical production that helped to create gender-political opinion in the period? The answer to both questions is men.[50] Working in the context of a professional transvestite theatre, Dekker and Middleton's *Roaring Girl* transforms a real-life woman into a humorous theatrical *zani*, a dramatic fiction whose generically determined role is simply to help her *inamorati* get past the blocking devices of a particularly miserable *senex*. Such representation purposely counteracts any feminist threat that the real Mary Frith may have embodied.

IV

hic puer, et studio uenandi lassus et aestu,
procubuit faciemque loci fontemque secutus;
dumque bibit, uisae correptus imagine formae
spem sine corpore amat, corpus putat esse, quod unda est.[51]

So when I gaze into the mirror of this early modern text is the truth of female subjectivity reflected back at me? Can I discern here a true image of its authors' intentions? Does *The Roaring Girl* reveal her gender-political allegiances? Sadly, no – and here I want to turn to one last trope of reflection as I set my criticism against the Ovidian verses above.

When I stare into *The Roaring Girl* I do not see an accurate reflection of Dekker and Middleton's attitudes towards proto-feminist agency. I simply see my own ideas about their beliefs returned back at me. Like Narcissus, I fall in love with this insubstantial reflection and scrawl my critical graffiti all over the text. Herein, perhaps, lies the most fundamental problem with Hamlet's mirror. If theatre does not constitute a simple reflection of society and the acts of players are complex legislative acts, how are we supposed to interpret them 'correctly'? What can twenty-first-century critics accurately discern when they examine historically distanced performance texts? The short answer is: I don't really know – or at least I don't want to be prescriptive about any particular result of doing it. The over-arching philosophical project of this volume is to explore the significance of post-structuralist criticism on the theory of mimesis. Writing about the post-structuralist itch to deconstruct, Ross C. Murfin has observed:

> [A]ny work of literature that we interpret defies the laws of Western logic. In the views of poststructuralist critics, texts don't say 'A and not B.' They say 'A and not-A,' as do texts written by literary critics, who are also involved in producing creative writing.[52]

My reading of *The Roaring Girl* is not the single correct and definitive interpretation of this text – neither is that of Jean Howard. There's much to be said for the gestalt rabbit/duck image that Norman Rabkin had so much fun with in relation to *Henry V*.[53] In conclusion then, I will simply offer a comment on the play by means of an observation once made by Jonathan Swift: "Satire is a sort of glass, wherein beholders do generally discover everybody's face but their own; which is the chief reason for that kind of reception it meets in the world, and that so very few are offended with it."[54]

Chapter Seven

1. William Shakespeare, *Hamlet*, The Norton Shakespeare, ed. Stephen Greenblatt and others (New York and London: W.W. Norton, 1997), III.ii.15–22.
2. As will become clear in the course of this essay, however, taking this speech as a manifesto that describes theatrical representation as a straightforward act of social reflection is only really possible if we look at Hamlet's speech through an entirely inappropriate lens – that of stage Naturalism. Self-consciously realistic or naturalistic acting (by which I mean acting that deliberately attempts to re-create the behaviour of the social and psychological world from which it comes) is often misunderstood to be the dominant mode of theatrical representation. However, the importance of psychological realism and naturalistic acting in European theatre is hugely exaggerated (largely because of the recent appropriation of these techniques by the cinema and television industries rather than as a result of any persistence with these models in the theatre). Most theatre historians concede that the desire for actors to 'imitate' life in a realistic manner is a mere blip on the radar of European acting – occupying, at best, a few decades in the last two and a half thousand years of theatrical activity. Hamlet is a deceptive fellow who knows 'seems' a lot more than he lets on – and there is more to what *seems* to be a reflection on the mimetic nature of acting than meets the eye here. As I intend to demonstrate, the apparent simplicity of this statement can only satisfy us if we are prepared to accept a mixture of historical anachronism and scientific impossibility.
3. In actual fact, mirrors do not need to be perfectly smooth – and are considered to reflect light perfectly if their irregularities are of a magnitude smaller than the wavelength of the light being reflected (the wavelengths of visible light are of the order of 5×10^{-5} cm).
4. Jonathan Miller, *On Reflection* (London: National Gallery Publications, 1998) pp. 11–12. Here and in the entire opening section of my essay I am greatly indebted to the work of Miller, whose recent work on reflection in Art History has significant implications for my argument.
5. See Miller, *On Reflection*, p. 59.
6. Ibid., p. 86.
7. Ibid., pp. 84–6.
8. As Miller observes: "In certain respects it's factually incorrect to insist that mirrors reflect things the wrong way round. If I stand facing myself in the mirror with my arms stretched out east and west, whenever I waggle my eastward hand I can't help noticing that it's the eastwardly extended reflection which waggles *its* hand. And vice versa. So there is *no* reversal from side to side. But wait. Although there is no visible reversal within the two dimensional plane of the mirror, as soon as we take the *third* dimension into consideration there *is* a reversal – only we are so accustomed to it that we don't notice. In facing the mirror, which I have to do if I want to reflect my front, my nose points due north, whereas my *reflected* nose is pointed in the other direction – due south. And *this* is where the apparent reversal from right to left happens. Looking at my reflection, I 'see' it as a real person facing in the opposite direction to me, at

the same distance *behind* the mirror as I'm *in front* of it. Now, if I *imagine* myself facing in the same direction as my reflection *seems* to be facing, I have to rotate my imagined self through 180 degrees, and when I do so, my *right* hand is now on the same side as my reflection's left. Hey presto – reversal. But this is *not* the result of some optical magic inherent in *mirrors*. On the contrary, it's the straightforward, though sometimes puzzling, consequence of the fact that in order to see the reflection of what we call the *front* of something, it must be rotated about its vertical axis so that its recognisably different front now *faces* the reflective surface, which then gives back an image of that aspect." Ibid., p. 91. The sections of Miller's book that outline the cognitive processes that give rise to the illusion of reversal in reflections are fascinating and make use of a series of very illuminating visual illustrations of the physical and cognitive processes at work. Ibid., pp. 91–5.

9. See ibid., p. 39.
10. This phenomenon can be said to account for much of what we interpret as 'anxiety' in early modern texts – such as in the instances where an undercurrent of cultural conservatism undercuts the apparent radicality of a text, one obvious example of which is those moments in early modern drama where a subtext of misogyny problematises the apparent proto-feminist empowerment of female characters (such as Rosalind's uneasy patriarchal account of the dynamics of heterosexual companionate marriage during her wooing of Orlando – a homily that is very obviously informed by the discourses of cuckoldry). It is precisely this phenomenon that has led critics to consider that Shakespeare's "*maleness* [...] makes it inevitable that his female characters are warped and distorted [...] that [he] did his best to be a true reflecting glass, but that contemporary society's limited understanding of women combined with his own male viewpoint have skewed the resulting picture" (see nn. 332 and 333 below), p. 3.
11. On the technical limitations in the craft of mirror making see Miller, *On Reflection*, p. 107. On the discovery of plate glass see p. 114 and on the emergence of flat mirrors in the mid-seventeenth century see p. 72.
12. In the exhibition curated by Miller at the National Gallery in London in 1998, few unambiguously flat mirrors are represented without deliberate foreshortening or other significant optical distortion prior to the mid-seventeenth century. Almost all of the flat mirrors depicted appear in northern Italian dynastic portraits of the sixteenth-century and even here they can often be seen to distort their subjects, such as the *Portrait of Anna Eleonora Sanvitale* by Bedoli, dating from 1562, which significantly reduces the girl's size so as to fit her within the mirror's frame. It is not until the mid-seventeenth century that a wide range of more accurate flat mirrors is represented right across Europe: 1650 (Ter Borch, *Woman at a Mirror*); 1656 (Velázquez, *Las Meninas*); 1660–5 (the Delft School, *An Interior, with a Woman Refusing a Glass of Wine*); 1662 (Hoogstraten, *A View down a Corridor* – a supposed mirror); and 1663 (Metsu, *Woman Reading a Letter*). These paintings are reproduced in Miller, *On Reflection*, pp. 89, 148, 77, 18, 81 and 100 respectively.
13. See Miller, *On Reflection*, pp. 54–5.
14. Reproduced in ibid., pp. 107 and 45 respectively.
15. In Vasari's *Lives of the Great Artists*, the debate between sculpture and painting is presented as a quarrel between Giorgione and a group of anonymous sculptors at the time of Verrocchio's sculpture of a bronze horse (cited in Miller, *On Reflection*, p. 115).
16. Convex mirrors such as these continued to be widely used well into the seventeenth century and are depicted in later artworks such as Matham's engraving of *Pride*

(reproduced in Miller, *On Reflection*, p. 160).

17. Domenic Mancin, *The Mirrour of good Maners. Conteining the foure Cardinal Vertues, compiled in Latin by Dominike Mancin, and translated into English by Alexander Barclay* (London: Iohn Cawood, 1570).
18. Laurence Saunders, *A trewe mirrour or glase wherin we maye beholde the wofull state of thys our realme of Englande, set forth in a dialogue or communicacion betwene Eusebius and Theophilus* (1556); Guillaume de la Perriere, *The Mirrour of Policie, a worke no lesse profitable than necessarie for all Magistrats (translated from Le Miroir Politique)* (London: A. Islip, 1598); Anon, *The Mirrour of Allegiance; or, a Looking-Glasse for the English, wherein they may reade their duty towards God and their King, and how to carry themselves in the taking or refusing of Oaths and Covenants* (London, 1647).
19. William Rankins, *A Mirrour of Monsters, wherein is … described the … vices … caused by the … sight of Playes* (London, 1587).
20. Lucas Wagenaer, *The Mariners Mirrour, wherin may playnly be seen the courses, heights, distances, depths, soundings, flows and ebs … risings of lands, rocks, sands and shoalds, with the marks for th' entrings of the Harbouroughs, Havens and Ports of the greatest part of Europe; their several traficks and commodities: together with the Rules and instruments of Navigation. First made and set fourth in divers exact Sea-Charts, by that famous navigator L. Wagenar … and now fitted with necessarie additions for the use of Englishmen by A. Ashley. Herein also may be understood the exploits lately atchived by the right honorable the L. Admiral of England with her Maties Navie, and some former services don by that worthy Knight Sir F. Drake* (London, 1590); and William Iohnson Blaeuw, *The Sea-Mirrour containing, a briefe instruction in the art of navigation; and a description of the seas and coasts of the Easterne, Northerne, and Westerne Navigation* (Amsterdam: W.I. Blaeuw, 1625).
21. Anon, *The Life and Death of that matchless mirrour of magnanimity and heroick vertues, Henrietta Maria de Bourbon, Queen to that blessed King and Martyr Charles the First* (London, 1669); William Roper (son-in-law of Sir Thomas More), *The Mirrour of Vertue in Worldly Greatnes; or, the life of Sir Thomas More* (Paris, 1626); John Falconer (Jesuit), *The mirrour of created perfection. Or The life of the most Blessed Virgin Mary Mother of God* (Saint Omer: English College Press, 1632); and Robert Boreman, *A Mirrour of Mercy and Judgement; or, an Exact true narrative of the life and death of Freeman Sonds … who … for murthering his elder brother … was arraigned and condemned at Maidstone, executed there …* (London: Thomas Dring, 1655).
22. Anon, *A Looking-Glass for Ladies; or, a mirrour for married-women, lively setting forth the rare constancy, chastity, patience and purity of Penelope, the wife of Ulisses, etc.* [a ballad] (London: 1680); and James Bland (Professor of Physic), *An Essay in Praise of Women: or, a Looking-glass for ladies to see their perfections in, etc.* (London: E. Curll, 1736).
23. William Baldwin, *A myrrour for magistrates Wherein may be seen by example of other, with howe greuous plages vices are punished: and howe frayle and vnstable worldly prosperity is founde, even of those whom fortune seemeth most highly to fauour* (London: Thomas Marshe, 1563); William Baldwin, *The Last parte of the Mirour for Magistrates* (London, 1574); Thomas Blenerhasset, *The Seconde part of the Mirrour for Magistrates, conteining the falles of the infortunate Princes of this Lande. From the Conquest of Cæsar, vnto the commyng of Duke William the Conquerour* (London, 1610); and Andrew Horne, *The Booke called the Mirrour of Justices, made by A.H. with the book called The Diversity of Courts and their Jurisdictions* (London, 1646).

24. Robert Abbot (Bishop of Salisbury), *A Mirrour of Popish Subtilties ... discouering sundry wretched ... euasions and shifts which a secret cauilling Papist in the behalfe of one Paul Spence Priest ... hath gathered out of Sanders, Bellarmine, and others, for the auoyding and discrediting of sundrie allegations of scriptures and Fathers, against the doctrine of the Church of Rome, concerning Sacraments, the sacrifice of the Masse, Transubstantiation, Justification &c* (London: T. Creede for T. Woodcocke, 1594); Thomas Gery, B.D., *A Mirrour for Anabaptists, in three Rational Discourses, that may put the blush upon them* (London, 1660); Anon, *The Catholick Mirrour, or, a Looking-Glasse for Protestants. Wherein they may plainly see the errours of their Church, and the truth of the Roman Catholick* (Paris, 1662); Gabriel Gerberon, *The Mirrour of Christian Piety. Wherein is considered ... the chain of Catholic truths, of predestination, and of the Grace of God, and their alliance with the liberty of the creature* [translated from Gabriel Gerberon's *Miroir de la piété chrétienne*] (London: Langley Curtiss, 1679).
25. Baldwin, *A myrrour for magistrates*, sig. Air.
26. Lisa Jardine, *Still Harping on Daughters* (London and New York: Harvester Wheatsheaf, 1983), p. 2. Jardine was taking issue with the work of Juliet Dusinberre and Anne Barton.
27. Ibid., p. 3.
28. Ibid.
29. See Jean Howard, 'Sex and Social Conflict: The Erotics of the Roaring Girl', in *Erotic Politics: Desire on the Renaissance Stage*, ed. Susan Zimmerman (London and New York: Routledge, 1992), and 'Power and Eros: Cross-dressing in Dramatic Representation and Theatrical Practice', in Jean Howard, *The Stage and Social Struggle in Early Modern England* (London and New York: Routledge, 1994). In these essays Howard sets her analysis of Moll Cutpurse against a range of material including Shakespearean heroines such as Rosalind and Portia as well as the cross-dressing controversy outlined in the *Hic Mulier* and *Haec Vir* pamphlets of 1621.
30. Howard, 'Sex and Social Conflict', p. 179.
31. The servants in typical love-comedy plots from Menander onwards do not always marry once they have helped the young lovers to get over the blocking devices of the older generation. Consequently, it could easily be argued that it is only the twentieth-century feminist desire to see Moll Cutpurse as the central character of this play that has caused such an imbalance in the way that she is generically viewed.
32. See Howard, *Power and Eros.*
33. See Howard, 'Sex and Social Conflict', pp. 179–87, esp. pp. 184 and 185.
34. Gustav Ungerer, 'The Viol da Gamba as a Sexual Metaphor in Elizabethan Music and Literature', *Renaissance and Reformation* (New Series) VIII (1984), pp. 79–90.
35. Christopher Simpson, *The Division-Viol, or, The Art of Playing Ex tempore upon a Ground. Divided into Three Parts* (London, 1667), p. 2 (quoted in Ungerer, 'Viol da Gamba', p. 80).
36. Simpson, *Division-Viol*, p. 7 (quoted in Ungerer, 'Viol da Gamba', p. 80).
37. The translation of this sonnet is my own. The sonnet was first published in 1572 (in a corrected edition of Jean Louveau's French translations of Giovan Francesco Straparola's riddles *Le piacevoli notti*). Larivey's edition (that first rendered Straparola's riddles into sonnets) was enormously popular and went through eleven volumes between 1572 and 1615. It is here reproduced from *Les Facetieuses Nuits de Straparole traduites par Jean Louveau et Pierre de Larivey*, ed. P. Jannet (Paris, 1857), vol. ii, p. 325 (quoted in Ungerer, 'Viol da Gamba', p. 81). In Straparola and Louveau, both the

subject and the object of the poem appear to be male (giving 'his thighs' and so on). Larivey consequently transposes the sexual orientation of the poem towards a heterosexual mode, yet still retains the essence of phallic penetration.

38. See Pierre Guiraud, *Dictionnaire historique, stylistique, rhétorique, étymologique de la littérature érotique* (Paris: Payot, 1978), p. 31.
39. The metaphor is evident in Pericles' comments to the daughter of Antiochus concerning the incestuous relationship that she has with her father: "You are a fair viol, and your sense the strings, / Who, fingered to make man his lawful music, / Would draw heaven down and all the gods to hearken; / But, being played upon before your time, / Hell only danceth at so harsh a chime" (William Shakespeare, *Pericles*, I.i.82–6). It is also employed in the induction to John Marston's *Malcontent*, in which Slinko refuses to sit between William Sly's legs and objects: "the audience will then take me for a viol da gamba and think that you play upon me" (*The Malcontent*, induction, ll. 19–20). The character Saviolina, in Jonson's *Every Man out of His Humour*, also displays an amusing desire to *become* her *own* viol, so that she will have the pleasure of being 'played upon' by the gallant (Fastidius Brisk) who woos her (Ben Jonson, *Every Man out of His Humour*, III.ix.78ff.). The figure also features in Donne's poem 'A Lady and her Viol', in which the instrument is given a masculine gender by a male lover who is jealous of the attention that the object of his own sexual desires affords her viol. See John Donne, *The Poems of John Donne*, ed. E.K. Chambers (London, 1896), vol. ii, p. 269. All of the above examples (and a range of others in French and Italian literature) are cited in Ungerer, 'Viol da Gamba', pp. 79–90.
40. Howard, 'Sex and Social Conflict', p. 175.
41. Ibid.
42. Ibid. The Saint Sebastian idea set out in full in James M. Saslow, 'The Tenderest Lover: Saint Sebastian in Renaissance Painting: A Proposed Homoerotic Iconology of North Italian Art 1450 – 1550', *Gai Saber* 1, (1977), pp. 58–66.
43. The different modes of representation are complex at this moment and need to be teased out. Although the boy actor playing Mary Fitzallard is at this juncture dressed in clothing that is suited to his real or actual sex, I would argue that – operating as he does as a female character within the conventions of a straightforward romantic disguise plot – he is *not* primarily 'read' by his audience as a *boy* in this scene. In my own practical experience of directing this play with an all-male cast, the *hetero*sexual valences of this moment certainly come out very strongly in performance (regardless of the transvestite tradition). Howard's claims about the 'one-sex' model are also further undermined here by the fact that Mary Fitzallard is dressed as a young *pageboy*. As Peter Stallybrass has observed, much recent criticism has somewhat blurred the distinctions between boys' and men's genitals, with the former being "peculiarly distorted [and enlarged] by being thought of as THE phallus". See Peter Stallybrass, 'Transvestism and the Body Beneath: Speculating on the Boy Actor', in Zimmerman (ed.), *Erotic Politics*, p. 68. Mary Fitzallard certainly lacks the phallic *puissance* that is sometimes erotically attributed to Moll (although Moll is also, in my opinion, an unambiguously female character, and those who consider her as male or hermaphroditical fall into the category of the comically reviled in the play).
44. Anon, *Muld Sacke: or the Apologie of Hic Mulier* (London, 1620), sig. B1r.
45. Mary Beth Rose, 'Women in Men's Clothing: Apparel and Social Stability in *The Roaring Girl*', *English Literary Renaissance* 14 (1984), p. 374. See also the various references to sexual incontinence and prostitution in Anon, *Hic Mulier: or, the Man-Woman;*

being a Medicine to cure [...] *the Staggers in the Masculine-Feminines of our Times. Exprest in a brief Declamation* [...] (London: John Trundle, 1620).

46. Mark Breitenberg, *Anxious Masculinity in Early Modern England* (Cambridge: Cambridge University Press, 1996), p. 151.
47. Ibid.
48. I am rather fond of the Paris example. For an early modern illustration of my point one needs only to turn to the decision of supporters of the Earl of Essex to commission the Chamberlain's Men to perform a *play* about Richard II prior to their rebellion against Elizabeth in 1601 – a decision that prompted the response: "I am Richard II; know you not that?" from Elizabeth.
49. See Jonas Barish, *The Anti-Theatrical Prejudice* (Berkeley, CA: University of California Press, 1981) for a detailed analysis of the fears and anxieties that lead most critics of theatre to dismiss it in this way.
50. The recent work of scholars such as Clare McManus and Melinda Gough on elite female performance in the court masque has had a significant effect upon our understanding of female influence on all theatrical performance in the early years of the Stuart monarchy, and has drawn significant attention to the ways in which the gender-political context of early modern drama was changing during this period. However, I still consider *The Roaring Girl* to have taken place in a professional theatrical context of unquestioned male dominance; that the real-life Mary Frith was taken to court and punished for playing her lute and singing songs on the public theatre stage is evidence enough of this fact.
51. Ovid, *Metamorphoses*, Book III, ll. 413–17. My translation of the Latin is as follows: 'In this place, tired from the heat and hunting, the boy reclined, drawn to the spot both by its beauty and the spring that it contained, but when he wanted to quench his thirst, another thirst arose in him – and as he drank he beheld a beautiful reflection and was captivated by it; but he loved an idea without form and what he thought to be a body was only water...'
52. Ross C. Murfin, 'Deconstruction and *Hamlet*', in *Hamlet: Case Studies in Contemporary Criticism*, ed. Susanne L. Wofford (Boston, MA and New York: Bedford, 1994) p. 286.
53. Norman Rabkin, 'Rabbits, Ducks and *Henry V*', *Shakespeare Quarterly* 28 (1977), pp. 279–96.
54. Jonathan Swift, 'Preface', *The Battle of the Books* (London, 1704).

CHAPTER EIGHT

Mimesis, resistance and iconoclasm: resituating The Revenger's Tragedy

Adrian Streete

I

IN A SEMINAL ARTICLE first published in 1980 on Thomas Middleton's play *The Revenger's Tragedy*, Jonathan Dollimore argues that the philosophical distinction between metaphysical transcendence and immanence is crucial for any understanding of early modern literary theory and drama. Specifically, Dollimore sees the discussion of mimetic theory in the sixteenth and seventeenth centuries in terms of a much older structural tension between competing Platonic and Aristotelian categories. As he observes: "The distinction between the metaphysical reality which is transcendent, and that which is immanent, remains at the centre of Western theology and philosophy, especially in the period under discussion."[1] Inspired by both Humanism and Reformed theology, early modern English thinkers were, essentially, putting a contemporary spin on what was an ancient Greek problem. To this end, and drawing on the work of Philip Sidney, Fulke Greville and Francis Bacon amongst others, Dollimore argues persuasively for a conflict during the period between what he calls "idealist mimesis versus empiricist mimesis".[2] In terms of early modern dramatic practice, he sees this conflict as being especially pertinent. For example, by looking at the ways in which *The Revenger's Tragedy* deals with the question of mimesis, Dollimore argues that the play both subverts and parodies idealist mimesis (associated with providential discourse), while at the same time finding no comfort in an emergent empiricist account of 'reality'. Put plainly: in the play "there is no ideal metaphysical order, transcendent, or immanent".[3]

Dollimore's argument, expressed both in this article and, more widely, in his book *Radical Tragedy*, has proved both influential and persuasive. More broadly, it offers an account of early modern conceptions of mimesis that leads to a memorable characterisation of the "sensibility" of the age as "that of a subversive black camp".[4] But, attractive as such a reading might be, I think that there is also an inherent danger of overplaying the decadent, self-conscious artificiality of a play like *The Revenger's Tragedy*. In large part, this is achieved by correspondingly underplaying the explicit political violence that structures both this play and the genre more generally.[5] Whatever else happens in a revenge tragedy, the secular figure of authority, whether it is a king, prince or duke, is nearly always the focus for violent attack, and more often than not is killed. In dealing with this radical political act, and also with the bloodbath that generally ensues, to a degree it makes sense to say that this excess must become self-conscious parody: how else might the eight dead bodies that litter the stage at the end of a play such as *The Revenger's Tragedy* be explained? The older critical alternative, which understood the dramatic and narrative thrust of plays in terms of a traditional affirmation of 'order' and political status quo, scarcely seems credible today.

Like most other revenge tragedies of the period, the structural teleology of the genre is fuelled by a violent interrogation of various forms of absolutism. This particular connection has been explored by a number of critics.[6] One of the most important of these critics, Franco Moretti, finds that the examination of absolutism in Elizabethan and Jacobean tragedy can be aligned with creation of a "public" that "assumed the right to bring a king to justice".[7] He goes on to argue that the genre itself "disentitled the absolute monarch to all ethical and rational legitimation. Having deconsecrated the king, tragedy made it possible to decapitate him."[8] From a historical perspective, absolutism is understood as a process giving way to the 'deconsecration of sovereignty', a shift that, in itself, also seems to imply what might be called an anticipatory political logic. In other words, radical political discourse is part of a *telos* that achieved its apogee in 1649. For Moretti, it is not so much the institutions of absolutism that this drama exposes: rather, it is "its culture, its values, its ideology".[9] The reasons behind this claim impact upon the symbolic capital of absolutism:

> Here the legitimacy of social power derives from a form of divine investiture. Power is founded in a transcendent design, in an intentional and significant order. Accordingly, political relations have the right to exist only in so far as they *reproduce that order symbolically*. [...] Sovereignty is a power that, having its origin *in itself*, is thereby released from any control; it is 'self determined', as Hegel will say. Sovereignty is a *universal* power, reaching and defining every part of the body politic, whose destiny is therefore enveloped within it.[10]

In the plays that Moretti examines, such as *Gorboduc*, *King Lear*, *Measure for Measure*, *Macbeth* and *Hamlet*, the legitimacy of this transcendent sovereignty is devastatingly undermined. As he summarises: "Fully realized tragedy is the parable of the sovereign inserted in a context that *can no longer understand it*. It is a text that lacks an adequate interpretative function and in which the final 'judgement' must be enormously poorer than that on which it is passed."[11] In contradistinction to Dollimore's self-reflexive reading of the genre, Moretti sees tragedy in anticipatory terms, as containing a radical potentiality that it cannot yet quite account for. In viewing tragedy as anticipating a secular political moment that deconsecrates the sovereign, paradoxically tragedy is collapsed into a transcendent reflection of a politically inevitable/desirable reality, albeit one understood from the historically retrospective viewpoint of the critic. Such a view obviously has implications for any understanding of mimesis: a shift from mimesis as 'parodic reflection of reality' to mimesis as 'anticipation of a desired reality', perhaps?

The work of Jonathan Dollimore and Franco Moretti offers competing views of early modern theatrical mimesis as irreducibly parodic or irredeemably anticipatory. But in this chapter I want to argue for a reading of mimesis that builds on this work yet which also departs from it. I suggest that it is possible to combine Dollimore's focus on the fraught connection between immanence and transcendence with Moretti's interrogation of absolutist political forms. But I want to suggest a different theoretical endpoint for this combination. Rather than finishing in parody or anticipating future realities, I argue that the endpoint of the kind of early modern representative practices examined here is violent mimetic iconoclasm. Furthermore, this is an iconoclasm that finds expression in the theatre because the roots of early modern debates surrounding both absolutism and iconoclasm foreground the deeply fraught mimetic status of signs. As I will show, many important strands of early modern political theory that dealt with questions of absolutism and rebellion consistently fall back on a mimetic conception of kingship and authority that pivots between notions of immanence and transcendence. The fact is that revenge tragedy re-emerges in England during the latter part of the sixteenth century, a time when many early modern political thinkers were deeply engaged in debating the mimetic and political function of the literal body of authority, the secular ruler.[12] Put simply, if the secular ruler was God's representative on earth, and if that secular ruler was attacked, was the assault not also an explicit attack upon God? To answer in the affirmative in this instance, as many in the period did, would appear to reinstate the mimetic distinction between the immanent and the transcendent that Dollimore seeks to problematise. Linking the secular body of the king with the divine body of God implies a mimesis of transcendence. Alternatively, to insist on the distinction, as another group of early modern thinkers maintained, would seem to deny the possibility of mimesis altogether. If the king has no connection with the divine then what exactly does a king signify? This chapter will argue that this constitutive tension leads to iconoclasm, and that the mimetic practice of early modern revenge tragedy can be understood as theatrical iconoclasm in practice. By examining early modern political discourse and the ways it conceives of authoritative figures such as the king and the Father, I end by offering a reading, via William Shakespeare's *Hamlet*, of *The Revenger's Tragedy* in the light of these observations.

II

For many years, political theorists have been debating the emergence of theories of resistance against tyrannical rulers during the Reformation.[13] For some scholars, resistance theory is Lutheran in inspiration and development. Others have pointed to Calvinist groups such as the French Huguenots as the real progenitors of political resistance. Perhaps the most influential example of the former view is found in Quentin Skinner's study, *The Foundations of Modern Political Thought.* Here, Skinner argues that, when it comes to judging the origins of political resistance during the Reformation, we should look not to the work of John Calvin but to that of Martin Luther. Specifically he argues that as they developed a number of Luther's political insights, Lutherans such as Philip Melancthon, Justus Jonas and Gregory Brück, and texts such as the famous

Magdeburg Confession of 1550 initiated a politically radical Reformism and specifically a defence of religious resistance.[14] As Skinner notes: "By contrast with the Calvinists, the Lutherans found little difficulty in defending the idea of active resistance to their lawful overlord."[15] It is certainly true that there were many Lutheran thinkers who actively supported this kind of resistance by developing certain aspects in the work of medieval thinkers such as William of Ockham and Marsilius of Padua. In the case of the famous Magdeburg Confession, for example, the Lutheran pastors of that city went so far as to direct their resistance at the Emperor himself, Charles V. Skinner's views have proved to be significant to the extent that they have instituted a certain reluctance to see Calvinism as politically radical at all. Understood in this way, Calvinism is often viewed as a politically quiescent movement. However, there is a body of scholarly opinion that disagrees with the Skinner line on this issue. In the work of Carlos Eire, Christopher Elwood and Ralph Hancock it is Calvinism, not Lutheranism, which provides the political engine of resistance theory. For these scholars, one crucial point divides Lutherans from Calvinists over the question of rebellion.[16] Moreover, this is also the point that Skinner underplays. Crucially, as Eire argues, in terms of political structures "The Lutherans never broke completely with the older notion of all power being divinely ordained."[17] In other words, the office and the person of the secular ruler are inseparable because the authority upon which the legitimacy of both rests is God given. As Luther put it in 1523: "If the governing authority and its sword are a divine service … then everything that is essential for the authority's bearing of the sword must also be divine service."[18] Therefore, according to this absolutist logic, any attack on the secular authority is ultimately an assault upon God. This may not seem like much of a distinction when thinking about questions of rebellion. But it was to prove absolutely crucial in the context of sixteenth-century theology and politics. Indeed, what makes Calvinist theory in this respect so distinctive and so suggestive is that Calvinist thinkers *did* insist precisely upon the metaphysical division of office and person that a Lutheran standpoint would not allow. Yet, as I will show, this division is far from straightforward and is in fact replete with difficulty. Early modern political thought, like early modern theology, does not lend itself to easy distinctions.

According to the logic of those Calvinists writing on resistance, dividing the office and person as conceptual categories makes it both possible and permissible to attack the corrupt person whilst still maintaining the integrity of the office.[19] In one respect, this appears to be a logical extension of Calvinist metaphysics. Calvinism is remarkable for the way in which it insists upon the division between man and God by contrasting the transcendent magnificence of the deity with abject, fallen, immanent humanity.[20] Understood in this way, thinkers such as John Knox, Theodore Beza, Pierre Viret, Peter Martyr, Philippe du Plessis-Mornay, Hubert Languet, François Hotman, George Buchanan, Christopher Goodman and John Ponet cannot be seen either as cranks or as crypto-Lutherans.[21] So although they undoubtedly drew upon Lutheran ideas and writings, they might also be said to represent a very distinct development of certain theoretical precepts in the thought of John Calvin himself. Calvin may not have been a political radical, but that did not stop his followers from developing a radical conception of political resistance.[22] Indeed, in developing theories of resistance against tyrants, these thinkers also pressed the distinction between person and office to breaking point. To put it slightly differently, it is not just in the work of the Classical republican theorists and Italian humanists that it is possible to find the development of what Robert Weimann has called "an intense and quite revolutionary principle of legitimation, in which the dualism of subject and object was religiously, ethically, and philosophically sanctioned".[23] The distinctions that it made may have been fine ones, but Calvinist resistance theory was a political movement in its own right. Indeed, one of the prime reasons that Queen Elizabeth I viewed Calvinism with such caution was the connection that she made early in her reign between Calvinism and resistance.[24] It is certainly the case that the ideas of these Calvinists were known in early modern England, particularly amongst the Sidney circle, as David Norbrook has shown.[25] And Alan Sinfield has persuasively read Shakespeare's *Macbeth* in the light of George Buchanan's writings on monarchical tyranny and rebellion.[26] More prosaically, it was possible during the reigns of Elizabeth and James to find a defence of rebellion in the marginal notes of the popular Geneva Bible, notes that emanated from the Reformed English and Scottish diaspora who fled to the Continent during the reign of Mary Tudor, and who included men such as Ponet, Knox and Goodman.

Mary's reign was also the catalyst for perhaps the most notorious resistance tract of the period, John Knox's *The First Blast of the Trumpet against the Monstrous Regiment of Women*. It is most commonly the misogyny of this text that garners scholars' attention. But of equal importance are the political arguments Knox uses, both here and elsewhere, to justify rebellion. As he apparently said to Mary Queen of Scots when discussing this tract with her, if princes "exceed their bounds", then "they may be resisted, even by power".[27] This is contentious enough, but consider the reasoning behind this assertion. Knox says: "God craves of Kings that they be, as it were, foster-fathers to His church" because, as he puts it, "this subjection … is the greatest dignity that flesh can get upon the face of the earth".[28] Whether this amounts to a Calvinist distinction between office and person or not is a moot point. However, what is noticeable is the fact that the ruler is a "foster-father", a substitute figure of authority, not one who shares a direct bloodline with his 'sons'. Emphasising the distance, slight though it may be, between secular ruler and the divine makes an attack upon that ruler more palatable. This kind of logic is further explained by John Ponet who writes as follows in *A Shorte Treatise of politike power*: "for as much as ther is no exprese positiue lawe for punishment of a Tyranne among christen men, the question is, whether it be laufull [*sic*] to kill such a monster and cruell beast couered with the shape of a man".[29] For Ponet, the tyrannous ruler is an unlawful image, "couered with the shape of a man", who must be destroyed. Of course, all political writing during this period makes metaphorical connections between the secular ruler and the divine. But the point is that resistance theorists of whatever religious persuasion foreground this metaphorical inheritance as a justification for rebellion. Ponet and Knox do not say, as James VI and I does in his *Basilicon Doron*, that a king is made "a little GOD to sit on his Throne, and rule ouer other men".[30] Whereas the justification of absolutist forms relies upon the political synthesis provided by metaphorical formulations such as King James's, resistance theorists are much more likely, explicitly or implicitly, to fall back on the political disjunction afforded by figurative discourse: the king is *like*, as opposed to the king *is*. Again, this separation may seem like so much quibbling and not really a substantive political difference. But what Ponet and Knox's suggestive texts point towards is the possibility that the "foster-father" and the "cruell beast" are essentially parasitic upon the absolute authority of the divine father. If the king is only *like*, then it is equally only a short conceptual leap to stating that the king is *un*like: to put it slightly differently, that authority, such as it is, is achieved not through direct divine ordination as it is for James, but through a strange form of secular mimesis. By saying that the office and person of the secular ruler are in fact distinct entities, resistance theorists like Ponet and Knox seem to be edging towards a form of conceptual Nominalism whereby the perceptual and linguistic gap between the corrupt world of fallen signs and the ever distant realm of metaphysical referentiality is insisted upon to such a degree that the one can draw no authority from the other. If the secular ruler can draw no direct authority from the transcendent status of his office then it would seem to follow that God no longer ratifies the immanent realm of human politics: in the place of divine ratification, the image and mimetic imitation. For a religion that made much of Catholicism's supposed idolatry of the sign, this conclusion is fraught, if hardly surprising. Indeed, it is possible to make an even more startling link. Whether the attack was upon the idolatrous statue or the corrupt tyrant, the logic behind that attack was essentially the same. As Carlos Eire has noted: "It can be argued ... that by consistently urging the people to hate idolatrous worship and abstain from it, Calvin was implicitly advising civil disobedience."[31] The status of the image was about more than abstract theory: in the case of resistance theory and iconoclasm, questions of mimesis were explicitly questions of political authority.

It is true to say that Christian theology has always been predicated on a tension between image and word. But during the Reformation, the doctrine of *sola scriptura* coupled with the Mosaic prohibition on figurative representations of the divine meant that this tension became a source of political dislocation. In England, the most well-known and well-documented manifestation of this dislocation was the iconoclastic assault on religious images and representations. If representations of the divine on earth impugned God's transcendent majesty, then it was incumbent upon the godly to remove or destroy the offending images, a task that many undertook with great zeal. Both literary scholars and historians have done much interesting work on the various political and religious impulses that underpin this movement. For example, Michael O'Connell has recently argued that iconoclasm emerges from "a clash between religious systems, one based on an incarnational structure of religious understanding and the other resting on the logocentric assumptions of early modern humanism empowered by print culture".[32] Protestantism was no different to any other form of orthodox Christianity in stressing the importance of the incarnation, the doctrine that God became man in order to save mankind. Nevertheless, the problem for the Reformers was that this doctrine is singularly ill suited to a purely logocentric or mimetic exposition. For example, this is what John Calvin has to say on the idolatrous impulse: "Daily experience teaches that flesh is always uneasy until it has obtained some figment like itself in which it may fondly find solace as in an image of God."[33] As with the earlier quotation from Knox, again we notice that the inheritance of the immanent flesh is foregrounded in favour of the transcendent spirit.[34] But it is also interesting to note that the separation of flesh from spirit is the basis upon which idolatry can be avoided. Still, Calvin cannot completely disavow the mimetic. As he goes on: "only those things are to be sculptured or painted which the eyes are capable of seeing: let not God's majesty, which is far above the perceptions of the eyes, be debased through unseemly representations".[35] Even Calvin seems to accept that imitation and metaphor are unavoidable. How else can fallen humankind signify, either visually or verbally, without falling back in some way upon image or metaphor, each of which is potentially idolatrous? As O'Connell observes, the incarnation implies "the belief that God, in taking on a human form, became subject to representation as an image".[36] As with resistance theory, iconoclasm demonstrates a constitutive tension between doctrine and practice, between the word and the representational expression that it implies, between immanence and transcendence. Pursuing this strand of Protestantism to its logical conclusion, there is a separation of word from thing, flesh from spirit, office from person, a separation that also implies a negation of the mimetic. In a sense, then, iconoclasm offers Protestantism a default position from the difficulties of the mimetic.

So if Lutheranism instituted a political and theological realignment of the human subject in relation to both divine and secular authority, Calvinism went further by foregrounding that distinction at the level of the sign. In terms of both iconoclasm and political theory, this shift also raised the possibility that the fallen world is constructed of nothing more than images and that mimesis is nothing more than a desperate attempt to reinstate some kind of metaphysical connection between divine and human. For example, in book four of his *Vindiciae contra Tyrannos*, which was published in England in 1588, Armada year, as *A Short Apologie for Christian Souldiours*, Hubert Languet noted that "we should cut short any prince, inuading the kingdome of Christ, any tyrant afflicting his own people, any king throwing downe the props and stayes of his common wealth".[37] The reference to the kingdom of Christ is quite deliberate. By aligning the rule of the king with the kingdom of Christ, the Father necessarily slides further away from the realm of man. Against a backdrop of absolutist political ideology, resistance theory looks to divide office and person, thereby seeking to justify rebellion against the Father.[38] Nevertheless, to kill a king is to commit resolutely and violently to the frailty of the flesh. To put it another way, this justification of regicide implicitly relies upon the ideological import of iconoclasm: the two cannot be seen in isolation. Moreover, in the context of the cultural dislocation between image and word engendered by the Reformation, it is noticeable that this iconoclastic impulse should foreground the constitutive status of both Father and son as iconoclastic signs. No matter how hard it tries, Reformed religion always falls back upon the image, and therefore upon a mimetic understanding of the world caught *between* immanence and transcendence. This difficulty can also be seen operating in the work of John Calvin.[39] Commenting in the *Institutes* on the part of the second Commandment that refers to visiting "the iniquity of the fathers upon the children", Calvin observes:

> it is to be understood that the Lord's righteous curse weighs not only upon the wicked man's head but also upon his whole family. Where the curse lies, what else can be expected but that the father, shorn of the Spirit of God, will live most disgracefully? Or that the son, forsaken by the Lord on account of the father's iniquity, will follow the same ruinous path? Finally, that the grandson and great-grandson, the accursed offspring of detestable men, will rush headlong after them?[40]

For Calvin, lineage, and especially patriarchal lineage, is to be understood as a curse. The law of the ever distant Father is, he says, "no brief and simple revenge, but one that will extend to the children, the grandchildren, and the great-grandchildren, who obviously become imitators of their father's impiety".[41] According to Calvin, the subject is caught between the trauma of a law that he is forced to imitate and the reality that this curse perpetuates an iconoclastic chain of imperfect signification.[42] As with the other Protestant theologians examined here, Calvin restates the tension between logocentric inheritance and the imperfection of signs in terms of the individual subject's relation to an authoritative Father figure. But perhaps the most interesting fact of all is that Calvin returns us to the imperative towards revenge.

As I have mentioned, the rise of reformed religion and the development of revenge tragedy are virtually synonymous in early modern

England.[43] Nearly all of these plays deal with the deposition or murder of a tyrannous figure and many of them, including *The Revenger's Tragedy*, display modes of signification that are often violently iconoclastic. So in what follows, I want to argue for an iconoclastic reading of *The Revenger's Tragedy*, one that foregrounds the profoundly unsettled nature of Reformed signs, both verbal and mimetic. It is not that the play ends in parody or that it necessarily anticipates future political systems. Rather, it demonstrates the failure of reformed theology to completely reform signs, to construct a discursive system predicated upon a complete disjunction between word and thing. By examining *The Revenger's Tragedy* via *Hamlet*, focusing on the literary and political status of the Father and the son, I aim to show how the mimetic inheritance of Reformed theology might be manifested in the play's violent iconoclasm. To this end, André Green's observation on the sacred and the tragic is apposite. He says:

> One cannot forget that the sacred, which is the implicit aim of the tragic, is not … a primary reference, or an ultimate one … but is itself the memory, the recall of an act that it commemorates, the murder of the primal father. The sacred as the fundamental expression of the religious is inseparable from the prohibition that establishes a particular category of objects to which sexual reverence is due because in them the presence of the dead man is signified. The dead man is given once more the power that death took away, a power to which homage must be paid in order to obviate any possible hostile act of revenge on his part.[44]

This is not to suggest that there is some kind of sublimated religious discourse in operation in *The Revenger's Tragedy*. It is to suggest, though, that the play, with its deeply uneasy juxtaposition of images and words, offers an interesting comment on the failure of the Reformed movement to completely reform signs. All language, verbal or visual, carries a political charge during the period, because, as one scholar has put it, "Symbols … create social worlds and regulate communal life."[45] It is only by understanding these symbols in their political and mimetic contexts that we can recover a sense of the political authority invested in them. Or rather, only by understanding the *failure* of these systems can we recover a sense of the political fragility that underpins the revenge genre.

III

In *Hamlet* the audience has to wait until Act Five of the drama to get a glimpse at the skull beneath the skin; but in *The Revenger's Tragedy* the skull is unapologetically revealed to the audience as the play begins. This is just the first of a number of well-known and self-conscious borrowings from *Hamlet* in the later play.[46] But unlike in *Hamlet* where the sight of Yorick's bones leads the Prince into a philosophical disquisition on mutability, the presence of the skull at the start of *The Revenger's Tragedy* is part of a complex strategy of memorialisation that self-consciously reflects the practices of the earlier play, but which also radically reinterprets those practices. Just as *Hamlet* has rightly been seen as the progenitor of *The Revenger's Tragedy*, so *Hamlet* retains its own shadowy begetter in the shape of the text known as the 'Ur-Hamlet', an earlier version of William Shakespeare's great tragedy.[47] The exact status and authorship of this ur-text are of secondary importance. What is relevant, however, is the signifying function of the relationship between the 'Ur-Hamlet', *Hamlet* and *The Revenger's Tragedy*. It might be possible to view this bond as a familial triad: the 'Ur-Hamlet' as ghostly 'father' of *Hamlet* and *The Revenger's Tragedy* as offspring of Shakespeare's play. Because the latter two plays are indebted to their predecessor they are also forced to acknowledge their parentage, their dramatic lineage, through similarities of language, theme and plot. However, the two later texts signify in their own right and as such also evince a strenuous textual and thematic attempt to grapple with this lineage, to re-write the story they were bequeathed.

This tension between memorialisation and generation is crucial in both *Hamlet* and *The Revenger's Tragedy*. Significantly it manifests itself at a structural level in terms of a familial triad that mirrors the relationship between the texts described above. For example, in *Hamlet* the triad consists of Old Hamlet, Hamlet and Claudius. Interestingly, the Ghost's injunction to Hamlet, "Remember me" (I.v.91), only serves to highlight the ambiguity of this masculine triad.[48] In the first place, it is only by hearing the Ghost's story that Hamlet (and the audience) understands that what has come to pass since his father's death is essentially a false narrative that goes against the 'normal' narrative of monarchical succession. Claudius should not be where he in fact is. It is for this reason that the Ghost's tale runs against the narrative thrust of the play itself. It is a retrospectively recounted story that, until he acts upon it, only really signifies in Hamlet's memory.[49] The Prince says that he will "wipe away all trivial fond records" from "the table of my memory" and that the Ghost's "commandment all alone shall live / Within the book and volume of my brain, / Unmix'd with baser matter" (I.v.98–104). But until he translates memory into the signifying realm of action, Hamlet is unable to generate a narrative that will counter Claudius's. The false father will continue to dominate and the ghostly father will remain dis-membered.

Largely because it builds upon *Hamlet*'s foundational presentation of these issues, there is arguably no play that takes these concerns further during the period than *The Revenger's Tragedy*. As it opens, the audience is presented with three separate yet interrelated 'bodies': Vindice, the skull of his dead lover Gloriana and the ruling body. Vindice desires revenge on the Duke for poisoning Gloriana:

> Duke; royal lecher; go, grey-hair'd adultery;
> And thou his son, as impious steep'd as he;
> And thou his bastard, true-begot in evil;
> And thou his duchess, that will do with devil:
> Four excellent characters.
>
> (I.i.1–5)

This complex representation, drawing as it does on both the Vice and *memento mori* traditions, situates Vindice at the very outset as both a part of the world he describes and as a metadramatic malcontent who attempts to locate himself outside this realm in order to comment upon it. This distinction (if that is what it is) will become more and more critical as the play progresses but at this stage Vindice's primary objective is to pass sardonic judgement on the body politic. And 'body' is the key word here. An early modern audience familiar with the official Church homilies would also have been familiar with one of the most ubiquitous political metaphors of the Tudor and Stuart ideological machine which stated, in the words of one of these homilies, that "the whole body of every realm, and all the members and parts of the same, shall be subject to their head, their king".[50] But what the audience are presented with at the beginning of the play is a representation that, in a similar way to resistance theory, undermines this popular political metaphor. Furthermore, in Vindice the audience have an anti-ideological propagandist who destabilises the essentialist rhetoric implicit in this metaphor. If the body is shown to be politically unstable then so, it follows, are the 'characters' that inhabit those bodies. Moreover, if 'character' is shown not to be an essence then the body becomes a signifier that may have various contingent meanings written upon it.

Vindice desires vengeance on the Duke for poisoning his lover Gloriana[51] and for destroying his father. As the play begins, Vindice enters carrying the skull of Gloriana. The iconography of the skull, the early modern emblem of death *par excellence*, seems fairly straightforward. Yet it is worth remembering that death is what we commonly expect at the end of a revenge tragedy. Unlike Hamlet who enters with the memory of his dead father and who ruminates on the skull in the final act of the play, Vindice actualises memory, making death a shockingly present iconic image from the outset. It seems that revenge is not a position to be worked towards so much as an element more pervasively constitutive of this culture.[52] Interestingly, this realisation is strikingly paralleled in Alex Cox's 2002 film version of the play, which opens with Christopher Eccleston's Vindice emerging from a bus full of corpses, and then paying a visit to the local charnel house to collect Gloriana's skull. By starting with the carnage that should properly conclude any self-respecting revenge tragedy, the film implies that this play's tragic practice is anything but straightforward. In the play, Vindice says this of the Duke:

> O, that marrowless age
> Would stuff the hollow bones with damn'd desires,
> And 'stead of heat, kindle infernal fires
> Within the spendthrift veins of a dry duke,
> A parch'd and juiceless luxur. Oh God! – one
> That has scarce blood enough to live upon,
> And he to riot it like a son and heir?
>
> (I.i.5–11)

The physical decrepitude of the Duke is particularly noticeable, but even although he has "scarce blood enough to live upon", he is still able to "riot it like a son and heir". This more than anything else seems to be what rankles with Vindice. As he continues: "O, the thought of that / Turns my abused heart-strings into fret" (I.i.12–13). Vindice's sense that the Duke is occupying *his* rightful place seems to be the key to the complex interplay between body and revenge in these lines. He sees the Duke as a dangerous patriarchal figure that he must destroy. Yet his description of the Duke as a "son and heir" not only confuses this aim, it also draws a curious parallel between revenger and patriarch. As Vindice notes sardonically: "old men lustful / Do show like young men, angry, eager, violent, / Outbid like their limited performances" (I.i.34–6). The Duke is almost too masculine and too angry. In many respects, it seems that he possesses those very qualities that the revenger lacks. As Vindice says of his own position: "My life's unnatural to me, e'en compelled / *As if I liv'd now when I should be dead*" (I.i.120–1, my emphasis). As Vindice means 'Vengeance' and as vengeance must inevitably end in death, the inversion in this line is doubly ironic.

So while the Father retains his symbolic centrality in the processes of identity formation, the signifying chain he institutes is predicated upon, and reproduces, terrible iconoclastic violence. To this end, consider this passage from John Calvin's popular *Sermons ... on the Epistles of S. Paule to Timothie and Titus*, first published in 1579. In the first sermon, Calvin offers a fascinating analysis of the genealogy of the term 'Father':

> This name *father* is so honorable, that it belongeth to none, but to God onely. Yea in respect of our bodies. And therefore, when we say, that they which have begotten vs, according to the flesh, are our fathers, it is an vnproper kind of speech: for no mortall creature deserueth this so high and excellent dignitie: yet so it is, that God of his singular goodnesse aduaunceth men, to this so high a steppe, that he will that they be called fathers: and he doth it to this end and purpose, that they should acknowledge them selues to be so much more bound vnto him.[53]

As Calvin makes clear, the role of Father is only grudgingly bequeathed to fallen humankind. Because it is only ever a fallen, fleshy and immanent copy of God's masculinity, the name of the Father represents, at best, a surrogate title and, at worst, traumatic abandonment. In effect, this form of subjectivity is predicated upon a prohibition of the name that structures early modern society: Father, pater, Deus. As Leo Bersani has argued:

> The fascination of our civilization, from Job to Kafka, with an absolutely impenetrable Law which refuses to allow itself to be obeyed is perhaps ... the displaced version of a uniquely human distress: the distress of being inhabited, and even constituted, by the wholly inaccessible and wholly inescapable, alien and alienating, objects of our desires.[54]

Under the influence of Reformed theology, it seems that, even if the status of Father is given in order that man might be "so much more bound vnto him", this cleaving to God does not offer stability. As Calvin explains in another sermon: "when we thinke we are well disposed to serue God, there is always some thing, I cannot tell what, that holdeth vs backe".[55] Like the Father, God signifies as an absent (mimetic) presence.

With Lussorioso, the Duke's son, in prison, Vindice gets his opportunity to kill the Duke, to take his resistance to its logical conclusion. The revenger explains to his brother:

> the old duke,
> Thinking my outward shape and inward heart
> Are cut out of one piece (for he that prates
> His secrets, his heart stands o' th' outside)
> Hires me by price to greet him with a lady
> In some fit place, veil'd from the eyes o' th' court
>
> (III.v.8–13)

Here, Vindice acts as ironic anatomist both of himself and of his intended victim. In the case of the Duke, this verbal anatomy ("His heart stands o' the outside") stands in ironic counterpoint to the terrible physical violence that will be visited upon him shortly. Hippolito asks "where's that lady now?" (III.v.28) and Vindice replies "O, at that word / I'm lost again, you cannot find me yet" (III.v.28–9), reaffirming the connection between Gloriana and Vindice's subjectivity. He has placed her skull atop a mannequin and put poison on the lips of the 'bony lady' (III.V.121), hoping to lure the Duke into kissing it. He outlines his rationale:

> Now to my tragic business; look you, brother,
> I have not fashion'd this only for show
> And useless property; no, it shall bear a part
> E'en in its own revenge.
>
> (III.v.99–102)

In Vindice's theatre of death, theatricality is invoked in an ironic parody of the world-as-stage topos, a parody that implicates the gaze of the audience as they try to distinguish the lineaments of the dialectical struggle between representation and 'reality'.

In *The Revenger's Tragedy*, this gap is mediated by and through the iconoclastic image of the skull that 'writes' as effectively as any verbal sign.[56] Vindice and his brother succeed in tricking the Duke into kissing

Gloriana's skull, which they have poisoned. As the Duke lies dying, Vindice says to him, "Look, monster, what a lady hast thou made me / My once betrothed wife" (III.v.166–7). In attacking the false Father with the skull, the potent symbol of the sexual fulfilment he was never able to attain, the son highlights, in Leo Bersani's words, the terrible way in which, in the arena of violent Oedipal desire, "objects of desire become agents of punishment".[57] By making the Duke kiss the body of Vindice's lover, this act symbolises the reasons behind his personification as Vengeance. Indeed, when Vindice says to the Duke "What? is not thy tongue eaten out yet? Then / We'll invent a silence" (III.v.194–5), the inversion becomes sharper. The Duke has been silenced, verbally poisoned by the lady, and now holds an analogous position to her. The silent, iconoclastic body of Vindice's lover subverts the body of patriarchy by taking away its voice, its ability to confer names upon subjects. To put it differently, by writing voicelessness upon the Duke's body, the skull enables us to see that the political rhetoric of patriarchal signification is not as iconoclastically robust as it seems.

Both the sons avenge the father, something that Hamlet does not get to do until his dying moments. They also force the Duke to watch his Duchess cuckolding him with his bastard son. Vindice says to Hippolito:

> Brother,
> If he but wink, not brooking the foul object,
> Let our two other hands tear up his lids,
> And make his eyes, like comets, shine through blood;
> When the bad bleeds, then is the tragedy good.
> (III.v.201–5)

These are extraordinary lines. In the first place, they profoundly disrupt a certain political and symbolic expectation. James VI and I famously wrote in *Basilicon Doron* that kings "are as it were set (as it was said of old) vpon a publike stage, in the sight of all the people; where all the beholders eyes are attentiuely bent to looke and pry in the least circumstance of their secretest drift".[58] The gaze according to James is a one-way process and it objectifies the populace as they regard the authoritative Other. But in *The Revenger's Tragedy*, the Duke does not share the privileged signifying status of the monarch. Vindice's insistence that the Duke's gaze "shine through blood" inscribes the Duke as the primary spectator of the action he watches (his bastard son with his wife). The gazed-at becomes the gazer. He becomes objectified as the intended audience of the representation and the audience in the theatre become the objectifying Others in relation to his own personal drama. As Philip Armstrong puts it, "Theatre … perpetually contaminates the position of pure spectatorship, precipitating its audience into (the) action."[59] Vindice's actions not only politicise the play's mimetic practice, they show both audiences that representation is ultimately an unstable basis for Law. Vindice's political iconoclasm disrupts the mimetic basis of authority. His self-mocking comment, "When the bad bleeds, then is the tragedy good", serves to highlight that any claims in this play for art as a 'representation of reality' are disrupted by the mimesis of political iconoclasm. The 'reality' of this play, such as it is, always lies further on, elsewhere.

In Act Five, the play proceeds hastily to a violent denouement. Vindice is hired by the Duke's son to kill Piato, Piato being the name Vindice assumed when working for him. Vindice gets around the problem of having effectively to kill himself in a wonderful *coup de théâtre*. He dresses the dead Duke's body in Piato's clothes and stabs him. Vindice ruminates on the ridiculousness of the situation in which he finds himself. Regarding the Duke's body dressed in Piato's clothes he says:

> I must kill myself. Brother, that's I; that sits for me; do you mark it? And I must stand ready here to make away myself yonder – I must sit to be killed, and stand to kill myself.
>
> (V.i.4–7)

In these lines, Vindice identifies with his 'mirror image' and says that he will 'kill' it, as in fact he does. As Michael Neill puts it: "it is as if Vindice too were facing the image of his Death".[60] It is a remarkable moment. The linguistic split in Vindice's speech parallels the visual division on the stage between the subject of enunciation (the dead body) and the enunciating subject (the revenger). Indeed, this is perhaps the nearest the play gets to a complete iconoclastic divorce between the word and the image.[61] After stabbing the dead body, Vindice says in an important aside:

> This much by wit a deep revenger can,
> When murder's known, to be the clearest man.
> We're furthest off, and with as bold an eye
> Survey his body as the standers-by.
>
> (V.i.92–5)

Vindice's use of the collective pronoun "We're" attempts to locate him and the audience as omniscient spectators to this act. They are all supposedly "standers-by" regarding what has happened and is happening on stage. Yet surely the audience's role is more problematic than the revenger allows at this point?

Vindice continues to personify himself as Vengeance, a form of dramatic disguise. He also desires that the audience acknowledge him as 'one of them', standing by, observing, detached. But his dramatic disguise 'Piato' has been displaced on to the Duke. More than this, in 'killing' the Duke, he has also 'murdered' Piato, his alter ego. We might say that the audience is gazing at Vindice, who is gazing at his alter ego, his mirror of self, and refusing to acknowledge it as such. Vindice can only be "a deep revenger" if he has someone or something to avenge. Yet he has carried out every act of revenge that he set out to accomplish: the trauma he has suffered has, structurally at least, been accounted for.[62] When he regards the Duke/Piato, what he sees staring back at him can only ever be, like revenge tragedy, a representation constituted by and through violence. Vindice's alter ego, the Duke, positioned him as a traumatised subject for the nine years that he planned his revenge. Yet, the Duke's death is also the revenger's death. For where the Father generates progeny, all that Vindice generates is resistance and violence: an iconoclastic surplus of meaning that fuels the discourse of revenge drama but which eventually becomes non-meaning. The brutally farcical ending of the play, with the brothers gleefully confessing their crimes and being hastily taken for execution, would appear to confirm this. In this play, representation, fuelled by a culture that symbolises revenge as an unremitting mimetic chain, is predicated upon a division between word and image. But although the play, like all revenge tragedies, destroys the tyrant and ends with a slaughter that would seem to affirm such a division, nonetheless this division is problematical. Vindice ultimately signifies 'Vengeance' and, in broader terms, revenge tragedy. Yet the one lineage he cannot avenge is the violent lineage of the mimetic tradition to which he belongs.[63] As he signifies in (mimetic) violence, so he dies by (mimetic) violence. For these reasons, perhaps the play's iconoclastic impulse, and that of Reformed theology more generally, should be read not as a disavowal of the image as such, but as a manifestation of what Jean Joseph Goux calls "*sanctified emptiness*".[64] It is useful here to recall Calvin's words on the sins of the Father: it is "no brief and simple revenge, but one that will extend to the children, the grandchildren, and the great-grandchildren, who obviously become imitators of their father's impiety". In *The Revenger's Tragedy*, the tragedy of the revenger is revenge. For as Vindice declares at the end of the play in a final expression of iconoclastic immolation: "'Tis time to die when we are ourselves our foes" (V.iii.110).

Chapter Eight

I am grateful to David Dwan and Caroline Sumpter of Queen's University, Belfast, for their comments on this essay.

1. Jonathan Dollmore, 'Two Concepts of Mimesis: Renaissance Literary Theory and *The Revenger's Tragedy*', in *Themes in Drama: Drama and Mimesis*, ed. James Redmond (Cambridge: Cambridge University Press, 1980), pp. 31–2.
2. Ibid.
3. Ibid., p. 38.
4. Jonathan Dollimore, *Radical Tragedy: Religion, Ideology and Power in the Drama of Shakespeare and his Contemporaries*, 2nd edn (London and New York: Harvester Wheatsheaf, 1989), p. 149.
5. See, for example, Andrew Hadfield's recent article 'Shakespeare and Republicanism: History and Cultural Materialism', *Textual Practice* 17 (2003), pp. 461–83, which argues that the political methodology of cultural materialism does not adequately account for the complex forms of early modern political discourse.
6. For a good overview, see Rebecca W. Bushnell, *Tragedies of Tyrants: Political Thought and Theater in the English Renaissance* (Ithaca, NY: Cornell University Press, 1990).
7. Franco Moretti, *Signs Taken for Wonders: Essays in the Sociology of Literary Forms*, trans. Susan Fischer, David Forgacs and David Miller (London and New York: Verso, 1988), p. 42.
8. Ibid.
9. Ibid., p. 43.
10. Ibid., pp. 44–5.
11. Ibid., p. 55.
12. In this chapter I focus solely on Protestant resistance theory. But it is important not to disregard those theories of resistance that have a Catholic provenance, and with which there is some important overlap. For an overview of this topic, see J.H.M. Salmon, 'Catholic Resistance Theory, Ultramontanism, and the Royalist Response, 1580–1620', in *The Cambridge History of Political Thought 1450-1700*, ed. J.H. Burns (Cambridge: Cambridge University Press, 1991), pp. 219–53.
13. For an overview, see Robert M. Kingdon, 'Calvinism and Resistance Theory, 1550–1580', in Burns (ed.), *Cambridge History of Political Thought*, pp. 193–218.
14. Quentin Skinner, *The Foundations of Modern Political Thought, vol. 2: The Age of Reformation* (Cambridge: Cambridge University Press, 1993), pp. 193–238.
15. Ibid., p. 194.
16. Carlos M.N. Eire, *War against the Idols: The Reformation of Worship from Erasmus to Calvin* (Cambridge: Cambridge University Press, 1986); Christopher Elwood, *The Body Broken: The Calvinist Doctrine of the Eucharist and the Symbolization of Power in Sixteenth-Century France* (New York and Oxford: Oxford University Press, 1999);

Ralph C. Hancock, *Calvin and the Foundations of Modern Politics* (Ithaca, NY and London: Cornell University Press, 1989).

17. Eire, *War against the Idols*, p. 302.
18. Martin Luther, 'Temporal Authority: To What Extent It Should Be Obeyed', in *Martin Luther's Basic Theological Writings*, ed. Timothy F. Lull (Minneapolis: Fortress Press, 1989), p. 677.
19. Eire, *War against the Idols*, p. 302.
20. See Hancock, *Calvin and the Foundations*, pp. 105–9.
21. Hubert Languet was not a Calvinist in the strict doctrinal sense, but worked for influential Calvinists throughout his career.
22. See the controversial final sections of Book Four of John Calvin's *Institutes*; these sections have given rise to no end of dispute as to the extent of Calvin's political radicalism. John Calvin, *Institutes of the Christian Religion*, ed. J.T. McNeil, trans. Ford Lewis Battles (London: Library of Christian Classics, 1961), pp. 1518–21.
23. Robert Weimann, *Authority and Representation in Early Modern Discourse*, ed. David Hillman (Baltimore, MD and London: Johns Hopkins University Press, 1996), p. 2.
24. For example, in John Calvin's 1559 letter to Elizabeth I's Secretary of State, William Cecil. In this letter, Calvin sought to distance himself from theologians like his friend John Knox who were at the forefront of developing theories justifying political rebellion against both civic magistrates and, famously in Knox's case, female monarchs. See *Letters of John Calvin Selected from the Bonnet Edition* (Edinburgh: Banner of Truth Trust, 1980), pp. 211–13.
25. David Norbrook, *Poetry and Politics in the English Renaissance* (Oxford: Oxford University Press, 2002), p. 84.
26. Alan Sinfield, *Faultlines: Cultural Materialism and the Politics of Dissident Reading* (Oxford: Clarendon Press, 1992), pp. 95–108.
27. John Knox, *On Rebellion*, ed. Roger A. Mason (Cambridge: Cambridge University Press, 1994), p. 178.
28. Ibid., p. 179.
29. John Ponet, *A Short treatise of politicke power, and of the true Obedience which subiectes owe to kynges and other ciuile Gouernours, with an Exhortation to all true naturall Englishe men* (Menston: Scholar Press, 1970), sig. G3r.
30. James VI and I, 'Basilicon Doron', in *Political Writings*, ed. Roger A. Mason (Cambridge: Cambridge University Press, 1994), p. 12.
31. Eire, *War against the Idols*, p. 288.
32. Michael O' Connell, *The Idolatrous Eye: Iconoclasm and Theater in Early Modern England* (New York and Oxford: Oxford University Press, 2000), p. 58.
33. Calvin, *Institutes*, p. 108.
34. Here, we might bear in mind the crucial distinction that St Paul makes in Romans between the flesh and the spirit. Paul's Epistle to the Romans was perhaps the most important biblical text for the Reformed movement, especially in relation to the question of political resistance. In more general terms, Paul emphasises that man should aim to live according to the Spirit, noting in Romans 8 that "if ye liue after the flesh; yee shall die" (Rom. 8: 13). This is an example of what Calvin has to say on Romans 8 in his *Commentary on Romans* published in 1540: "The kingdom of the Spirit is the abolition of the flesh. Those in whom the Spirit does not reign do not belong to Christ; therefore those who serve the flesh are not Christians, for those who separate Christ from His Spirit make Him like a dead image or corpse." John Calvin, *Calvin's*

New Testament Commentaries: Romans and Thessalonians, trans. Ross Mackenzie (Michigan: William B. Eerdmans Publishing, 1995), p. 164. This is an extraordinary passage. Even in his assertion of the Spirit, Calvin raises the spectre of the flesh and, more suggestively, the death of the King. And in one important respect, this is precisely what resistance theory also insists upon.

35. Calvin, *Institutes*, p. 112.
36. O'Connell, *Idolatrous Eye*, p. 10.
37. Hubert Languet, *A Short Apologie for Christian Souldiours* [...] (London: Iohn Wolfe, 1588), STC 15207, sig. B7v.
38. In *Moses and Monotheism* Sigmund Freud notes that, in introducing the idea of the Son of God as expiator of his Father's death, Pauline Christianity is in effect predicated upon a displaced sacrifice, "an obviously tendentious distortion, difficult to reconcile with logical thinking" (p. 140). Freud goes on: "The Mosaic religion had been a Father religion: Christianity became a son religion. The old God, the Father, took second place: Christ, the Son, stood in His stead" (p. 141). Because of this, Freud concludes, "the new religion was a cultural regression as compared with the older Jewish religion". Sigmund Freud, *Moses and Monotheism*, trans. Katherine Jones (Letchworth: Garden City Press, 1939), p. 142.
39. See O'Connell, *Idolatrous Eye*, pp. 51–2, on the important 'first generation' of iconoclastic Reformers, such as Andreas Bodenstein von Karlstadt and Huldrych Zwingli.
40. Calvin, *Institutes*, p. 386.
41. Ibid., p. 384.
42. This Calvinistic dualism is a good example of what Mark Breitenberg has recently called "anxious masculinity". Breitenberg argues that in the early modern period this anxiety is "a necessary and inevitable condition that operates on at least two significant levels: it reveals the fissures and contradictions of patriarchal systems and, at the same time, it paradoxically enables and drives patriarchy's reproduction of itself". Mark Breitenberg, *Anxious Masculinities in Early Modern England* (Cambridge: Cambridge University Press, 1996), p. 2.
43. For a good recent overview of the genre, see Stevie Simkin (ed.), *Revenge Tragedy* (Basingstoke: Palgrave, 2001).
44. André Green, *The Tragic Effect: The Oedipus Complex in Tragedy*, trans. Alan Sheridan (Cambridge and London: Cambridge University Press, 1979), p. 235.
45. Elwood, *Body Broken*, p. 7.
46. All references are to *The Revenger's Tragedy*, ed. R.A. Foakes, The Revels Plays (Manchester: Manchester University Press, 1980). See, for example, at I.i.116–18, I.iv.56–64, II.i.118, II.ii.91, III.v.163 and V.i.19.
47. For a recent, sceptical reading of the 'Ur-Hamlet', see Emma Smith, 'Ghost Writing: Hamlet and the Ur-Hamlet', in *The Renaissance Text: Theory, Editing, Textuality*, ed. Andrew Murphy (Manchester and New York: Manchester University Press, 2000).
48. All references are to William Shakespeare, *Hamlet*, ed. Harold Jenkins (Surrey: Thomas Nelson, 1997).
49. As Francis Barker has observed in a complex discussion of the play, Hamlet's great difficulty is that he must negotiate with the fantasy of representation, a fantasy that inscribes Claudius as "a questionable copy of a copy of the king" (p. 35) but which also, through its focus on memory, displaces the Ghost of Hamlet's Father by opening "a gap within 'natural' self identity 'itself.'" (p. 37). For Barker, Hamlet's representational politics "provide the organising metaphors for the impossibility of memory as

such" (p. 41). Francis Barker, *The Culture of Violence: Essays on Tragedy and History* (Manchester: Manchester University Press, 1993), pp. 35, 37, 41.

50. 'The Third Part of the Sermon of Obedience', in *Certain Sermons or Homilies Appointed to be Read in Churches in the Time of Queen Elizabeth of Famous Memory* (London: Society for Promoting Christian Knowledge, 1843), p. 121.
51. As has often been noted, calling Vindice's dead lover Gloriana is a striking ploy bearing in mind that this was one of the noms de plume of the recently deceased Elizabeth I.
52. On this point, see Michael Neill, *Issues of Death: Mortality and Identity in English Renaissance Tragedy* (Oxford: Clarendon Press, 1998), pp. 1–48.
53. John Calvin, *Sermons of M. John Caluin, on the Epistles of S. Paule to Timothie and Titus. Translated out of French into English by L.T.* (London: G. Bishop, 1579), pp. 9–10.
54. Leo Bersani, *The Freudian Body: Psychoanalysis and Art* (New York: Columbia University Press, 1986). The complete quotation runs as follows: "The mythology of the Oedipus complex presents this monstrous and unavoidable impossibility as a *goal* of human development, as if the primary Oedipal identification constituted a way of transgressing aggressiveness rather than the psychic operation which makes it permanent. The post-Oedipal superego legalizes pre-Oedipal aggressiveness; it transforms object-loss into object-interdiction, and thereby makes us permanently guilty of those very moves of consciousness by which objects of desire become agents of punishment" (p. 97).
55. Calvin, *Sermons … to Timothie and Titus*, p. 992.
56. There is an obvious connection between the hidden Protestant God who nevertheless sees all, and the early modern conception of death that touches everyone regardless of status, sex or age. See Neill's *Issues of Death.*
57. Bersani, *Freudian Body*, p. 97.
58. James VI and I, 'Basilicon Doron', p. 4.
59. Philip Armstrong, 'Watching *Hamlet* Watching: Lacan, Shakespeare and the Mirror/Stage', in *Alternative Shakespeares*, vol. 2, ed. Terence Hawkes (London and New York: Routledge, 1996), p. 229.
60. Neill, *Issues of Death*, p. 84.
61. There are a number of other purely verbal moments like this such as Vindice's "What brother, am I far enough from myself?" (I.iii.1) and his odd comment on Piato at the end of the play: "Tis well he dies, he was a witch" (V.iii.119).
62. It is noticeable that in the final act it is a 'mask of revengers' that kills Lussurioso and three other unnamed nobles after performing a dance. It is not specified in the play's stage directions who kills whom. This apocalyptic ending signifies the way in which Vindice becomes reinscribed within the traditional practices of revenge tragedy. He is no longer a "deep revenger" but returns to being a constitutive part of the processes that he tries so hard to appropriate for himself throughout the play.
63. As the New Testament God states: "Vengeance is mine: I will repay" (Romans 12: 19).
64. Jean Joseph Goux, *Symbolic Economies: After Marx and Freud*, trans. Jennifer Curtiss Gage (Ithaca, NY: Cornell University Press, 1990), p. 147.

CHAPTER NINE

"There must be something heard":[1] *John Donne's aural universe*

Jonathan Holmes

THE AIM OF THIS ARTICLE is to consider John Donne as performance poet equipped with a sophisticated arsenal of various performative strategies, themselves predicated on a complex understanding of Neo-Platonic mimesis. I interpret the phrase 'performance poet' both in the sense of a writer of performative identities, following the terminology of speech-act theory established by J.L. Austin and refined in the 1990s by Judith Butler,[2] and also, more simply, in the sense of a poet writing for performance, in this case musical performance. I will explore the ways in which these varying resonances operate within his poetry, and will place them within a broader understanding of the relationship of poetry to the world of the English Renaissance. In other words, this article will articulate an investigation of Donne's work through the concept of mimesis.

Almost two hundred poems by Donne survive. Many (although not all) of these exist in manuscript, and most manuscripts seem to have been circulated after about 1615; as far as can be known, this seems to be some time after the date of composition of most.[3] In contrast, only five poems with Donne explicitly stated as the author were printed during his lifetime (one probably without his approval).[4] Three of these were occasional poems: elegies written for specific events. Other textual evidence of Donne's poetic output stems mainly from editions of his work published after his death.[5] It seems reasonable, then, to agree with generations of critics in stating that Donne did not write poetry for publication.

The consequent problems of dating and, in some cases, attributing his work have led to a sustained critical reliance on the fragmented traces of a colourful life. This life has in itself become a further commonplace of both writing and teaching about this author. This is a writer more than commonly dogged by reputation. The notorious tensions in this biography – the cleric who was also a poet of sexual appetite; the Catholic background of the man who became Dean of St Paul's; the courtier, soldier and man of the Church – were seemingly fascinating also to his contemporaries. Isaak Walton's *Life* (the first biography of a contemporary historical person to be published in English) appeared within eight years of his death, and ran to four editions in Walton's own lifetime. In additon to this, within two decades of his death editions of his poetry, prose, sermons (by far the largest section of the Donne corpus) and letters had all been published – broadly, all the material we now have. Donne's immediate public after-life was characterised by an interest in his biography and work unmatched until the twentieth century.

Rather than offer an alternative interpretation of the poems based on a new interpretation of the life (a well-worn methodology of limited value with this poet), my intention is to situate an understanding of Donne's project in writing poetry within the context of ideas of mimesis worked through in one of the most varied and extensive corpuses of any writer of the period.

The statistic cited earlier – that only five of Donne's poems made it into print in his lifetime – is not actually wholly accurate. Several more poems also were printed, as lyrics accompanying musical scores published in books of airs. All of these would later form part of the collection posthumously published as *Songs and Sonets* [*sic*]. Apart from a fragment of one poem published just before his death, nothing from this volume was otherwise printed in Donne's lifetime.[6]

Books of airs – collections of songs printed usually at the initiative of the composers – were an influential vogue of the early seventeeth century. None were printed before John Dowland's *First Booke of Songs or Ayres* in 1597, and the vogue ended just as suddenly in 1622 with John Attey's *First Booke of Ayres* (the next such collection was not printed until 1652). Between 1597 and 1622, however, thirty-seven such books were printed.[7] The acknowledged masters of the form were John Dowland, Alfonso Ferrabosco and Thomas Campion, although there were many other composers of note working in the genre. In terms of productivity the peak years for the vogue were 1609–12. In these three years alone eleven books of airs found their way into print, compared with only nine printed between 1612 and 1622. It is in the years 1606–12, when the vogue was at the height of its popularity, that all of Donne's printed lyrics appear – the first in Alfonso Ferrabosco's 1609 *Ayres*, others in editions by Dowland, William Corkine and Orlando Gibbons, all in 1612.[8]

This was an intermediate period of Donne's life, when he was without employment and had not yet taken Holy Orders. The years 1611–13 also saw the publication of four of the earlier mentioned authorised poems: 'Upon Mr Thomas Coryats Crudities', *The First* and *Second Anniversaries*, and the 'Elegy upon the untimely death of the incomparable Prince Henry'. Donne's entire printed poetic output therefore covers the years 1609–13. It is around this time also that he considered publishing an edition of his poetry; a letter to his close friend Henry Goodyer in 1614 asks him to find and return any manuscript copies of Donne's poems he can lay his hands on:

> I am brought to a necessity of printing my Poems … I apprehend some incongruities in the resolution; and I know what I shall suffer from many interpretations: but I am at an end … By this occasion I am made a rhapsoder of mine own rags, and that cost me more diligence to seek them than it did to make them.[9]

Whether, as seems to be implied, Donne is printing for money, or whether, as others have supposed, he is publishing as a form of confession before entering the Church[10] (he took orders in 1615), what seems certain is that this period represents the closest Donne ever came to being a professional author.[11]

To move toward a more comprehensive understanding of Donne's view of his work it is necessary to see his songs as an important part of that view. Songs form the largest section of Donne's small print output. Although there is no evidence to suggest that he oversaw their publication directly, it is unlikely that he was either unaware or disapproving of it. Moreover there are at least indirect connections between Donne and the composers responsible for setting his words: Ferrabosco was the regular collaborator with Ben Jonson on his masques and songs, and, while this of course does not guarantee a personal relationship with Donne based on his friendship with Jonson, it makes it implausible that he would not have known of Ferrabosco's work. John Dowland was, with Gibbons, the most celebrated composer of Donne's day, and also the most famous lutenist. One of his patrons was Lucy, Countess of Bedford, also patron of Donne and Jonson. Lucy Bedford was a celebrated lutenist in her own right, and was fond of bringing those who received her patronage together.[12] Again, while there is inadequate evidence to presuppose a personal relationship between Donne and Dowland, it is highly improbable that they would not have known of each other. Additionally, Donne seems to have been an enthusiast of this vogue and its principal exemplars; the only book of English poetry we know for certain to have been in his library was a collection of the work of the poet/composer Thomas Campion.[13]

Although the biographical links between Donne and such prominent musicians are typically incomplete, it is reasonable to assume that, given his strict control over the publication of his poetry and his closeness to the circle of major lutenists and composers, he would have both known and approved of the setting of his words to music. It is, however, a big leap from this to a confident assertion of Donne as performance poet in an active and deliberate sense. For this we need to examine the evidence of Donne's writing itself, and to reflect on the intellectual culture of early-seventeenth-century London.

In 'The Triple Foole', Donne talks of the experience of hearing his poetry set to music. Just when he has successfully "tamed" and "fettered" his "paines" in verse,

> Some man, his art and voice to show,
> Doth Set and sing my Paine
> And, by delighting many, frees againe
> Griefe, which verse did restraine.[14]

And so the double fool of sentiment and expression becomes triple by virtue of the musical addition. It seems clear by this poem that the setting of Donne's poems to music was not uncommon and, despite his protestations, perhaps also not an unpleasant experience – it delights "many". Several contemporary settings of Donne songs exist in addition to those printed; in general, they are personal copies of an original circulated in manuscript.[15] In total, there is evidence that between fourteen and eighteen of the *Songs and Sonets* were set to music in Donne's lifetime. Many of these are in songbooks privately compiled by women. As with the printed music it seems clear that the object was performance; instrumental parts are included, pasted sideways on to the page or in shorthand, making the whole difficult to read linearly but so designed that "in performance, the book was placed on a table so that singers and/or instrumentalists, seated around, were able to share the same copy".[16] These are documents for performance, not reflection. The arrangement is usually for alto, tenor or counter-tenor with lute, sometimes with viol (the standard arrangement for airs of the time).

Just as more manuscripts of Donne's work exist than of any other poetic contemporary, so also more examples of songs with Donne lyrics exist than of any other English poet of the period[17] with the exception of Fulke Greville. Additionally, no fewer than eight contemporary composers of the period are responsible for setting Donne's work, demonstrating his popularity amongst musicians and making a list of his musical collaborators sound like a who's who of Renaissance English music. John Dowland, William Corkine, Alfonso Ferrabosco, Orlando Gibbons, Henry Lawes, Giovanni Coperario, John Hilton and John Wilson all set Donne's work to music in his lifetime. Even although it was extremely common for the work of poets to be set to music, no other poet or playwright of the Renaissance received such widespread attention from musicians.[18] Interestingly, whereas the popularity of Donne's work in manuscript increased dramatically due to his fame as Dean, there seems to have been no attempt in print to capitalise on this popularity. Although Donne songs were undoubtedly successful, as the quantity of 'cover versions' testifies, the fact that they are not reprinted after 1615 suggests strongly that Donne is involved in their publication: manuscript copies, uncontrolled by the author, in contrast proliferated.

The poem 'Break of Day', first printed as part of the 1633 edition of Donne's works, and from the second edition of 1635 included as part of the *Songs and Sonets*, received the most attention from composers. The poem is remarkable in itself for being written from a female point of view. It expresses the longing to continue a romantic and sexual encounter typical of Donne, but phrases this wittily from a woman's perspective. In 1612 it was printed as the lyric to music by three of the most celebrated writers of music alive in England at the time: William Corkine, John Dowland and Orlando Gibbons.[19] Again, such Renaissance 'cover versions' were rare – the only other example I have found is a setting of another Donne poem, 'The Expiration', by two composers at different times. In addition to the three parallel-printed songs, there is also an anonymous manuscript version, and a later setting by Henry Lawes, making this among the most popular lyrics of the period. No other song comparable in popularity received the simultaneous attention of three major composers, and no other is written from a female point of view. To have three versions of the same song printed in the same year is both unheard of and extremely significant; moreover it is clear from the scores that Gibbons was working with knowledge of Dowland's version (and not the other way around).[20]

The audience for musical scores both in print and manuscript was principally other musicians; hence the textual layout. These included professional lutenists and singers attached to the court, to the theatres or to aristocratic households, but also the amateur audience of genteel or aristocratic individuals educated in music. Of these latter, by far the majority would have been women, for whom singing and training in the art of lute playing was central to a courtly education. This can be supported not only by the considerable number of dedications to young, aristocratic, female musicians among books of airs, but also by the fact that all surviving private songbooks compiled from circulated manuscripts of the period are made by young gentlewomen.[21] The majority of those performing these scores on an amateur basis were women. Male amateur singing and playing, by contrast, was considered unmanly, as Henry Peacham makes clear: "I might run into an infinite sea of the praise and use of so excellent an art but … I desire not that any noble or gentleman should prove a master in the same or neglect his more weighty employments."[22]

The non-professional audience for the three editions of 'Break of Day', printed in 1612, would be predominantly female. While Corkine's version is for voice and viol, therefore implying performance by two people, Dowland's is arranged for a lute and four voices, and Gibbons's madrigal is in five parts. All of these imply very different performance experiences of an intimate and sexually suggestive text. In all cases the score emphasises treble and counter-tenor voices, implying performance by women or boys, supported by a single bass (either instrumental or vocal). Given the context described above, it seems possible that these songs were written not only from a female perspective, but for female voices in private performance.[23]

In 'Break of Day', Donne is thinking of voice theatrically, as character; the poem takes on a female persona. But if the theory regarding the poem's readership is correct, he takes this move one step further than any playwright in conceiving the poem's performance by an actual female voice, rather than by a boy. Indeed, whether or not the text was explicitly prepared for performance, the fact remains that a poem written by a man for a female voice became the most frequently arranged song in the English Renaissance, and was both arranged for and in all likelihood sung by women.

The coincidence of dates, and the sudden burst of interest in the piece, suggests that it was not in circulation before 1611–12, and was perhaps written close to that date. 'The Triple Foole' implies that Donne was used to seeing his texts set, and indeed almost expected this to happen. The earliest printed song with Donne lyrics – Ferrabosco's setting of 'The Expiration' – appeared in 1609, making this in fact the earliest appearance in print of anything by Donne. By 1612, then, Donne had seen his work circulated in manuscript, and had seen and possibly heard musical settings of his lyrics. From manuscript evidence it seems that other settings of his poetry were also in circulation at this point. Furthermore, it is clear that he was as attached to the close-knit world of Renaissance music as he was to that of poetry, as his library records, family background and friendships testify.

In addition to all this, it is clear that he had already written for music in his youth, writing epithalamia, or marriage songs, while he was at Lincoln's Inn in the 1590s, and while he held the post of Master of the Inn Revels in 1593. After his ordination he would again write for music, this time in the form of hymns, several of which survive. Walton, in his *Life*, writes that "he [Donne] did also shorten and beguile many sad hours by composing other sacred Ditties",[24] and goes so far as to record the occasion of composition of at least one such hymn:

> I have rather mentioned this Hymn [to God the Father] for that he [Donne] caused it to be set to a most grave and solemn tune, and to be often sung to the organ by the choristers of St. Paul's church, in his own hearing; especially at the evening Service, and ... did say to a friend 'The words of this Hymn have restored to me the same thoughts of joy that possest my soul in my sickness when I composed it ... Harmony added to this Hymn has raised the Affections of my heart, and quickened my graces of zeal and gratitude; and I observe that I always return from paying this publick duty of Prayer and Praise to God with an unexpressible tranquillity of mind and willingness to leave the world.[25]

If, as seems likely, John Hilton's manuscript score to this hymn is a version of that referred to by Walton, then we have evidence of the hymn as performed, and an account, probably embellished, of its reception. Donne's poetic career was bookended by writing for music, so there seems little reason, given the evidence we have, for supposing that the interim period – approximately that of the *Songs and Sonets* – was different.

Whoever was responsible for categorising these fifty-five poems under this title for the 1635 edition it remains true, as many have observed, that there is not a single actual sonnet among them. It therefore seems logical that there should be an equivalent paucity of actual songs. Interestingly, there are, however, three important precedents for a collection with this title. The first is the famous 1557 anthology of poetry and song, *Songes and Sonettes*, printed by Richard Tottel and commonly known as *Tottel's Miscellany*.[26] Then, in both 1588 and 1611, the composer William Byrd – probably the most significant of the sixteenth century – published collections of *Psalmes, Songs and Sonets*. He too omitted to include actual sonnets in either volume, rather using the word in its archaic sense of 'little sound', or song. Byrd held a monopoly on printed music in the latter half of the sixteenth century, and was Orlando Gibbons's predecessor and master as Organist of the Chapel Royal (the most prominent official music post of the time). Byrd, like the young Donne, was Catholic in a Protestant world, and was working at the Chapel Royal on his second collection of *Psalmes, Songs and Sonets* at exactly the time his associate Gibbons was preparing his setting of Donne's poem that would later be anthologised under the same title. We therefore have well-known contemporary and historical precedents for a collection of verse using the word 'sonet' as synonymous with 'song', and in all cases using the word 'song' actually to refer to a text designed for musical accompaniment.

Following this, John Hollander among others has pointed out that, while Donne's *Songs and Sonets* look nothing like sonnets, they do look very much like songs.[27] Moreover, in the few letters in which Donne referred to his poetry, the only time he uses an actual descriptive noun to refer to it, that noun is "song".[28] Indeed, within the *Songs and Sonets* themselves he frequently refers to "songs", "hymns", "verses" and only once – in 'The Triple Foole', of all poems – to "poetry".[29] Hollander – who on the whole does not approve of the theory that the collection is of actual songs – also talks of what he calls "expressive titling"; i.e. titles that indicate the theme of the poem: not a common phenomenon in poetry prior to this collection, but a constant feature of song titling. Finally, he approaches the notorious issue of Donne's 'rough metre': the critical commonplace that Donne's prosody is uniquely irregular and uneven among Renaissance writers, a view popular ever since Ben Jonson remarked that, because of it, his friend "deserved hanging". Hollander notes that many of Donne's poems establish a metrical sequence only to work against it when it returns in the second stanza; iambs become trochees or even dactyls, simple monosyllabic lines find awkward polysyllables, and so on. Of this, Hollander remarks: "Composers like Dowland who set a great variety of texts would always work out a setting for the initial stanza and cheerfully ignore the lack of fit in subsequent ones ... with Donne this situation is frequent and strongly marked."[30] It could also be argued that Donne's idiosyncratic metre and rhyme schemes in fact come into their own when framed by a strong musical time signature and emphasised by the techniques of fugal imitation and counterpoint central to the Renaissance air and madrigal: Dowland and Gibbons both place what in Donne are irregularly stressed words in perfect counterpoint between three or more voices, thus drawing a listener's attention to them easily and simply. When this is combined with techniques of word-painting (as described below), the result is a convention of textual emphasis just as effective as any used by the poet. Finally, the extent to which Donne applied sub-genres of songwriting – from the aube (of which 'Break of Day' is a typical example) to the lament – to his own work suggests someone working consciously within the confines of song.

A connected concern with Donne's poetry is its famous 'metaphysical' difficulty. As Elise Bickford Jorgens writes:

> Many features of the metaphysical style made poetry very difficult to set to music. One of these features was the personal character of metaphysical verse. Where the Elizabethan song lyricist wrote at length of idealised or universal situations, the metaphysical poet was far more likely to write about personal experience ... since musical setting lends abstraction or distance from direct statement, it was difficult for a composer to adopt an appropriate stance toward poetry of this kind. At best, he was compelled to seek a way for singer and persona to be identified.[31]

The last sentence here recalls 'Break of Day': what better way of identifying singer and persona than to suit the speaking or singing voice to your audience? Further, the reliance of Jorgens's argument on types of narration and characterisation is at best naïve: the notion that narrative voice of whatever style hampers or helps the setting of words is disproved by reference to almost any genre of song in English at any time from the Renaissance to the twenty-first century. Ian Spink, writing from an analysis of the music, begins by agreeing with Jorgens that: "The ayres consistently explore the same group of thematic preoccupations (grief, desire, self, inexpressibility) with subtle changes in emphasis effected through tropological and formal literary orderings."[32] This, however, arguably makes the poetry of Donne more, rather than less, suitable for musical setting:

> As poetry, the ayres use strategies that deny the power of the word to express metaphysical states; as music, the ayres collaborate with these literary strategies through the semantics of musical media … In the ayres' lyrics, the correspondence between the musical and literary expression depends on the inexpressibility topos, which permits the literary approximation of metaphysical states such as divinity and harmony or grief and love.[33]

In short, poetry that is, in particular, semantically and syntactically complex, such as that of Donne, can be enriched, rather than obfuscated further, by virtue of musical setting. The music can have the effect of commenting on the words, either to explicate meaning or to create a parallel experience. Donne's own perspective on this, if 'The Triple Foole' is to be believed, was that music "frees againe" the meanings his verse "did restraine". This is consonant also with Walton's reportage of his views on the 'Hymn to God my father', a poem which delights in many-layered punning of an intimately autobiographical nature in each of its three verses.

The beginning of the air vogue saw also an unprecedented sequence of attempts by the composers to theorise their own artform. In 1597, the year Dowland printed his first *Booke of Ayres*, the madrigalist Thomas Morley published *A Plain and Easy Introduction to Practical Music*. In it he writes:

> If therefore you will compose in this kind [madrigal] you must possess yourself with an amorous humour (for in no composition shall you prove admirable except you put on and possess yourself wholly with that vein wherein you compose), so that you must in your music be wavering like the wind, sometime wanton, sometime drooping, sometime grave and staid, otherwhile effeminate.[34]

The music, in short, must be "like unto the passion which [it] express".[35] On the most obvious level this leads to adherence to the established convention of word-painting. This involves using an established repertoire of musical techniques to underline textual meaning, ranging from using high or low notes when the text uses tropes of high- or lowness, to long, slow harmonies for sadness and so on. There are plentiful examples of this in the settings under discussion: Gibbons, for example, on the line "Ah, dear heart, why do you rise?", writes the melody in such a way that it rises by step from F to A. More tellingly, in the next line, "The light that shines comes from your eyes", the melody rises abruptly by a minor sixth interval on the word "comes", before descending by step down to note A, from where it began. This interval is heard again on the word "come" in the first tenor's imitation in bar nine, the alto in bar ten and the soprano in bar eleven. Such a striking interval has the almost comic effect of sexual climax through the sudden rising sixth and subsequent slow descending step motion, an innuendo entirely consistent with Donne's punning style in the poem.[36]

It was not long, however, before such techniques were being openly criticised. Thomas Campion in 1601 responded: "Such childish observing of words is altogether ridiculous, and we ought to maintain as well in notes, as in action a manly carriage, gracing no word, but that which is eminent."[37] Campion was instead in favour of the music maintaining its own formal integrity, existing in parallel harmony to the words.

Whether the technique observed was closer to Morley or to Campion, composers were highly conscious of expressing meaning through their music. Rather than conforming to Jorgens's description of 'abstract' rather than 'direct' expression, the music used in these songs is as deliberately expressive as the poetry. Indeed, in a period that was just beginning to devise the musical terminology we are familiar with today, the language of music and that of poetry was still to a large extent the same. A poet-composer such as Campion, when talking of strophes, antistrophes, iambs, dactyls and so on, could as well have been describing music as poetry.[38]

Where Morley's advice becomes more complex, however, is in his instruction to "possess yourself wholly with that vein wherein you compose". You should feel that of which you write. This takes music into the area of direct expression and representation of meaning and emotion, akin to Stanislavskian acting in its understanding of mimesis. Much of the difficulty critics have with the connection of music with poetry is based on the assumption that a setting distances the poem's expressive directness. Donne's poetry is famous for such directness (hence the seeming inability to get away from biographical reading), and so the idea of his poetry having a musical dimension seems contradictory. If, however, the musician/composer approaches the poem much as an actor approaches a speech, then this paradigm of directness is in fact reversed and the poem becomes more, rather than less, immediate – a model borne out, as we have seen, both by Donne's responses to the setting of his Hymn, and in his lines in 'The Triple Foole'. To understand this further, it is necessary to first revisit the complex field of Renaissance music theory.

In 1603 Thomas Robinson published *The School of Musicke*. In it he writes: "Musicke is none other than a perfect harmonie, whose divinite is seene in the perfectnesse of his proportions."[39] Music is imitative not just in an artistic sense of representing feeling, but in a more fundamental sense of an intrinsic echo of the Divine. This notion is central to Donne's understanding of both music and the voice. In the 1624 sermon that gives this chapter its title, Donne is absolutely unconditional in his prioritisation of the aural and oral worlds:

> The last and powerfullest proof of all, which is the power of miracles; not this weak beginning, not this powerful end, not this Alpha of creatures, not this Omega of miracles, can imprint in us that knowledge, which is our saving knowledge, nor any other meanes than a voyce; for this knowing is believing. And how should they believe, except they heare? Says the Apostle. It must be vox, a voyce.[40]

In another sermon, preached the same year, Donne reiterated that "there was not only a word, the word, Christ himself … but a voyce". In 1618 Donne made clear also the priority of the voice and the ear over other senses, in particular that of sight: "The Organ that God hath given the natural man is the eye; he sees God in the creature. The Organ that God hath given the Christian is the ear; he hears God in his Word."[41] Most unequivocal of all is Donne's belief in the concept of the Christian Calling, expressed most clearly in a sermon given in 1626: "Christ … came to call. Now this calling implies a voice, as well as a word; it is by the word; but not by the word read at home … nor by the word submitted to a private interpretation, but by the word preached according to his Ordinance." To read is mortal, to speak divine. The model is not interaction between receptor and text, but between direct, present addresser and direct, present addressee. The Word is the word spoken, not the word read. For Donne, this is not just a Christian conceit. The voice is not only divinely, but metaphysically, endowed with truth, for it is the vehicle of the soul; "breath is speech, but breath is life", and so the voice becomes Christ in man:

> In nature then ... the soule of man hath this image of God, of God considered in his Unity; intirely, altogether, in this, that this soule is made of nothing, proceeds of nothing. All other creatures are made of that pre-existent matter, which God had made before, so were our bodies too; But our soules of nothing. Now, not to be made at all is to be God himselfe: Onely God himselfe was never made. But to be made of nothing; to have no other parent but God, no other element but the breath of God, no other instrument but the purpose of God, this is to be the Image of God. For this is nearest to God himself, who was never made at all, to be made of nothing.[42]

The belief that the voice is the vehicle of the soul goes back to Aristotle, with whom Donne was certainly familiar. In *De Anima*, Aristotle writes that "voice is the sound of the ensouled thing".[43] Donne is speaking both philosophically and spiritually; the essential part of man is sound, expressed at its best as a '*musica carmen*', a love song between God and man. As Stanwood and Asals comment:

> Art as expressed as praise and prayer is one measure of our life's sojourn – a sojourn that is soon finished, yet endless, containing all of eternity. The life of man finds its speech in art – in the word of God – at the meeting place where expressive sound has a harmony that is both human and divine.[44]

Importantly, this harmony is also at the time scientific. Renaissance music theory, like its poetic counterpart, was derived from disparate classical and medieval sources. Most influential by far among these were the Neo-Platonic treatises of Boethius and of St Augustine. Augustine comments upon the divine ordering of the universe in a passage that anticipates Donne in the sermon just quoted:

> What is the origin of this [harmony]? From where do all these things come if not from that supreme and eternal origin of rhythms and similarity and order? If you take these things away from the earth, it will be nothing. Therefore God has created the earth, and it was created from nothing.[45]

Pythagoras had initially propounded the notion that the universe emitted a form of cosmic sound as it moved. In his work on the structure of musical intervals and harmonies – still very much the basis of all Western composition – he posited that, as all bodies emit sound when in motion, so must the spheres of the heavens. From this came the much-vaunted concept of the music of the spheres, subsequently adopted by both Plato and, with some adjustments, by Aristotle. By the time of Boethius the idea had been refined somewhat, and he was able to posit three subdivisions: *musica mundana* (the harmony of the universe); *musica humana* (the internal ordering of human biology); and *musica instrumentalis* (musical composition). The relationship of *humana* to *mundana* was that of micro- to macrocosm, while *instrumentalis* was imitative of both. The position of the voice in all this was unique, as it existed on the boundaries of *humana* and *instrumentalis*, as well as being the indication of divine presence. As Henry Chadwick, in the commentary to his translation of Boethius's *De Institutione Musica*, writes:

> Cosmic music is a leading Platonic/Pythagorean theme, that is, the fitting together of the heavens, the harmonic ratios and intervals being the principle controlling the distances between the planets. For this doctrine the *Timaeus* offered classical authority. According to Porphyry's commentary on the *Timaeus*, the Platonists hold that the physical universe is constructed on the model of musical concords in harmonic ratios which are part of the fabric of the world-soul.[46]

The mathematical ratios governing the difference between the intervals of an octave, a fourth and a fifth, were those governing the orchestration of the cosmos. Musical composition, then, was a direct reproduction of the harmony of the universe. As Robinson went on to explain in 1603:

> Musicke is none other than a perfect harmonie, whose divinite is seene in the perfectnesse of his proportions, as, his unison shewth the unitie, from whence all other Springeth, next his unitie, his third (which is the perfectest concord in all music) representeth the perfect and most holie Trinitie; his fift (the most perfect consonance in all musicke, for that it is the very essence of all concords) representeth the perfection of that most perfect number.[47]

The importance of correct composition was that it used for its material the very elements of the divine universe, and brought man closer to God.

The European Renaissance saw the first substantial challenges to the

Aristotelian view of the universe. The work of Copernicus, Tycho Brahe, Johannes Kepler and finally Galileo paved the way for the now-familiar heliocentric cosmography. Donne was an enthusiastic follower of the new astronomy, and eagerly embraced the principles it espoused. This included placing the Sun at the centre of the cosmos, which for Donne had the effect of moving heaven further away from the "stupid centre": the Earth.[48] In *The First Anniversary*, printed in 1612, he wrote:

> And new Philosophy calls all in doubt,
> The Element of fire is quite put out
> The sun is lost, and th'earth, and no mans wit
> Can well direct him where to look for it.[49]

The lines refer not only to the realigned universe, but also to the increased scepticism as to the validity of separating matter into four elements; Kepler had disproved the existence of an element of fire during the previous decade.

Donne and Kepler were almost exact contemporaries (Kepler was born a year before Donne, and also died one year before the Dean). By the early 1600s they knew each other's work well; as well as evidence of Keplerian thought in Donne's poetry and correspondence and the copies of the scientist's books kept in his library, Donne referred to Kepler directly in his prose tract *Ignatius: His Conclave*, published in 1611. Kepler's own copy of this same work contains amused marginalia concerning these references, and the two men eventually met during Donne's travels abroad with the Earl of Doncaster in 1619.

Despite Kepler's revolutionary views of the structure of the universe, however, he intriguingly continued to defend the doctrine of the music of the spheres. In his masterpiece, *Harmonices Mundi*, he writes:

> Accordingly the movements of the heavens are nothing except a certain everlasting polyphony (intelligible, not audible), with dissonant tunings, like certain syncopations or cadences (wherewith men imitate these natural dissonances). Which tends towards fixed and prescribed clauses – the single clauses having six terms (like voices) – and which marks out and distinguished the immensity of time with these notes. Hence it is no longer a surprise that man, the ape of his creator, should finally have discovered the art of singing polyphonically, which was unknown to the ancients, namely in order that he might play the everlastingness of all created time in some short part of an hour by means of an artistic concord of voices

> and that he might to some extent taste the satisfaction of God the workman with his own works, in that very sweet source of delight elicited from this music which imitates God.[50]

That Donne was persuaded of this is evident in both poetry and prose. In his poem 'Upon Sidney's Translation of the Psalms', he writes:

> They tell us why, and teach us how to sing;
> Make all this All; three Quires, heaven, earth and spheares;
> The first, Heaven, hath a song but no man heares,
> The spheares have Musicke, but they have no tongue,
> Their harmony is rather danc'd than sung.[51]

He expresses similar views in one of his earliest sermons, preached in 1616:

> The correspondence and relation of all parts of Nature to one Author, the concinnity and dependence of every piece and joynt of this frame of the world, the admirable order, the immutable succession, the lively and certain generation and birth of effects from their Parents, the causes: in all these, though there is no sound, no voice, yet we may even see that it is an excellent song, an admirable piece of musicke and harmony, and that God does (as it were), play upon this Organ in his administration and providence by naturall means and instruments.[52]

This idea of a divine Organ is found again in the poem on Sidney's translation, in the post-Boethian notion of the "third Quire":

> But our third Quire, to which the first gives eare
> (for Angels learne by what the church does here)
> This Quire hath all. The Organist is hee
> Who hath tun'd both God and Man, the Organ we.[53]

Like Kepler, Donne combined the ancient belief in the music of the spheres with the modern, controversial notion of a heliocentric universe. Music was direct imitation of the divine voice of the universe, played upon the organ of an individual soul and expressed through the voice. The realignment of the universe made little impact on Donne's philosophy, based as it was on the fundamental equivalence of interior and exterior, on man as, famously, "a little world made cunningly" contained within a universe the size of a teardrop. Donne's universe was decentred without Copernicus, because God has no centre. For Donne, God expresses Himself through sound and through the harmonies of the universe. The individual acts as a receiver and transmitter for the Word, which is finally expressed through an oral and aural understanding of the Calling.

Donne's notion of the individual as "Organ", as divine instrument, also has its precedent, this time in the writings of St John Chrysostom. In his *Exposition of Psalm XLI*, Chrysostom writes:

> If you like, you may yourself become a cithara, mortifying the members of the flesh and making a full harmony of mind and body. For when the flesh no longer lusts against the Spirit, but has submitted to its orders and has been led at length into the best and most admirable path, then you will create a spiritual melody ... here there is no need for place or for season; in all places and at all seasons you may sing with the mind ... one may also sing without voice, the mind resounding inwardly. For we sing, not to men, but to God, who can hear our hearts and enter into the silences of our minds.[54]

Donne's own commentary upon the Psalms, the poem on the Sidney translation, echoes this understanding of humanity as a literal instrument of God, the divine musician. The Christian organ, as Donne says, is the ear. God's word is transmitted through the ear to the soul, which resides in the breath of the lungs and of speech. Following ancient and contemporary theological, musical and scientific thought, Donne's was emphatically an aural universe.

We are here dealing principally with aural mimesis: representation through sound. In utter contradistinction to the twentieth-century belief that music is not directly mimetic, in Donne's thought the most literal mimesis is neither linguistic nor pictorial but musical, for here is a direct and actual representation of the mind of God and the workings of the universe. This in turn leads to the predominance of voice, speech and music in his work, whether poetry, prose, correspondence or sermon.

In thinking thus, Donne is at one with received Neo-Platonist thought, handily expressed by Stephen Halliwell in a paraphrase of Plotinus:

> If levels of reality are partial models, images or imprints of that which lies above them in the ontological hierarchy, in the case of the human soul this process is an especially active engagement in mimetic assimilation. For the philosopher this is to be understood above all as the goal, by this date shared by pagan and Christian thinkers, of fashioning oneself 'in the likeness of God'.[55]

Throughout the *Songs and Sonets* Donne draws a remarkably constant symmetry between all aspects of creation, each a version and mirror of the other. In this way, eyelids eclipse the sun, tears drown the world, a sigh causes a storm, and so on. Donne is condensing the levels of Neo-Platonist mimesis and simultaneously effacing the established relationship between micro- and macrocosm. Instead of beginning at the centre – the original platonic Form, or the mind of God – and moving out through layers of imitation, Donne's decentred universe posits an absolutely simultaneous and harmonious equivalence between all created things. As he says in a sermon delivered in 1628:

> There is not so poor a creature but may be thy glasse to see God in. The greatest flat glass that can be made cannot represent anything greater than it is: If every gnat that flies were an Archangel, all that could but tell me that there is a God; and the poorest worm that creeps, tells me that ... All things that are, are equally removed from being nothing; and whatsoever hath any being, is by that very being, a glass in which we see God, who is the root and the fountain of all being.[56]

Furthermore, this view of the world can be seen as directly imitative not only of the divine mind, but also of that mind's own processes of creation. As Barbara Lewalski has written: "The theory, which informs many of Donne's poems, is grounded upon the proposition that the divine poet not only may but must imitate God's own method of creation.[57] Halliwell goes on to talk of the mimetic nature of the act of creation itself:

> The Aristotelian tenet tells us that all human techne (all productive craft, including such activities as medicine) follows principles comparable with or analogous to those of nature, above all in two respects, the orderly imposition of a form on matter and the operation of final causes.[58]

The section of Aristotle referred to by Halliwell is principally part 2 of *The Physics*. Donne's knowledge of Aristotle was extensive; he is a regular character in the sermons, usually referred to simply as 'The Philosopher'. In a sermon given in 1626 he makes explicit reference to this same principle of *The Physics*:

> A carpenter builds not a house, but that he first sets up a frame in his own mind, what kind of house he will build ... whatsoever is made, in time, was alive in God, before it was made, that is, in that eternal idea and pattern which was in him ... of all things in Heaven and earth, but of himself, God had an idea, a pattern in himself before he made it.[59]

The human process of creation is mimetic of the divine process, an idea evident also in Sidney's *Defence of Poetry*, in which the poet becomes "another nature"[60] through the act of writing. Not only is the act of creation mimetic, then, but in creating music – specifically vocal music – the created thing becomes a direct reproduction, a microcosm, of the universe itself. The voice as principal medium for this music is essential, as it is the vehicle of the soul and therefore bears the "seal of God".[61] Donne's post-Copernican view of the equality of created things means that the Neo-Platonic distance between forms is concatenated; there is only one step from the divine mind to the thing that mind produced.

The purest and closest activities the good Christian can do, then, are to preach the word and to mimic the universe in music: in other words, to write sermons and songs (especially, of course, hymns). As he says: "the scriptures are God's voice, the Church is his echo; a redoubling, a repeating of some particular syllables, and accents of the same voice".[62]

Moreover, this view of the operations of mimesis is also, in Donne's thought, traceable in reverse; the existence of the image presupposes the existence of the model:

> How do we see in a glass? The old writers in optiques said, that when we see a thing in a glass, we see not the thing itself, but a representation only; All the later men say, we do see the thing itself, but not by direct, but by reflected beames. It is a useless labour for the present, to reconcile them. This may well consist with both, that as that which we see in a glass assures us that such a thing there is (for we cannot see a dream in a glass, nor a fancy, nor a chimera), so this sight of God, which our Apostle says we have in a glass, is enough to assure us that a God there is.[63]

It is here that we approach the usefulness of art; by its very existence and dependence on theories of mimesis it presupposes a creator of whom to be mimetic, as "the whole frame of the world is the Theatre, and every creature the stage, the medium, the glasse in which we may see God".[64]

More particularly than this, Donne also theorises the kinds of speech, of manifestations of the Word, that can be encountered. In 1621 he made this explicit: "In man there are three kinds of speech; *sermo innatus*, that inward speech … he thinks something. And then *sermo illatus*, a speech of inference … And lastly, *sermo prolatus*, that speech by which he manifests himself to other men."[65] In the same sermon he extrapolates this division further by linking these three modes of speech to the trinity – the first (*innatus*) is the "eternal, natural word"; the second (*illatus*) is the "decree of sending Christ"; the third (*prolatus*) is Christ's "speech of manifestation". There is an obvious link here with the Boethian trinity of *musica mundana*, *humana* and *instrumentalis*. In Donne, *prolatus* is a manifestation of the urge of *illatus* to reveal *innatus*, just as *instrumentalis* is the expression of *mundana* through *humana*.

This trinity of speech is included in a further mortal trio, which he calls the "three witnesses of Spirit, and Water, and Blood". These correspond to the remaining three elements of air, water and earth (fire having been discredited by Kepler), and are made manifest in the form of "preaching, and baptism, and communion". In turn, these are combined with the "three faculties of the soul; the reason, the memory, the will". It becomes clear throughout the 1624 sermon from which these extracts are taken that these are synonymous with the original trinity of *innatus* (memory), *illatus* (reason) and *prolatus* (will).[66] The reference points of this sermon also make it clear that Donne is taking as his text St Augustine's *Confessions*, particularly his reflections on 'Time' and 'Memory', in which he posits that the vocabulary of past, present and future is useless. Instead, we should be aware of three subjective linguistic tenses: memory, awareness and expectation. Augustine writes:

> If the present were always present, it would not pass into the past: it would not be time, but eternity. If then, in order to be time at all, the present is so made that it passes into the past, how can we say that this present also 'is'? The cause of its being is that it will cease to be. We cannot say that time exists except in the sense that it tends towards non-existence.[67]

Donne also came to believe in the illusory status of linear time, as he did of distance; such matters were simple aspects of perception. The aim of any truly exemplary life was simply to be close to God, "for this is nearest to God himself … to be made of nothing", or, as it is elsewhere expressed, "Some lovely, glorious nothing".[68] This requires a refusal of both absolute temporality and absolute distance:

> This, no tomorrow hath, nor yesterday,
> Running it never runs from us away,
> But truly keepes his first, last, everlasting day.[69]

This again echoes the Augustinian concept of an endlessly iterable – but not eternal – present.

In total, these Donneian trinities awake a third – faith, hope and charity – which in turn make 'a trinity of trinities', what Donne calls the "nine witnesses". This was the divine order of the universe itself: eight spheres and the earth; in music theory, the eight notes of the octave, which, as Robinson explicates, are themselves divided into the trinity (the 'perfect' third) and the fifth (representing the five wounds of Christ). Donne's theory of witnessing also presupposes an auditor, 'the supernatural way'[70] of hearing: a present witness to receive the Word – "there must be something heard". The Word is unavoidably performative, in the sense of a manipulation of personae and identity, but more profoundly and more essentially in the necessity of a living, present voice and witness. It is this actual presence which differentiates the performed poem from that designed to be silently read: the latter operates on a communication model placing the reader as overhearer, with the poem addressing a projected addressee, while performed poetry implies actual presence, a physical addressee, a witness, as Donne says. It is the latter model that much of Donne's song both implies and requires.

Theologically, scientifically, philosophically and formally, Donne's varied output rests on an extraordinarily consistent concept of words in performance. At no time in his life is there any indication that this complex and sophisticated belief was questioned or abandoned – in fact, the evidence for it only grows as his career develops. This evidence is, as we have seen, to be found in letters, sermons, prose works and the image systems and structure of the poems themselves. Although Donne was a sparing publisher of any of his work in any genre, the fact that the number of his songs – with music – printed in his lifetime outnumbers any other form of publication, and is equalled only by the later publications of his sermons, is telling. Although, as with almost every aspect of this writer's life, any final conclusion about his practice must contain speculation, it seems clear that by far the most likely theory as to the design of many of the poems we know as *Songs and Sonets* must include music. The next step in the development of this theory would of course be to locate a method that would identify with some certainty which of the collection fall into this category.[71]

This hypothesis in turn both points to and is supported by an unusual and complete theory of mimesis, one predicated on a thorough knowledge of those texts to first propound the concept and later defend it, and one articulated within a remarkably thorough system of doctrinal thought. This system itself constitutes one of the most extensive workings-through of the relationship between artefact and world in the English Renaissance. It is also a system hitherto ignored by commentators, so convinced have we become of an entirely unsubstantiated theory of the purpose of Donne's poetry, one based on long-since outmoded New Critical ideological assumptions of the primacy of silent reading in the study. This system can now be brought to the fore by a belated appreciation of John Donne as performance poet.

Chapter Nine

1. John Donne, Sermon given at St Paul's Cathedral, 1624, in *The Sermons of John Donne*, 10 vols, ed. George Potter and Evelyn M. Simpson (Berkeley, CA: University of California Press, 1962), 6: 133–4. My thanks to Tom Davis and to Peter Hinds for carefully reading and insightfully commenting on drafts of this article, and to Litha Efthymiou for her patient assistance with musical analysis of the songs.
2. See, amongst others, Judith Butler, *Gender Trouble* (London and New York: Routledge, 1990).
3. See Peter Beal, *Index of English Literary Manuscripts*, vol. 1, part 1 (London: Mansell, 1980), esp. pp. 245–7. Beal identifies sixty-nine manuscripts containing more than twenty poems by Donne, the largest containing 169 (probably in preparation for the 1633 *Poems*), and a staggering 4,100 other extant manuscripts of Donne poems circulating prior to 1640. The probable later date of most of these manuscripts (after 1615) suggests that Donne's celebrity as a high-profile cleric led to a boom in interest in his earlier poetry.
4. These publications are: 'Upon Mr Thomas Coryats Crudities', printed as part of *The Odcombian Banquet* (London, 1611); *An Anatomie of the World (The First Anniversary)*, printed in 1611; *On the Progresse of the Soule (The Second Anniversary)*, printed in 1612; and 'Elegie upon the untimely death of the incomparable Prince Henry', printed in 1613 as part of Sylvester's *Lachrymae Lachrymarum.* The possible unauthorised publication was of 'The Broken Heart', printed a few months before Donne's death in *A Helpe to Memory and Discourse.*
5. Principally Marriot's 1633 and 1635 collected editions of Donne's poems, both entitled simply *Poems, by J.D.* The second of these groups the poems in their now familiar order. It is not known by whom these editions were compiled.
6. See n. 4 (above).
7. Details of these can be found in Edward Doughtie (ed.), *Lyrics from English Airs* (Cambridge, MA: Harvard University Press, 1970).
8. Alfonso Ferrabosco, *First Booke of Ayres* (1609); John Dowland, *A Pilgrimes Solace* (1612); William Corkine, *The Second Booke of Ayres* (1612); Orlando Gibbons, *First Set of Madrigals and Motets* (1612).
9. Letter to Henry Goodyer, 14 Dec. 1614, in *John Donne: Selected Letters*, ed. P.M. Oliver (London: Carcanet Press, 2002). Helen Gardner points also to a lesson for lyra violl in Corkine (no.22), which she identifies as 'The Bait'. The lesson is entitled 'Come live with me and be my love', and so could easily be an instrumental version of the

Marlowe poem 'The Passionate Shepherd to his Love', to which 'The Bait' is a response. It is likely, as Gardner observes, that the same melody served both versions, and so the lesson would be designed to suit both.

10. See R.C. Bald, *John Donne: A Life* (Oxford: Clarendon, 1970), particularly Chap. 9.
11. The major prose works printed during his lifetime, with the exception of the *Devotions* and collections of sermons (obviously written later), were also published at this juncture.
12. There are letters from Donne to Jonson and others regarding these meetings. See, for example, Bald, *John Donne*, p. 196.
13. See Appendix IV, 'Books from Donne's Library', in Geoffrey Keynes, *A Bibliography of Dr John Donne, Dean of St. Paul's* (Oxford: Oxford University Press, 1973), esp. p. 266.
14. Donne, 'The Triple Foole', in *The Complete Poetry and Selected Prose of John Donne*, ed. Charles M. Coffin (New York: Modern Library, 1952), p. 15, ll. 13–16.
15. Manuscripts of Donne poems with accompanying music, or otherwise identified as songs, include Coprario's 'The Message' (Tenbury Ms. 1019), 'Sweetest Love I do not go' (Tenbury Ms 1018, Add Ms. 10377), 'Go, catch a falling star' (Egerton Ms. 2013), 'Community' and 'Confined Love' (both in Add. Ms. 10377), Thomas Ford's setting of the first two stanzas of 'The Lamentations of Jeremy' (Christ Church Ms. 736.8), and Lawes's version of 'The Apparition' (Edin Ms. Dc. 1 69).
16. R. Bennett, *A History of Music* (Cambridge: Cambridge University Press, 1982), p.19. See also Donald J. Grout and Claude V. Palisca (eds), *A History of Western Music* (New York: Norton, 1960), p. 217.
17. Not including playwrights – Ben Jonson, for example – whose work in masque and courtly entertainments led to the composition (usually with Ferrabosco) of a large number of occasional songs. See Beal, *Index of English Literary Manuscripts*, for details of Donne manuscripts.
18. Musical settings exist for work by almost every major English literary figure of the Renaissance, many of whom – Wyatt, Surrey, Sidney, Shakespeare, Jonson, Marlowe, Ralegh, etc. – clearly also wrote intending their poems for musical accompaniment. Indeed, so popular was the practice of setting contemporary poems that it is difficult to believe that by the seventeenth century writers were not at the very least considering the possibility that their circulated work would eventually be set.
19. Dowland and Gibbons use almost identical texts of a verse of 'Break of Day' absent from the 1633 *Poems, by J.D.* The verse is, however, present in no fewer than 45 separate manuscripts of the full poem compiled in or shortly after Donne's lifetime. See Helen Gardner (ed.), *Elegies and Songs and Sonnets* (Oxford: Clarendon, 1965), pp. 34–6 and p. 127. In their respective editions Gardner and Grierson both claim this first verse to imply a male speaker, but there is nothing in the text to suggest this. Major editions of Donne include the verse conditionally, while all commentators on and editors of Dowland conclude that the verse is Donne's.
20. See John Harley, *Orlando Gibbons and the Gibbons Family of Musicians* (Aldershot: Ashgate, 1999), pp. 85–90. Gibbons quotes from and reworks part of Dowland's score in a collection published in November 1612; Dowland's book was printed six months earlier. Gibbons's dedication states that none of his music was written prior to the summer of 1612.
21. There is also a large quantity of paintings of the time depicting young women playing lutes, few of which appear allegorical. See, for example, Gentileschi's *Woman Playing a Lute* and Titian's *Pastoral Consort.*

22. Henry Peacham, quoted by Edward Jones, *The Performance of English Song, 1610–1670* (Pinkerton: Garland, 1989), p. 30. Peacham was friend to several noted musicians of the time, including Dowland.
23. The tendency for lute playing by women to be seen as both a ladylike accomplishment and subtly erotic is parodied by Shakespeare in *The Taming of the Shrew*, III.i. Renaissance educationalists were strongly in favour of female singing at all stages of adolescence, whereas boys, though trained to sing in early childhood, soon moved away from this to more 'learned' pursuits. See Helen Jewell, *Education in Early Modern England* (Basingstoke: Macmillan, 1998). Donne's own education prior to him entering university at eleven is unclear: he was educated at home, and probably, as Bald surmised, was influenced substantively by his uncle John Heywood, playwright, musician and master of St Paul's choir. It is likely therefore that Donne had some early musical training.
24. Isaak Walton, 'Life of Donne', in *Lives* (4th edn, 1675), ed. George Saintsbury (Oxford: Oxford University Press, 1926), p. 66.
25. Walton, 'Life of Donne', p. 62.
26. *Songes and Sonettes, written by the ryght honorable Lorde Henry Haward late Earle of Surrey, and others* (Richard Tottel, 1557).
27. See John Hollander, *Vision and Resonance: Two Senses of Poetic Form* (Oxford: Oxford University Press, 1975), p. 47.
28. Letter to Goodyer, 1608, in Oliver (ed.), *Letters*, p. 30.
29. In the entire corpus of Donne's poetry he uses variants of the word 'poem', 'poetry', 'poesy', etc. only eight times, compared with thirty instances of the word 'song'.
30. Hollander, *Vision*, p. 47.
31. Elise Bickford Jorgens, *The Well Tun'd Word: Musical Interpretations of English Poetry, 1597–1651* (Minneapolis: University of Minnesota Press, 1982), p. 14.
32. Ian Spink, *English Song, Dowland to Purcell* (London: B.T. Bashford, 1974), p. 55.
33. Ibid.
34. Thomas Morley, *A Plain and Easy Introduction to Practical Music* (London, 1597), p. 291.
35. Ibid., p. 294.
36. I am grateful to Litha Efthymiou for this observation.
37. Thomas Campion, *Observations in the art of English Poesie* (London, 1601), p. 24.
38. Moreover, the development of print culture itself is closely tied to music: as Tessa Watt remarks: "Any study of the impact of printing in England must take account of the fact that one of the first widespread and widely affordable forms of the printed word was the song." See her *Cheap Print and Popular Piety* (Cambridge: Cambridge University Press, 1991), p. 11.
39. Thomas Robinson, *The Schoole of Musicke* (London, 1603), p. 7.
40. Donne, *Sermons*, 3: 133–4.
41. Ibid., 2.114.
42. Sermon delivered in 1629, ibid., 9: 82–9.
43. Aristotle, *De Anima*, II.9, ed. and trans. Hugh Lawson Tancred (Harmondsworth: Penguin, 1986).
44. P.G. Stanwood and Heather Ross Asals (eds), *John Donne and the Theology of Language* (Missouri: University of Missouri Press, 1986), pp. 44–5.
45. Augustine, *De Musica*, trans. and with an Introduction by Martin Jacobson (Stockholm: Almquist & Wiskell International, 2002), XVII: 57.

46. Boethius, *The Consolations of Music, Logic, Theology and Philosophy*, ed. and trans. Henry Chadwick (Oxford: Clarendon, 1981), p. 81.
47. Robinson, *Schoole*, p. 7.
48. Letter to Goodyer, April 1615, in Coffin, *Complete Poetry*, p. 385.
49. Donne, 'The First Anniversary', in Coffin, *Complete Poetry*, p. 191, ll. 205–9.
50. Johannes Kepler, *Harmonices Mundi*, transl. Charles Glenn Wallis (Chicago: University of Chicago Press, 1952), v.vii, p. 1048.
51. Donne, 'Upon the Translation Of The Psalmes By Sir Philip Sydney, And The Countess Of Pembroke His Sister', in Coffin, *Complete Poetry*, p. 255, ll. 22–6.
52. Donne, *Sermons*, 1: 289–90.
53. Donne, 'Upon the Translation Of The Psalmes', ll. 27–30.
54. St John Chrysostom, 'Exposition of Psalm XLI', in *Source Readings in Music History*, ed. and trans. Oliver Strunk (London: Faber, 1950), pp. 69–70.
55. Stephen Halliwell, *The Aesthetics of Mimesis: Ancient Texts and Modern Problems* (Princeton, NJ: Princeton University Press, 2002), p. 315.
56. Donne, *Sermons*, 8: 224.
57. Barbara Kiefer Lewalski, *Protestant Poetics and the Seventeenth Century Religious Lyric* (Princeton, NJ: Princeton University Press, 1979), p. 282.
58. Halliwell, *Aesthetics of Mimesis*, p. 352.
59. Donne, *Sermons*, 7: 60–1.
60. Philip Sidney, *An Apology for Poetry*, ed. Geoffrey Shepherd (Manchester: Manchester University Press, 1973), p. 101.
61. Donne, *Sermons*, 6: 158.
62. Ibid., 6: 223.
63. Ibid., 8: 222.
64. Ibid., 8: 224.
65. Ibid., 3: 292.
66. Ibid., 5: 148–9.
67. St Augustine, *Confessions*, trans. and ed. Henry Chadwick (Oxford: Oxford University Press, 1991) p. 231.
68. 'Air and Angels', in Coffin, *Complete Poetry*, p. 19, l. 6.
69. 'The Anniversary', in Coffin, *Complete Poetry*, p. 20, ll. 8–10.
70. Donne, *Sermons*, 6: 133–4.
71. The search for such a method constitutes part of my ongoing research into this topic.

Afterword

John Drakakis

THE OPENING SHOTS of Grigori Kozintzev's *King Lear* depict a mass of people converging purposefully upon a location where something is about to happen that will alter the trajectory of their lives. The scene is what Erich Auerbach might describe, as he did in his seminal book *Mimesis: The Representation of Reality in Western Literature* (1946), as "the beginning of a deep sub-surface movement, the unfolding of historical forces" for which:

> it is essential that great numbers of random persons should make their appearance; for it is not possible to bring to life such historical forces in their surging action except by reference to numerous random persons – the term being here employed to designate people from all classes, occupations, walks of life, people, that is, who owe their place in the account exclusively to the fact that the historical movement engulfs them as it were accidentally, so that they are obliged to react to it in one way or another.[1]

What Auerbach emphasises time and time again is that the 'imitation' of reality is something more than a simple replication in literary texts of the world of phenomena. Indeed, it is his claim that the literature of antiquity "was unable to represent everyday life seriously" precisely because it could only do so "in the low style, comically or at best idyllically, statically and ahistorically", the implication being that "these things mark the limits not only of the realism of antiquity but of its historical consciousness as well". For Auerbach, 'reality' consists of the dynamic interaction between phenomena and the historical forces – intellectual, economic, political, military, diplomatic – that both shape and are the products of "the variations in the depths of everyday life".[2] Auerbach had in mind much more than the superficial manifestations of "everyday life" in the literature of antiquity, and his emphasis upon questions of 'historicity' led him to focus less on matters concerned independently with emotions and psychology, and more upon the *differences* between the ancient world and the one with which he was familiar.

A.D. Nuttall's *A New Mimesis: Shakespeare and the Representation of Reality* (1983) revisits, in part, some of the issues raised by Auerbach and introduces the term 'culture' into the combination of historical forces that the latter sketches out. Nuttall maintains a clear historical focus but he gives special emphasis to the objective existence of a reality that it is one of the functions of art to represent. In response to Auerbach's claim that Homer's 'characters' live in a continuous present and have no historical awareness, Nuttall observes that the gods and goddesses in *The Iliad* "freely decide, think and emote", and that "Homer has these concepts and it is difficult to see where he could have got them from if it was not from human beings".[3] Nuttall's objective is a revitalisation of the concept of mimesis in the face of what he takes to be the linguistic formalism, and the attendant relativism, of post-Saussurean literary theory. He wants to move beyond the notion that a writer like Shakespeare is imprisoned in late-sixteenth- and early-seventeenth-century ideology – that "*their* perceptions are unconsciously conditioned but *we* can identify the conditions" – to suggest that he is "endlessly rebellious against this arrogant relegation".[4] He goes on:

> Even when one works with seemingly modern tools of thought, such as the concepts of cultural history, one finds that Shakespeare is there before one. The inference is obvious: the text refuses to relinquish what I have called 'the hope of truth'. Its level of *cognitive* activity is so high that later attempts to compass even the latent character of thought-categories find that its most radical moves have been anticipated by the poet.[5]

In his return to what is, in effect, a received way of talking about Shakespeare's texts, Nuttall plays down the role of the reader or auditor in shaping the text, producing meanings and providing a culturally overdetermined narrative of its concerns. Indeed, despite his invocation of Homer's performance of the epigrammatic claim that man "saw himself in the heavens before he saw himself directly"[6] Nuttall seems unwilling to cede the *mediating* power of the reader/auditor, or indeed of the complex network of genres implicated in language, preferring instead to resurrect an ameliorated version of the Romantic Shakespeare. These received ways of talking about Shakespeare are, in the words of Terry Eagleton, "too precipitous in what they take as read".[7]

The objections to the reactionary nature of Nuttall's 'new' mimesis notwithstanding, the 'truth' claims that he makes for literary texts need to be taken seriously. Now that we have moved beyond the heady rhetoric of an irreducible textuality that was characteristic of the initial stages of post-structuralism, we are in a position to probe more thoroughly the nature of the interplay between what many literary critics have come to label 'world' and 'word'. Valentine Cunningham's guarded respect for Cultural Materialism, for example, is founded upon its "steady refusal either to go back to a naïve historiography, one unalert to problems of textuality, of writing, of the story-telling aspects of history, or to rest content with history as mere reflection".[8] Indeed, while we might agree that we receive our impressions of the world textually in that it is through the process of meaning-production that we make sense of its complexities, we need to remind ourselves that "the real", as Cunningham defines it, "is never not just a construction in a text – not ever, and especially not in the worlds of power and victimisation, of colonising and persecution, where ideology impacts on the body, and bodies are tortured, minds deformed, men and women cut up, maimed, killed, and otherwise subjugated".[9] Whereas Nuttall seeks a context in the realms of 'culture' and anthropology, occasionally lapsing into an uncharacteristically simple-minded referential model of language, Cunningham returns us to an irreducibly *political* version of what he calls "the historical *realium*", a version that is not too far away from Auerbach's nuanced account of mimesis, but which in the final analysis fudges the complex connection between power, domination, persecution, subjugation, and its discursive representations.

Very little has been done to replace or update Auerbach's text, a fact that is surprising considering the sharp, but by no means uniform, linguistic turn that literary theory took in the 1970s. However, the situation is now beginning to change as scholars now begin to focus more coolly and deliberately upon what can be salvaged from the term 'mimesis' in the wake of the persistent emphasis upon the textuality, and the intertextuality, of 'history' and of narrative generally. If we comprehend the material world through language, to what extent does the medium itself shape or determine our perception of reality? Or, more perplexing, notwithstanding Cunningham's timely reminders of the material features of political power and its attendant horrors, how do we disentangle the material world from the discursive, generic, matrices of those imaginative texts whose primary function is the act of re-presentation itself? When Hamlet extols the virtue of the Players because they 'hold the mirror up to nature', we have to ask what is meant by a 'mirror' and what is meant by 'nature' in this context, and why Hamlet should be so interested in the *process* of representation? Hamlet's answer is that the mirror shows "virtue her feature, scorn her own image, and the very age and body of the time his form and pressure" (III.ii.22-4); in other words, it is both self-reflexive and analytical rather than simply referential. Moreover, Hamlet's 'form and pressure' of the time seems much less a description of timeless universal truth than a precise formulation of the historically specific function of re-presentation, what Auerbach categorises as 'the historical' that "comprises a great number of contradictory motives in each individual, a hesitation and ambiguous groping on the part of groups", and of "a situation that is subject to division below the surface [and that] is indeed almost constantly in danger of losing its simplicity".[10] In fact, this describes precisely Hamlet's predicament at the same time that it offers a gloss on his advice to the Players, and has the effect of turning the drama in upon itself as well as offering a glimpse of the complexities of the world that it aims to represent. This is not quite the same as reducing the act of representation to an ever-receding textuality, but nor is it a capitulation to the stubborn faith invested in the transparent relation between the world of words and the world of objects. It is, to borrow a Foucauldian formulation, a moment in the play "in which representation is represented at every point".[11]

And yet, questions of 'truth' are involved. There are some statements about the world that remain 'truer' than others, although this does not mean that they can be reduced to "the *eterne mutabilitie* of human nature, perennial, unhistorical variations of temperament",[12] or to the classical model of representation whose demise Foucault charts. If human beings are historical animals, then 'human nature', with its injunction to homogenise and to cause "the identical to appear in the disordered chain of representations" that is 'nature',[13] changes even as the 'form and pressure' of the times impose themselves upon them and it. And as Alan Sinfield has reminded us, narrative is the way in which we identify, homogenise and understand the world in which we live, but it is also the way in which we, or any social formation, produce ideology. Sinfield's refusal to reduce the motivations of a figure like Iago in *Othello* to the question of 'character', but to insist that it is "Venetian culture that sets the conditions of plausibility" for his behaviour, is another way of talking about the devices embedded in fictional texts that will allow us to detect their ideological purchase upon the facts of social existence. In speaking of 'stories' Sinfield argues that he is addressing "the production of ideology", and he goes on:

> Societies need to produce materially to continue – they need food, shelter, warmth; goods to exchange with other societies; a transport and information infrastructure to carry those processes. Also they have to produce ideologically … They need knowledges to keep material production going – diverse technical skills and wisdoms in agriculture, industry, science, medicine, economics, law, geography, languages, politics, and so on. And they need understandings, intuitive and explicit, of a system of social relationships within which the whole process can take place more or less evenly. Ideology produces, makes plausible, concepts and systems to explain who we are, who others are, how the world works.[14]

We can say that this is a 'truth' about the complex way in which societies work, and we can attempt to verify it empirically. It is an extrapolation of empirical observation, raised to a sophisticated theoretical level at which material forces are shown to interact with the processes of narrative that make them comprehensible. It stands firmly against Nuttall's 'truth' of an unchanging and permanent, though mutable, 'human nature', and its rhetorical force derives from its attempts to be inclusive, to address the unevenness of social reality rather than to discard awkward detail. It is, in short, a representation that points to other *structures* that underpin social existence and to which any disinterested account must pay attention. It also allows for differences of interpretation, for various alternative *readings* of the empirical evidence that Sinfield adduces. But it also, and crucially, addresses the very political complexities that Cunningham wishes to preserve in the face of a textuality that would suck 'history' itself into a dizzying and ultimately bottomless vortex. What for Sinfield, and for most materialists, stands between the world and language is a process of filtering for which the term 'ideology' continues to serve as an indispensable term, a means of inflecting language with the distributive realities of power that operate in specific ways at any given moment in history. In short, it promises a fuller explanation of the way the world works, and hence a more 'truthful' account, than that which relies on appeals to individual motivation and action, or to a stubbornly untheorised 'human nature'. But it also, crucially, folds into itself the process of representation. And it is this that Jonathan Dollimore addresses in the tension that he observes between 'idealistic' and 'realistic' mimesis during the Renaissance. He defines idealist mimesis as a "didacticism" that was "inherited as dramatic conventions from the morality tradition" and that "demanded that the universe be seen to be divinely controlled; that justice and order be eventually affirmed, conflict resolved, and the individual re-established within, or expelled from, the providential design". In contrast, realist mimesis as evidenced in the drama of the period, "was rapidly progressing as a form with empirical, historical and contemporary emphases – all of which were in potential conflict with this didacticism".[15] In short, 'truth' was not unitary or coherent, but multiple and contradictory. It changes as the emphases of 'history' change and those emphases are shot through with moral and ethical concerns, which taken together constitute what Foucault identified as 'the episteme' – the historically over-determined paradigm within whose aegis particular knowledges are generated, legitimised and sustained.

Whatever we might think of the historical accuracy of Foucault's conception of periodicity – and, in particular, his claim that in the Renaissance "the classical *discourse* in which being and representation found their common locus" with the result that, "in the profound upheaval of such an archaaeological mutation, man appears in his ambiguous position as an object of knowledge and a subject that knows: enslaved sovereign, observed spectator, he appears in the place belonging to the king"[16] – Robert Weimann's account of 'the archaeology of representation' as a 'decline' that is also "a moment of liberation, when language, recapturing its freedom and movement, is able to triumph once more",[17] returns us to the difficulty that immediately follows upon the renewed emphasis upon the formative power of language. Weimann's interest in mimesis can be traced back to his investigation of the processes of staging in his seminal book *Shakespeare and the Popular Tradition in the Theater* (1978) and he has returned to the issue of representation and its attendant difficulties periodically in response to the post-structuralist emphasis upon the irreducible nature of textuality. Weimann sets out to address the question of what is involved in the act of 'playing' on the Renaissance stage in which *locus* and *platea* were locked in a dialogue with each other. The advent of perspectival space, Weimann argues, found its objective existence in the stage *locus* that, he claims, is "a strategic approximation to the uses of perspectival form: it implicated the establishment of a topographically fixed locality".[18] He insists, rightly, that the growing predominance of what he calls "localized discourse" in the theatre of the period "must be viewed against the larger context of related representational practices in sixteenth-century culture" that accompanied "the decline of institutionally or metaphysically given types of authority" and that included "newly independent modes of authorisation, the spread of print and literature, as well as the new public platforms of theatrical entertainment".[19] What he calls "the ordering of the *place* of representation was complemented by a differentiation of the space *in* representation",[20] so that the act of performance itself could unravel, and demystify the "pictorial mode of symbolisation" by a process of assimilating "[the] thresholds between the imaginary world-in-the-play and the stage-as-stage" with the consequence of precluding "closure".[21] It is in the theatrical deployment of disguise, in which "the primary role … does not consume the uses of its own concealment", that a gap can be discerned "between impersonator and impersonated".[22] This is not unlike Walter Benjamin's analysis of the interruption of the '*gest*' in Brechtian performance, that is specifically designed to expose the *process* of representation rather than its object, and that effectively allows the performer to displace "the imaginary figure of the performed".[23] The effect of this process is an arresting of meaning that, in effect, undermines authority even as it discloses the mechanics of legitimation. The result is not a deconstruction of 'truth' so much as a historicisation of the conditions of its possibility, along with a reconfiguration of the *context* within which meaning emerges. In this way Weimann confronts post-structuralist theories of textuality by acknowledging the force of the linguistic turn, but, at the same time, resisting the vulgar attractions of an empirically referential model of mimesis, and, also, refusing to concede the claim that all meaning is irreducibly plural and indeterminate. For Weimann, meaning is multiply over-determined, and investigation of the act of representation itself involves what he calls a "dissociation between the mimetic element in representation and the work's meaning" that can only be approached "historically, against the background of earlier forms and functions in narrative".[24] This is, perhaps, another way of saying that 'the world' is mediated through a range of genres of discourse that make pure and uncomplicated reference impossible except on the most superficial of levels. Indeed, elsewhere he notes that although all systems of reference "can be of great and even crucial importance, any single one of them, when pursued exclusively on its own ground, fails to yield a compelling perspective on representation in the full range of its forms and functions". Weimann's ambitious objective is to "retrieve mimesis from the ashes of classicism and metaphysics" in the face of "the forbidding difficulties in our time to distinguish the copy from the copied".[25] Although focusing on a particular historical conjuncture, the Renaissance, and on a particular activity, theatrical practice, Weimann's own approach is informed by the challenge to mimesis proposed variously by the writings of Heidegger, Lacan and, latterly, Lacoue-Labarthe, all of which reverse the process of the traditional displacement of the emphasis upon what Lacoue-Labarthe calls 'the product' back on to the figure of the 'producer', the mimetician.[26]

This questioning of the veracity of 'the mirror' that has been so central to the concept of mimesis is the occasion for this adventurous collection of essays, ranging widely across the terrain of Shakespearean and Renaissance mimetic practice. Each essay selects a particular aspect of the general problem and the result is a provocative, wide-ranging reformulation of the problem by an exciting group of young scholars, keen to take up the gauntlet that Weimann himself threw down in his Afterword to the second edition of *Alternative Shakespeares* (2002). Each essay, in various ways, resists the sense that mimesis simply involves 'resemblance', the straightforward bringing forth, or disclosure, of substantive presence, and in doing so points towards a range of historically specific discomforts with received models of 'reality'. The self-reflexiveness of contemporary praxis, that finds an interesting analogue in the Renaissance itself, raises fundamental questions about the nature and process of representation, to the extent that the editors, Jonathan Holmes and Adrian Streete, can claim, and with absolute justification, that each of the essays (including their own) radically disrupts "the category of mimetic referentiality". The essays encompass detailed consideration of individual Shakespearean texts, as well as expanding this focus to engage with the post-colonial reception of categories of representation, and latterly go beyond the drama itself into other areas of Renaissance writing. As a collection, this is a timely and impressive intervention in an important area of literary studies that will generate further thought on a topic that, since Plato, has continued to perplex and stimulate philosophers and literary scholars alike.

Afterword

1. Erich Auerbach, *Mimesis: The Representation of Reality in Western Literature*, trans. Willard R. Trask (Princeton, NJ: Princeton University Press, 1974), p. 44.
2. Ibid., p. 33.
3. A.D. Nuttall, *A New Mimesis: Shakespeare and the Representation of Reality* (London and New York: Methuen, 1983), p. 165.
4. Ibid., p. 166.
5. Ibid., pp. 166-7.
6. Ibid., p. 165.
7. Terry Eagleton, *After Theory* (London: Allen Lane, 2003), p. 88.
8. Valentine Cunningham, *Inside the Reading Gaol: Post-modernity, Texts and History* (Oxford: Blackwell, 1994), p. 46.
9. Ibid., p. 47.
10. Auerbach, *Mimesis*, p. 20.
11. Michel Foucault, *The Order of Things: An Archaeology of the Human Sciences* (London: Tavistock, 1970), p. 307.
12. Nuttall, *New Mimesis*, p. 167.
13. Foucault, *Order of Things*, p. 309.
14. Alan Sinfield, *Faultlines: Cultural Materialism and the Politics of Dissident Reading* (Berkeley, CA and Oxford: Oxford University Press, 1992), pp. 31-2.
15. Jonathan Dollimore, *Radical Tragedy: Religion, Ideology and Power in the Drama of Shakespeare and His Contemporaries*, 3rd edn (Basingstoke: Palgrave, 2004), pp. 71ff.
16. Foucault, *Order of Things*, p. 312.
17. Robert Weimann, *Authority and Representation in Early Modern Discourse*, ed. David Hillman (Baltimore, MD and London: Johns Hopkins University Press, 1996), p. 190.
18. Robert Weimann, *Author's Pen and Actor's Voice: Playing and Writing in Shakespeare's Theater* (Cambridge: Cambridge University Press, 2000), p. 182.
19. Ibid., p. 184.
20. Ibid., p. 189.
21. Ibid., p. 192.
22. Ibid., p. 196.
23. Robert Weimann, 'Doubly Encoded Representations in Modern Drama and Fiction: Rupturing Co-ordinates of (Re)semblance and Meaning'. Unpublished ms. I am grateful to Professor Weimann for having allowed me to see parts of the typescript of this article.
24. Ibid.
25. Robert Weimann, 'Introduction: Representation and Mimesis: Towards a New Theory', *Symbolism: An International Annual of Critical Aesthetics* 6 (2004) (forthcoming).
26. Philippe Lacoue-Labarthe, *Typography: Mimesis, Philosophy, Politics*, ed. Christopher Fynsk (Stanford, CA: Stanford University Press, 1998), p. 90.

Index

Compiled by David Coleman